working on a dream

working on a dream

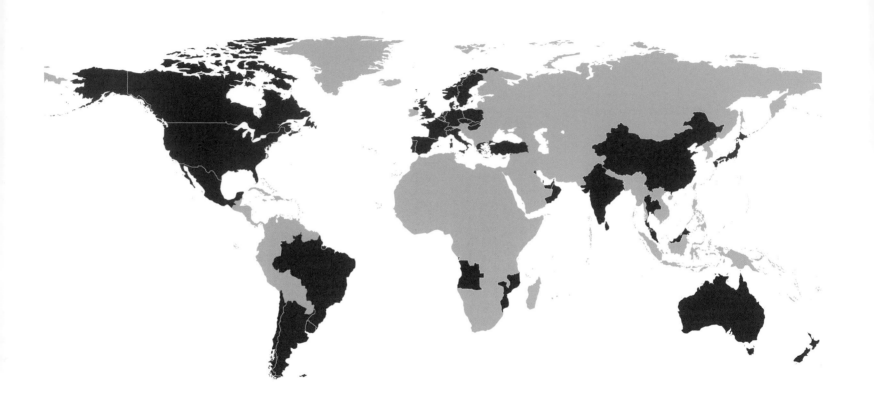

preface

Dear Reader,

The book you're holding in your hands is not just a book about the history of Randstad. It is much more than that. It is a document that shows how the employment world developed over the past fifty years, and how many groups of people and companies, who all had their own ideas, their own values and their own inspiration, came together in what is today one of the greatest companies of its type in the world.

The importance of what Randstad has reached should not be underestimated. Every day we provide work for over half a million people around the world. People of various ethnic backgrounds and religions, men and women, people with disabilities or other special needs. To our clients, we are a significant provider of the asset which is most critical for their success: their people. In doing so, we need to balance the interests of all our stakeholders. We call it "the simultaneous promotion of all interests".

To me personally, this is the essence of what a modern corporation should be about. It once started as a dream, but we make it a little bit more real every day.

We hope that you will enjoy reading the book, and that later you will go back and browse through it every now and then. In particular, we think that this book will be a source of inspiration, and hope that it will show you the many possibilities there are to improve the labor market.

Yours sincerely,

Ben Noteboom
CEO and Chairman of the Board of Randstad Holding nv

table of contents

This book includes two Randstad story lines. The first tells the history of Randstad in five chapters. The second tells fifty stories of (former) employees, clients, and other persons, which reflect Randstad's core values.

Amounts stated in euros give a rough indication of actual values. Historical Dutch guilder values were converted at the 2002 exchange rate, when one euro was worth approximately 2.20 Dutch guilders. Dollar amounts were converted at a more recent exchange rate (fall of 2009), and do not reflect actual values. Neither euro amounts nor dollar amounts have been corrected for inflation.

history

fifty stories

the Randstad dream

Back in 1960, the world of Randstad was no more than one old bicycle, two student rooms and 500 Dutch guilders. But Frits Goldschmeding, the founder, had big plans.

Flexible work was still a little-known phenomenon at the time, but Goldschmeding saw that flexibility could potentially play a much larger role in the labor market. It was a role that would benefit all parties concerned. Flexible working relations would allow employers to arrange staffing quickly, easily and in line with the economy, whereas employees could change jobs quickly, while gaining expertise and achieving personal growth as a result.

begins

The company was inspired by the goal of achieving flexibility for the labor market. Within 50 years, the thousands of Randstad entrepreneurs, the staffing consultants, together with their colleagues had realized the dream, not only for themselves, but for the clients, the candidates and for society itself.

This is a story about entrepreneurship, dedication and job satisfaction. It is a story that links the first perfect match in 1960 with the company's mission in 2010: *Shaping the world of work*.

a flair for
business

The labor market can be different and better, more flexible, and temporary labor is the means to achieve that. This was the dream of two young men, with which they started their Randstad Uitzendbureau staffing business in 1960. Competitors were lurking, but after less than ten years there was no denying it: Randstad was the best, and had the greatest ambitions. Within ten years, the young company had established branches in four countries. The dream was beginning to become reality.

N.V. RANDSTAD UITZENDBUREAU

let's start an
employment agency!

Imagine the scene. Early sixties, it is late at night, and the streets of Amsterdam are deserted. The distant sound of two excited voices is gradually getting louder, closer. Two students in their mid-twenties, dressed in dark, dignified suits, are cycling through the silent streets of the city, totally absorbed in their dialogue.

Frits Goldschmeding and Ger Daleboudt were both studying economics at Amsterdam's Free University, in those days a devout Christian stronghold of learning. Goldschmeding had just spent three months completing a dissertation on the subject of the staffing industry. Satisfied that his efforts had been rewarded with a good grade, he put away his books and thought no more of it. Until, that is, he bumped into Ger Daleboudt one night at the student club. When Ger asked Frits Goldschmeding how he had done on his dissertation, they became so engrossed in a discussion that they were still talking as they started to cycle home.

The subject for Goldschmeding's dissertation had been suggested to him by Professor F.L. van Muiswinkel, who had often wondered why it was that during peak business periods, companies

were able to rent almost anything – from machines to buildings to tools – except people. Van Muiswinkel wondered whether the American concept of employment agencies might also be of interest to companies in the Netherlands. A handful of temporary employment agencies already existed, such as the Algemeen Service Bedrijf (ASB), which had been established in 1949 in The Hague and was later taken over by Vedior, but they were few and far between. The professor sent his young student off in search of some answers.

Frits Goldschmeding went through the libraries of Amsterdam with a fine-toothed comb but was unable to find anything on the subject. Van Muiswinkel was not surprised; he had found just a single article on the subject in an American journal of economics, and a single sentence that had featured in a Citroën annual report, asserting that any company employing less than five per cent temporary staff was poorly structured. The professor quietly admitted that the lack of material available on the subject was, in fact, the very reason he had suggested it to his student. Goldschmeding rose to the challenge and three months later he had finished his thesis.

Left: Frits Goldschmeding (left) and Ger Daleboudt at an open house event at the A.J. Ernststraat head office in July 1970. The tandem is a reminder of the beginning of the Randstad adventure in 1960.

Right: The first Randstad 'head office' in 1960: a student room with a landlady at the Sloterkade wharf in Amsterdam.

An ASB branch in Amsterdam. In the nineteen-sixties and seventies, ASB would grow to be one of the largest competitors of Randstad in the Netherlands.

Goldschmeding was brimming with enthusiasm that night as he told Daleboudt what he had found. He explained that during peak business periods, companies were often forced to hire extra staff that would not be needed once the rush was over and would therefore hurt profits. Goldschmeding argued that flexible employment would help create jobs, and thereby increase prosperity. In short, flexible labor would act as a lubricant for the economy.

As they cycled along in conversation, Frits Goldschmeding decided it was time to do something with the idea of flexible employment; after all, he came from long line of entrepreneurs. His cousins ran a successful piano and pipe organ business in downtown Amsterdam, and in 1875, his grandfather started importing harmoniums, a domestic musical instrument popular at the time among members of the Dutch Reformed Church. His grandson Frits was the entrepreneurial type, and he recognized an opportunity when it came knocking. While still a student, he had approached the Amsterdam City Council and negotiated a plan allowing ex-prisoners to sell herrings from a cart upon their release, and as an undergraduate he had supported himself by selling shoe soles and car tires.

With entrepreneurial blood running through his veins, Frits Goldschmeding put his plan into words: "Let's start our own employment agency! I know a bit about it now and it would be a great way for us to earn some extra cash." He had meant it as a joke, but to his surprise, Daleboudt responded: "What a brilliant idea!"

Eagerly they cycled back to Goldschmeding's rooms on Sloterkade wharf, where they got his father's old typewriter out and typed the very first flyer for their new venture, 'Uitzendbureau Amstelveen' (*uitzendbureau*, pronounced 'out-send bureau', is Dutch for 'employment agency';

Amstelveen is a suburb of Amsterdam), a name conceived there and then in a nocturnal flash of inspiration. They would stencil copies of the flyers in college the next day and deliver them to various companies by hand since there was no money for stamps. Dawn was breaking as they raised their glasses and drank a toast to their great adventure.

if you're this persistent, **your staff must be good**

The Goldschmeding family had made its name in the Dutch-reformed community as a purveyor of home organs. By placing a television in the display window, the shop owner drew attention to his store in the nineteen-sixties.

Once the flyers had been distributed, Goldschmeding and Daleboudt got back to their regular business of being students; after all, they still had to study for exams. Two days later, the phone rang. To Goldschmeding's surprise, there was a potential client on the line: "Hello, is this Uitzendbureau Amstelveen? I have just read your flyer and was wondering if you happen to have a secretary who can take shorthand in French, German, Dutch and English?"

Goldschmeding's heart was racing, but he calmly replied that he would check the files to see if they had a suitable candidate. "I'll get back to you as soon as possible," he said. He put the phone down and immediately called his friend. "Ger, you'll never believe what I....," he started, but Daleboudt cut him short. "I have just registered our first temporary worker, one Ms. Honhoff!" When Goldschmeding asked if she could take shorthand in French, German, Dutch, and English, Daleboudt answered with a firm "Yes!," upon which Goldschmeding replied, "in that case, we've just clinched our first deal!"

Goldschmeding called the client back immediately and, with all the professional cool he could muster, informed him that they did, indeed, have a

suitable candidate for the job. He explained that Ms. Honhoff could start at 8:30 the next morning, and hung up before the client could ask any awkward questions. Unfortunately, paying the first temporary worker also created the first financial headache for the young entrepreneurs. Their student grants had long since been spent, so funding would have to be found elsewhere. They hunted high and low in search of credit; without result. The banks were not interested, they were too young, not experienced enough, and insufficiently creditworthy. It was only when both Goldschmeding's father and Daleboudt's father agreed to put up EUR 2,800 each by way of security that Uitzendbureau Amstelveen was granted a loan of EUR 1,800 from the Rotterdamse Bank. When the agency closed its first financial year 1960, profits amounted to the modest sum of EUR 4.12.

Frits Goldschmeding was nevertheless determined to make a success of the agency. He often went off in search of potential clients, either by bike or driving around in his little Volkswagen, and will always remember one client in particular. The company in question, located in a stylish, canal-side mansion in Amsterdam, had been advertising for two transcription typists for three weeks.

bureau randstad
v/h uitzendbureau „amstelveen"

TARIEVENLIJST

typiste nederlands	f 2.80	per uur
extra per taal	f 0.10	per uur
facturiste nederlands	f 2.90	per uur
extra per taal	f 0.10	per uur
facturiste (machinaal)	f 3.10	per uur
dictafoniste nederlands	f 3.10	per uur
extra per taal	f 0.30	per uur
steno-typiste nederlands	f 3.10	per uur
extra per taal	f 0.30	per uur
secretaresse	f 4.20	per uur
correspondente nederlands	f 3.10	per uur
extra per taal	f 0.40	per uur
telefoniste nederlands	f 2.70	per uur
extra per taal	f 0.20	per uur
polistypiste	f 2.90	per uur
stenciltypiste	f 2.90	per uur
statentypiste	f 3.00	per uur
relexiste	f 2.90	per uur
balanstypiste	f 3.10	per uur
ponstypiste	f 3.20	per uur
kracht boekhoudmachine	f 3.10	per uur
jongste bediende	f 1.90	per uur
administratieve kracht vanaf	f 2.60	per uur
ass. boekh. kracht vanaf	f 2.90	per uur
loonadministrateur	f 3.80	per uur
zelfst. boekh. kracht	f 4.10	per uur

19 63 *Memo-randstad was the first newsletter published by the young staffing agency. Issued quarterly, in carried news about recruiting and human resources policy. It also included tips about reducing typewriter noise or amplifying phone conversations, to allow for the participation of additional people. Printed on 9 x 15 cm sized paper (3.5 x 6 inch), every page of the newsletter could be torn off individually, allowing people to save particularly handy tips.*

memo-randstad

maandelijkse uitgave van n.v. randstad
uitzendbureau van kantoorpersoneel
hoofdkantoor, directie en administratie:
amsterdam oranje nassaul. 7 tel. 020-76 05 05 *

amsterdam-c tel. 020- 6 22 13 *
amsterdam-z tel. 020-73 76 66 *   rotterdam-c tel. 010-13 71 52 *
leiden   tel. 01710- 3 42 99   rotterdam-w tel. 010-25 47 20 *
's-gravenhage tel. 070-63 79 66 *   utrecht   tel. 030- 1 82 46 *

Minder schrijven

Wie veel correspondentie moet verwijzen kan gebruik maken van een geleidebriefje. Hierop behoeft slechts een x-je te worden geplaatst voor de te verrichten handeling (verzoeke: te raadplegen, onderzoek in te stellen en verslag uit te brengen, direct te beantwoorden en mij kopie te zenden, deze zaak verder te behandelen, etc.).

Dressed in his best suit, Goldschmeding went along to talk to the manager, but his efforts were in vain. The manager listened politely to Goldschmeding before announcing that he was not interested. "But you need two transcription typists; you don't have them and I do. You can hire them from me on a temporary basis and in the meantime continue searching at your leisure," Goldschmeding replied. The manager was equally resolute: "My dear man, we have never done anything like that before and we are not about to start now."

Two weeks later, Goldschmeding saw the same advertisement appear in the newspaper once more, and, once more, he went to see the manager. "Leave, right now!" was all the manager had to say. A short while later, when the ad appeared yet again, the stubborn economy student decided to try his luck one last time. This time, the manager was waiting for him at the top of the stairs. He pushed his visitor down the stairs, but Goldschmeding was not one to give up easily; he brushed himself off and returned to the manager's door. He knocked three times and

shouted, "You still don't have those two transcription typists!" "Well, I'll be damned," the man retorted. "You'd better come in. I guess if you're as stubborn as this your staff must be pretty darned good too. I'll need them by this afternoon."

The initial ups and downs did not go unrewarded. The number of agency staff gradually increased, to twenty by late 1961. With sales of EUR 81,067, Uitzendbureau Amstelveen's profits for 1962 came to EUR 7,866 – roughly two thousand times as much as In its inaugural year!

Frits Goldschmeding (2nd from left) was a member of the Cicero debating society of the L.A.N.X. fraternity. The photo was taken at an Amsterdam debating event.

seasonal peaks and sick leave

These exceptional figures, however, were not simply due to hard work. In the 1950s and 1960s, the world economy was booming, and that included the Netherlands. Employers were having great difficulty finding new staff. In fact, in the early 1960s, almost 99 percent of the Dutch labor force had work. This was an unprecedented high for the Netherlands and the labor market began to change accordingly. New groups of potential employees gained access to the labor market thanks to agencies such as Uitzendbureau Amstelveen, Stenotyp and Typistensociëteit. Interestingly enough, the great majority of temporary staff available were married women, many of whom lived in newly built suburbs like Amsterdam Buitenveldert and Ommoord in Rotterdam. The introduction of the contraceptive pill had made family planning possible and large families were becoming a thing of the past. Where the labor market was concerned, this meant that women had more time available for

things like work, and innovations in household appliances (vacuum cleaners, washing machines and refrigerators) helped free up even more time. Moreover, women wanted to enjoy the increased prosperity of the 1960s as much as their male counterparts did. Their participation in the labor market was nevertheless modest, often amounting to little more than a couple of hours a week, but companies were eager to make use of their availability during busy peak periods or to provide cover for staff on sick leave. Flexible work arrangements were ideal for such situations. As a rule, these women worked as secretaries, shorthand typists and punchcard operators, positions in which women were readily accepted in the male-dominated working environment. In this way, employment agencies were able to provide solutions for both supply and demand.

Some employment agencies, such as ASB, focused on an entirely different sector, providing

staff for industry and ports. These sectors were generally looking for men who could lend a hand for a few days when there was a shortage of permanent staff due to annual or sick leave. Initially, Uitzendbureau Amstelveen did not deal with these sectors since both Goldschmeding and Daleboudt had an academic background and little affinity with the world of industry. Uitzendbureau Amstelveen was providing most of its temporary staff to rapidly growing insurance companies, banks and healthcare institutions.

19 65 *The first advertising agency to work with Randstad was Nijgh & Van Ditmar. They introduced the slogan 'Randstad – voor de inspringkracht die er uitspringt', a word play roughly translatable as 'Randstad temporary employees – for stand-ins who stand out'. The slogan was repeated in all communications, from brochures and price lists to posters and display windows. The image shows one of the first branches.*

N.V. RANDSTAD UITZENDBUREAU

voor de inspringkracht die er uitspringt

Kruiskade 18
Rochussenstr. 397 b

Goed betaald tijdelijk werk? Bel Randstad: 137152

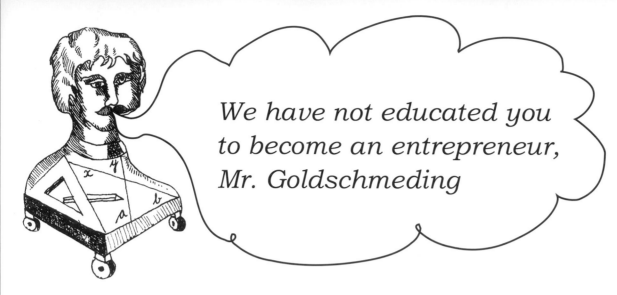

We have not educated you to become an entrepreneur, Mr. Goldschmeding

Goldschmeding and Daleboudt continued with their college courses and in 1963, both gained master's degrees in economics. Professors at the VU University in Amsterdam had carefully observed their passionate entrepreneurial spirit for some time. Following his graduation, Frits Goldschmeding was invited to speak with one of the professors. The professor congratulated him on gaining his degree and asked him about his plans for the future. He was surely not thinking of pursuing his business enterprise?! The professor began to lecture him about his education and his potential as an economist. "You must realize that we have not educated you in order for you to become an entrepreneur. You could have any position you wanted in a large company. Mr. Goldschmeding, let's be clear about one thing: the government does not finance universities in order for people like you to pursue a career as an entrepreneur."

The professor's 'sermon', however, had little effect on the new graduate. In fact, it seemed to encourage him to do completely the opposite. A couple of weeks after the graduation ceremony, Goldschmeding and Daleboudt swapped their student housing for a real office. The two managing directors and three members of staff settled in premises on Koninginneweg Road

near Vondel Park, in the affluent southern part of Amsterdam. They rented the front-facing rooms of a private residence, setting up office in the former living room on the first floor. From here the young graduates, aptly dressed in smart suits, began to manage their business. In 1964, their administrative staff set up office on the second floor, where the legs of the bathtub still protruded from the floorboards. The employment agency itself was situated on the ground floor and was traditionally furnished with stylish parquet flooring, curtains at

the window, and a couple of large green plants to complete the picture. This conventional style was in keeping with the young female staff and their card-trays (where all the employee information was recorded); they were all well turned-out girls of around 18 wearing skirts and blouses, their outfits finished off with neat pearl necklaces. Dressed in housecoat and slippers and with blue-tinted hair the landlady would deliver the mail to her tenants every morning, while they took turns at making tea and coffee in her kitchen.

Goldschmeding and Daleboudt now had a good foundation on which to build their ambitious plans. The agency had a forty-strong temporary staff for hire and a branch manager for the general management of the business side of things. A few months later, however, the branch manager left, and when a suitable replacement proved harder to find than expected, Goldschmeding decided to take up the position himself, albeit temporarily. In those early years, young Frits proved himself to be a hard worker who could always be found at his desk. He was acutely aware of the fact that anyone who had ambitions had to work hard in order to fulfill them.

Randstad's first head office on Koninginneweg Road in Amsterdam.

RANDSTAD UITZENDBUREAU

In 1963, the company, still in its infancy, opened branches in Leiden and Rotterdam. This, however, presented a problem, since they did not yet have a name for these new branches. Uitzendbureau 'Amstelveen' sounded somewhat strange in the cities of Leiden and Rotterdam, and the idea of naming every office after the city in which it was located was simply not practical. The managers decided to act upon the advice of a friend and marketing specialist who suggested the name Randstad Uitzendbureau. They thought that the name Randstad (for the urbanized area that includes the cities Rotterdam, Amsterdam, The Hague, and Utrecht) would more than cover the area they expected to serve.

The opening of new branches in Leiden and Rotterdam marked the first unwavering step taken by a company that now stood on a solid foundation. Goldschmeding and Daleboudt were now confident enough to start looking to the future and making plans. In 1963, they set their first target profit figures and even drew up a five-year plan. However, the company continued to face liquidity problems due to the rapidly growing sales. They decided that with significant share capital contributions from participants they would gain better financial control and be less dependent on bank loans.

Goldschmeding went looking for advice from someone with a business community background who would understand the ambitions of a small but determined company like theirs. Ideally, he would have liked someone wealthy, a millionaire perhaps, and one with both an interest in the sector and the desire to invest in it. It was, in fact, the manager of the Rotterdamse Bank in Amstelveen who put him in touch with Dick Schwarz. Schwarz had recently sold his perfume chemicals factory and thus had the necessary funds at his disposal. He had also just set up an innovative design agency, Total Design, with several business partners. Goldschmeding went to meet Schwarz at his fashionably furnished office on Amsterdam's Herengracht canal. As he tried to persuade Schwarz to invest in his venture, Goldschmeding was scrutinizing every inch of the stylish surroundings at Total Design, and he loved what he saw.

Likewise, the manager of Total Design admired and believed in these young entrepreneurs. He recognized in Goldschmeding in particular a drive that greatly appealed to him. Schwarz decided to loan Randstad EUR 90,909 at an annual interest rate of 6 percent. Moreover, he purchased a percentage of the shares himself. Eighty of the 125 shares were immediately divided between Goldschmeding and Daleboudt. Four of these shares were priority shares, which gave their holders extra voting rights. The two founders then sold the remaining shares to their parents and other family members, and with that, the financing was arranged. It was time to get down to some real work.

Total Design management in 1963. Clockwise:
Dick Schwarz, Friso Kramer, Benno Wissing,
Ben Bos, Paul Schwarz, Wim Crouwel.

GLORIFIED GANG MASTERS

The opening of the first subway in the Netherlands, on 9 February 1968 in Rotterdam, was a big event. Randstad immediately recognized the added value of heavily frequented subway stations, and the next day opened its Rotterdam Beurs branch.

Business was going well In the mid-60s, but this also resulted in Randstad coming up against prejudices for the first time. In those days, the concept of temporary staffing was very much frowned upon. What Randstad was doing – mediating between employers and employees – was generally associated with gang masters. They were usually shady characters who hung around in bars or railway stations recruiting people, preferably temporary manual laborers, to work for them. The gang masters would employ these recruits themselves before subsequently offering them to companies (usually in industry, the docks or the building trade) in exchange for considerable sums of money. They did not pay social security contributions, tax or insurance, yet earned for themselves a tidy fortune at the recruits' expense. When legal claims were filed against them, they would declare their company bankrupt, and continue under a new name as if nothing happened.

As reprehensible as their practices were, however, they filled a need. The rapidly growing economy in the 1960s was making it difficult for companies to find sufficient employees, and in order to meet the ever-increasing need for staff, employers found themselves turning, albeit reluctantly, to gang masters. Staff hired this way often earned

more than permanent staff, who were also having pension and health insurance premiums deducted from their salaries. This, of course, stirred up ill will among permanent staff and the unions, and feelings of dissatisfaction were strengthened further by government wage policy at that time. Salaries had been kept artificially low since the end of the Second World War in order to make the Netherlands attractive to investors. Thanks to the booming economy, however, the government felt obliged to abandon the guided wage policy; salaries simply had to be increased.

The government was equally aware that they had to put a stop to the activities being carried out by gang masters. In 1965, a new labor law was passed, which made it possible to regulate the placement of employees by bona fide private employment agencies. As a result of the Veldkamp Act, which was implemented in January 1966, staffing agencies were required to withhold social benefit contributions, and pay the employer contributions. A licensing system was introduced in 1970. In order to gain a license, employment agencies were obliged to meet certain conditions. This system is not entirely in line, however, with Convention 96 of the International Labor Organisation (ILO), which had been ratified by the

Netherlands. This international organization, which comprises government representatives, employers and employees, deals with international labor issues. ILO Convention 96 of 1949 stated that fee-charging employment agencies were considered undesirable and prohibited. This dismissive attitude towards employment agencies stemmed from the 1930s, when an economic crisis had caused mass unemployment. Many of those who were unemployed resorted to accepting work from unscrupulous individuals they met in bars and who subsequently caused them to work under appalling conditions in factories or dockyards.

Goldschmeding realized how important it was for Randstad that people knew they were dealing with a reputable company. The difference between them and shady gang masters had to be made crystal clear. Initial steps in the right direction were taken in 1964 when Randstad applied to become a member of the ABU (the Dutch association of temporary work agencies). Since its establishment in 1961, this trade federation had been trying in every possible way to make the position of temporary staff, bona fide employment agencies and companies using temporary staff more secure. Initially, the ABU refused to admit Randstad as a member. The

agency paid its temporary staff for annual and
sick leave, and that was not in accordance with
the principles of the branch organization. After
some hesitation, however, the federation decided
to allow the fast-growing and ambitious Randstad
company to become a member.

The Veldkamp Act also provided social security
rights protection for temporary employees.
The obligatory withholding of social security
contributions caused agency fees to increase
by almost thirty percent, and employment

agencies everywhere expected this to have fatal
consequences for the industry. Actually, the
opposite was true. Compulsory insurance and
the withholding of social benefit contributions
gave temporary employment legitimacy and a
social image that was held in high regard by many
clients. From 1966 onwards, requests for staff
poured in. In fact, with Randstad, the ABU had
found true brothers in arms. Together, they set
out to erase the glorified gang masters image
that society still held of employment agencies.
In 1968, the Netherlands had 110 employment

agencies, less than half of which were honest and
reputable. These agencies might have been in the
minority, but they did have a 90% share of the
market. The other 10% belonged to fraudulent
agencies run by gang masters who neither paid
benefits nor insured their agency staff.

Goldschmeding wanted more. It was obvious that
he was not a gang master, particularly when you
looked at the staff he provided, the majority of
whom had a university education. But Randstad
wanted to go one step further in order to

Ger Daleboudt and Frits Goldschmeding at the opening of the head office at Oranje Nassaulaan 16 in Amsterdam.

emphasize that difference. Goldschmeding had not forgotten his visit to Dick Schwarz at Total Design where they worked on strong designs for large companies such as KLM Royal Dutch Airlines and Royal Ahrend. This leading design agency appeared to be just what he needed to help him make that 'giant leap forward.'

KIJK, ZIJ HEEFT HAAR EIGEN PLAATS

OVER
OPZITTEN
EEN
MINISTER
SOCIALE
BESCHERMING

EN
N.V. RANDSTAD
UITZEND
BUREAU

BUREAU
RANDSTAD
HET
VEELZIJDIGSTE
UITZENDBUREAU
IN
HET
WESTEN
VAN
NEDERLAND

19 66 *In the nineteen-sixties, Randstad was accused of removing workers from the market who might otherwise have obtained a permanent job. The brochure 'Kijk, zij heeft haar eigen plaats' ('Look, she has a place of her own') refuted this accusation. People dispatched by Randstad formed a new segment of the professional population. People signing up with staffing agencies included women with young children, young men between school and military service, as well as experienced workers who were only available for a shorter period. In this way, temp workers fulfilled a valuable function in companies at times of sickness, temporary understaffing, or peak production periods.*

totally
different

Goldschmeding had become tired of the logo that the Nijgh & Van Ditmar advertising agency had made for Randstad; an 'r' shape from which a traditional typewriter carriage return lever appeared. The logo looked too much like those of their competitors, all bearing typewriters, pens, and globes. Randstad was different, and that *had* to be reflected in their logo!

Dick Schwarz was one of Randstad's shareholders, but also a partner at Total Design, where together with his brother Paul, he was responsible for the business side of things. Goldschmeding decided to approach Schwarz during a shareholders meeting in 1966. He had recently seen a particularly stylish desk that had been created for Ahrend by one of the designers at Total Design. He asked Schwarz if they might be able to design a house style for Randstad. Schwarz did some quick calculations before announcing that to design a logo would cost EUR 682, and that an additional amount of EUR 1,364 would be required to purchase the exclusive rights to the design. That was quite some investment, but young Goldschmeding agreed. After all, quality did not come cheap and the profits they had made in recent years justified the investment.

Total Design was by no means a run-of-the-mill design agency. Wim Crouwel, Benno Wissing, Friso Kramer, and brothers Paul and Dick Schwarz had set up their design agency in 1963. The name Total Design represented their goal, which was to create uniformity in every aspect of their clients' communication, from letterhead to packaging materials, from logos to interior design. As was typical for their generation, the designers were averse to middle-class small-mindedness, and bent on demonstrating the courage of their convictions by contributing towards a better world through their work. Total Design was the first Dutch design agency dedicated exclusively to developing and implementing corporate identity, which at the time was an entirely new concept in the Netherlands. It was a revolutionary design agency, and a revolution was exactly what Frits Goldschmeding wanted. He was looking for a design that was distinctive, a logo with which Randstad could, once and for all, break free from the negative image of employment agencies as gang masters.

Total Design manager Wim Crouwel, however, regarded their new client as small time and therefore introduced the 34-year-old Goldschmeding to their agency's most junior staff member,

Nijgh & Van Ditmar's promotional material gave a good representation of Randstad's work: typewriters, telephones, and envelopes indicated that this was a business that specialized in the provision administrative personnel.

37-year-old Ben Bos. A part-time student at the Amsterdam School for Applied Arts (later renamed the Gerrit Rietveld Academy), Bos attended lectures given by Crouwel, an obsessive art lover described by many as willing to work "25 hours a day and 400 days a year". He was, quite simply, a phenomenon. Bos held the strict-natured Crouwel in high regard. Indeed, his adage to the academy was that if he could please him, he would be well on his way to success. It was little wonder then that when Crouwel asked Bos to become head of studio at Total Design, he thought he had landed on cloud nine. He felt, in fact, that he had "landed a place with the gods", initially granting himself only the modest title of 'junior designer'. He believed that he had much to learn from his superiors.

Early in 1967, Bos went to introduce himself to Randstad at their new premises on Oranje Nassaulaan avenue. Before leaving, he checked his diary for details: Mr. Goldschmeding and Mr. Daleboudt, Randstad Uitzendbureau, seven branches. A frown appeared on his face; employment agencies were known to be run by rough, unscrupulous cowboys. He expected little of the visit and didn't really understand why his boss had accepted this particular client. As soon as he crossed the threshold, however,

it was clear he had been very much mistaken. Rather than finding 'unscrupulous cowboys', he was welcomed by two very respectable and well-dressed young men, one with fair hair neatly parted to one side, the other with short dark hair and stylish glasses.

Bos had hardly sat down before Goldschmeding eagerly began voicing his dissatisfaction with their current house style and explaining what he did and definitely did not want. To illustrate his point, he threw down a huge pile of papers showing examples of competitors' house styles. "These are the logos used by all our so-called 'competitors' in their stuffy, dim-lit offices with mock velvet and macramé furnishings and walls hung with Anton Pieck nostalgia. This represents everything I don't want!" he said. What Goldschmeding did want was something like the Mercedes logo – that was a good example of flawless design: crystal clear and immediately recognizable. Yes, that was what Goldschmeding was after. "Finding a good design takes time and effort," Bos explained. "The message you want to put across has to be used consistently and repeatedly. Only then does a logo become recognizable." Goldschmeding had in mind something simple like a circle or a square, but

19 67 *The sleek lowercase 'r', perfectly balanced by its mirror image: it looks as if this logo has been around forever. The power of a good logo is such that one might forget that there was a time that it did not exist.*

In 1967, Randstad chose to work with Total Design and designer Ben Bos. In this it departed from the explicit ads it used in its first seven years, and moved toward more abstract forms. The new logo nicely encapsulated the professionalism, reliability and accuracy of the new enterprise.

Randstad's new orientation expressed itself in all forms: not only was the stationery different, but the interior of the branches was also redesigned. In the nineteen-sixties, Randstad gained a significant head start over its competitors, taking on a corporate identity like those of leading Dutch companies such as KLM and Philips. Today, forty-three years later, Randstad is one of those leading companies.

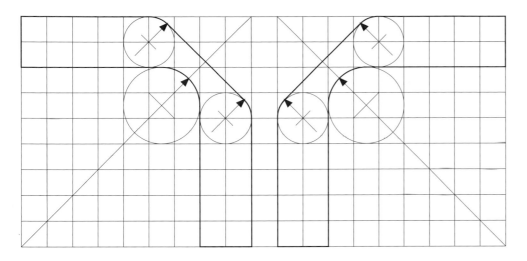

Bos explained to him that a simple shape could not be registered as a trademark. The new logo would therefore have to be a clear, simple shape, but with a strong, unique character.

Bos returned to his studio on Amsterdam's Herengracht canal to consider his challenge. How on earth did one design a logo for an abstract product that did not, in fact, have any shape at all? And how did you make sure that it also exuded status and reliability? He began to search for words that typified the field of temporary employment. He came up with 'administrative work', 'female-oriented', 'secretary' and 'typist'. Together with his colleague Elizabeth James, he set out to create an image based on these words. They discussed the options at length, but for the time being committed nothing to paper. They both felt certain that a logo was not something you could rush, but something that would simply 'evolve' in its own due course.

As the weeks went by, gradually an idea began to develop in Bos's mind. Why didn't they simply use a stylized 'r'? One morning, he picked up his sketchbook and with soft pencil strokes he began to draw an elegantly styled letter 'r' on the white paper. Keeping in mind the feminine character of

the temporary employment, he drew an elegant letter 'r' that was refined and decorative, yet also clear and precise. It was a start. Ben Bos went to get a cup of coffee, and when he came back he held out his sketchbook at arm's length and squinted to examine his creation. He was reasonably satisfied, but the letter 'r' appeared to be out of balance. He suddenly decided to place a second 'r' against the first one, but now in mirror image. At that moment, everything fell into place; the logo was balanced, the logo was complete.

Bos discussed the result with Elizabeth James and they both knew it was good! In fact, it was the only design they would present to Randstad. Dick Schwarz had informed Bos that the client wanted the entire name of Randstad Uitzendbureau to appear in the logo. He therefore tried out a number of variations such as both words in capitals, combinations of upper and lower case letters, both words in small letters, bold letters and narrow letters, and each time he held up his new logo alongside one of the combinations. It was soon obvious that 'randstad' was a better option than 'RANDSTAD' or 'Randstad', particularly in combination with the logo. Bos also noticed

Designer Ben Bos at his desk.

The new house style was visible everywhere: The photo shows the branch on Kalverstraat, one of the most important shopping streets in Amsterdam.

that both the words 'randstad' and 'uitzendbureau' were beautifully balanced and almost symmetrical in shape: 'randstad uitzendbureau'.

To use Bos's own words, the day of the presentation was "a coming together of the instinctive, artistic world of designers, and that of university-educated business entrepreneurs". He opened his presentation by stating that, "with its new house style, Randstad wishes to establish a clear profile for itself. Randstad is a serious, reliable partner within the business community. The core message is this: Randstad understands the responsibilities it has toward its temporary staff, those who contract their services, its suppliers, and its own people. This logo conveys that very message!" Without further delay, Bos revealed his design.

The elegantly styled 'r' was an instant success and Goldschmeding was extremely enthusiastic. He immediately recognized that this was exactly the house style he had been looking for. His intangible enterprise had become a powerful, recognizable personality, on the street, in mailboxes, on public transit posters, in the phone book, on invoices and at the office's very front door. He now knew for sure that with this, his dream could be turned into reality.

randstad
uitzendbureau

Ben Bos Total Design

randstad
zet 'n hoge (uur-)
prijs
op uw hoofd

randstad 1974
ndstad 1974 ra
stad 1974 rand
ad 1974 randst
1974 randstad

19 70 *This characteristic poster would be remembered as the 'Chinese girl'. The beautiful abstract hairdo gives the woman an Asian appearance. The colorful crown on her head symbolizes the high hourly rate she earns – Randstad flex workers will only earn the best.*

"Good morning, this is Randstad"

No time was lost in implementing the new house style. By now, branches of Randstad could be found not only in the Netherlands but also further afield. In March 1967, the first London branch opened its doors on busy Wigmore Street, a street just off London's main commercial thoroughfare, Oxford Street. Mr. Dilnot, general manager of Randstad Ltd, had managed to find a ground floor, open-fronted office space from which to run the branch. It was the ideal spot for an employment agency: it provided plenty of walk-in trade and was in close proximity to countless other businesses. The telephone never stopped ringing and was always answered by a polite, British voice saying, "Good morning, this is Randstad."

Initially, Goldschmeding had planned to use a different name for their branches in England. 'Randstad' meant nothing to the British and would not be easy to remember, he thought. There was no money for extensive market research, but Dilnot came up with an ingenious idea. He invited Goldschmeding out to a show at a London nightclub, where he had secretly bribed the female announcer. For the sum of 25 pounds, she had agreed to announce after every act that the artist was from "Randstad of Amsterdam". She kept this up for the entire evening and at the end of the show called out to the audience "and where do all tonight's artists come from?" The audience replied in chorus, "From Randstad of Amsterdam!" After that evening, all Goldschmeding's doubts were assuaged for good.

randstad

ganz europäisch
zéér europees
very european
très européen

19 69 *Within ten years, Randstad had established branches in four European countries (the Netherlands, Belgium, the United Kingdom, and Germany). Randstad thus distinguished itself from its Dutch competitors, which remained primarily in Holland. The four Monty-Pythonesque fingers on the poster emphasized this fact: very European.*

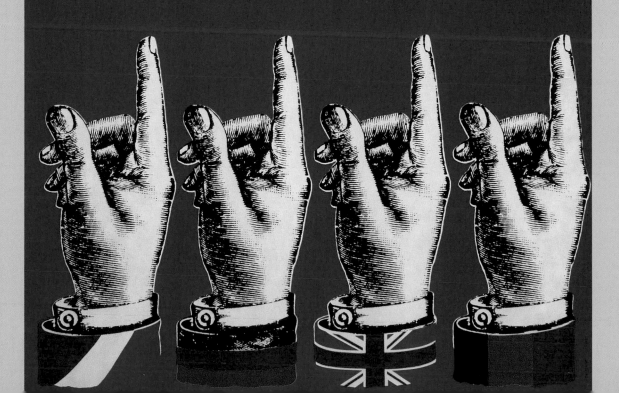

Lily pads

The branch on Wigmore Street was not Randstad's first foreign venture since they had already opened an office in Brussels in 1965. The move had been a logical step in the 'lily pad strategy' used by Randstad with regard to growth: you must fill your first pond with lily pads before you go looking for a new pond. By the mid-1960s, the Dutch 'pond' had become somewhat overcrowded. In those days, temporary staff amounted to just 0.1% of the Dutch labor market. An average-sized city such as Amersfoort had approximately thirty temporary staff to choose from, all of whom were registered at a single employment agency. A simple calculation was enough to convince Goldschmeding that opening more branches outside the main Dutch cities was not a viable proposition. This would only prove cost-effective once more than 1% of the Dutch labor force consisted of temporary staff. It was obviously time to look for new ponds outside the Netherlands.

The Belgian capital of Brussels at that time had a population of over one million, and it already had several employment agencies such as the American Manpower company, Swiss-based Adia, and the Belgian Daoust and Creyf's agencies. These agencies, however, were relatively small,

which left opportunities open for Randstad. If Randstad could gain access to 1% of the working population, it would be a worthwhile venture. They decided to take a chance. Advertising agency Nijgh & Van Ditmar, however, advised them to use a different name in Belgium. They suggested a name that comprised the French words for 'temporary staff' and 'work': Interlabor.

The Brussels branch began its life on the sixth floor of a 29-floor office block on Place Rogier under the direction of Charles Cancelier. He was a born salesman with a reputation for being able to sell ice to Eskimos in wintertime. His way of doing business, however, was rather different to what people were used to in the Netherlands. His favorite way of securing clients was by taking them out to dinner, declaring no less than three hundred restaurant visits in his first year alone. Shocked at the amount, Goldschmeding hastily arranged a meeting with Cancelier, but his concerns were soon dispelled. Over those three hundred dinners, Cancelier had successfully secured 295 clients.

The European economy was growing quickly in the 1960s, and Belgium was no exception. Companies were taking on all the staff they could

in order to expand their capacity, but if growth were to stagnate after 1965, they would end up facing the costly problem of overstaffing. The understanding that companies should not take on too many permanent employees was an excellent development in the Belgian market for the temporary staffing industry. Two years later, with the opening of a second branch in Antwerp, Interlabor was inundated with requests for temporary staff.

Fünf Uhr Tee

With their populations of between 500,000 and one and a half million, cities such as Brussels and Antwerp fitted perfectly into Randstad's lily pad strategy. Moreover, Belgium had several more such cities to choose from. Gradually, however, this 'pond' became overcrowded too. The next logical step was Germany, home to even larger cities, such as Frankfurt, Hamburg, and Düsseldorf.

In 1968, Randstad opened its first branch in Düsseldorf, a branch which specialized in providing temporary administrative, industrial, and technical staff. The international name Interlabor, however, was a problem in Germany. The name had not worked in England because 'labor' sounded like 'labor', as in 'Labor Party'. In German, on the other hand, 'Labor' means 'laboratory', an association that was equally undesirable. Randstad therefore decided to keep its original name for its branches in Germany, and it became Randstad Zeit-Arbeit.

This 'promised land', however, was far from perfect. The German market for temporary employment was highly complicated at the time due to stringent legislation. It was not until mid-1967 that the German high court decided that employment agencies did not violate regulations that prohibited labor mediation. The image of employment agencies remained a problem, however. In those days, people who did not aspire to full time 9-to-5 employment were frowned upon as non-conformists, and this notion carried over to employment agencies who utilized and reinforced these 'non-conformist' preferences. Randstad Zeit-Arbeit was one of the few serious and ambitious employment agencies that tried to maneuver itself around the strict German legislation. In summary, employment agencies were themselves required to employ temporary workers on a permanent basis. Each of these employees had to maintain at least two assignments lasting no more than three months, otherwise the activity would be regarded as agency work. This meant that employment agencies and their branch staff often struggled to meet the stringent requirements.

The man who would deal with this problem for Randstad was Werner Then. He had gained significant relevant experience during his career within the German conservative Christian Democratic Union (CDU) party. His patience would be tested from the day he started at Randstad. When he arrived at the branch in Düsseldorf on June 1st, 1968, he couldn't believe his eyes. The office was completely empty. There was no telephone, no furniture, no typewriter, and the assistant who was expected to come to the office simply had not reported for work. He decided to rent a room at the Düsseldorf Post Office so that he could get to work regardless. He set up an office together with Ger Daleboudt, who, thankfully, had come to Then's rescue from Amsterdam. Without any staff, he had to simultaneously fill the roles of bookkeeper, sales representative, consultant, and director. Some months later he received more support from Randstad in the Netherlands, and in early November he was able to swap his makeshift premises at the post office for a proper office on Graf-Adolf-Strasse.

From that moment on, there was no stopping Then. Not only did he open a branch in Frankfurt a month later, he was also elected president of the German national federation of employment agencies, the Bundesverband Zeitarbeit (BZA). Then was a natural when it came to entertaining people, arranging meetings, and providing information, a trait that helped make his *Fünf Uhr Tee* (German for five o'clock tea) sessions such a huge success. He regularly invited personnel managers from a wide range of companies to join him for a cup of tea and a short talk on some aspect of employment agencies and the concept of temporary work. The talks were always followed with an opportunity to discuss the profession in general. The *Fünf Uhr Tee* was held at the end of the working day and soon attracted an average of one hundred interested personnel managers every time. This was an absolute boon for the brand recognition of Randstad Germany.

randstad

appels voor de dorst

19 71 *In every city, Randstad branches are always situated at prime locations. This allows their display windows to serve as an ideal stage to attract the attention of passers-by. In 1971 this was done in an original way with the poster 'Randstad – Appels voor de dorst' (meaning 'a nest egg').*

In a number of branches, Randstad went even further: white-painted crates were on display there, with real apples inside. A person who could guess the combined weight of all the apples in the crate would be invited for an evening out, at Randstad's expense.

dining their way into the **french market**

Meanwhile, business was flourishing to such an extent in Belgium that in 1970, a second division of Interlabor was set up, Randstad Interim. The time now seemed right to start tapping into the French market. During one of his many business dinners, Charles Cancelier heard about an interesting takeover possibility in France. Through various business connections, he was put in touch with Mme Tridde, owner of the 'Votre Bureau' employment agency, one branch of which was located on the Boulevard de Sébastopol in Paris. In 1973, Randstad decided to take over her office as a way of setting a first modest step onto French soil.

France had recently introduced regulations for the French employment agency industry, which was still a relatively small sector. Before 1972, employment agencies and temporary work had suffered a particularly poor reputation. In fact,

in the 1960s, Philippe Foriel-Destezet, who had founded the Ecco employment agency (later renamed Adecco), faced prosecution for human trafficking. Fortunately, the French government later realized that employment agencies were not comparable to human traffickers, and finally decided to start taking the industry seriously. A law was passed in 1972, allowing employment agencies to operate, albeit under certain conditions.

The Votre Bureau takeover was, in fact, very straightforward for Randstad. Nevertheless, the official transfer was celebrated with typical French grandeur. The Randstad International management team took great pride sitting in the front row for the ceremony which was held at the Hilton Hotel. For that extra touch of class, Mme Triddle had invited a university professor to speak at the ceremony. In his speech, which lasted over an hour, the guest speaker presented a range of

complex management theories, all in highbrow French. For the Dutch guests, whose French was by no means fluent, his speech was quite impossible to follow. The professor's speech was followed by Mme Triddle's fast-spoken account of her role in the business. The management team had barely managed to pick out the words 'Votre Bureau' and 'Randstad' from this verbal waterfall, but when her speech was over, the takeover was complete. The management team looked at each other in amazement. Was this really what they had traveled all the way to Paris for?

Cancelier went on to manage the ten employees of Votre Bureau Randstad. He kept the head office informed of progress by phone, in writing and through meetings with the Internationaal Management Team (IMT), which had been appointed by Randstad in the early 1970s.

breakneck
growth

The bicycle ride that Goldschmeding and Daleboudt had made through Amsterdam that night back in the early 1960s now seemed like a lifetime ago. Within ten years, the plan they had light-heartedly raised their glasses to had grown into a full-fledged company with branches in the Netherlands, Belgium, England, Germany, and, as of 1973, in France. The company's fast growth testified to the entrepreneurial spirit and originality of its founders, and the decision to pursue an individual style demonstrated its strength.

The Randstad brand was now solid as a rock, but in spite of this, the former students were still a world away from where they wanted to be. In 1970, a licensing system was introduced in the Netherlands. That should have been a favorable development, but the requirements that had to be met in order to obtain a license were stringent and shifted constantly. In fact, it was becoming almost impossible to obtain a license. It almost seemed as if the government was using the new law to put employment agencies out of business. All of Randstad's foreign ventures were put on hold, although with the exception of those in Belgium they had been making little profit anyway. Every effort would now be needed to help maintain the position they had managed to establish in the market.

In 1970, a 'Teen and Twen Fair' was organized in Haarlem, and Randstad is represented with a booth. No typewriting contest here, but two race bikes, inviting people to race jointly as fast as they can. The team that made the fastest time, as indicated by the clock behind them, won – in other words, a matter of cooperation!

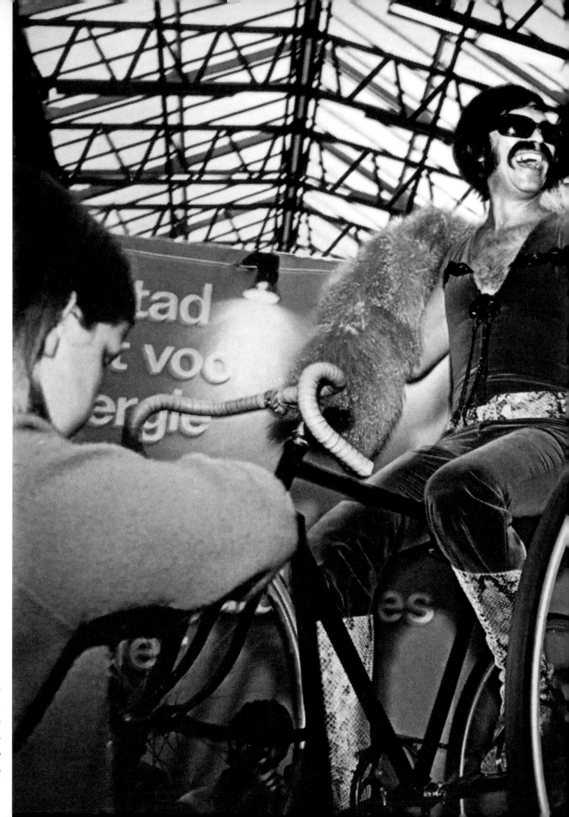

Randstad stories

Workpocket, Henk Janssen
else?, Daniel Aumer 03 the
04 discovery expedition,
the tree and the ballerina,
y Easter, Gemma Parry 07
Czech, Dutch, and English,
ife-changing experience,
s money, Laurent Herzog
solidarity, Tracy Robinson

I just get the Workpocket every year!

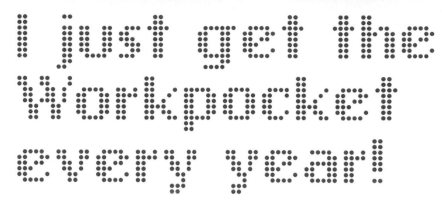

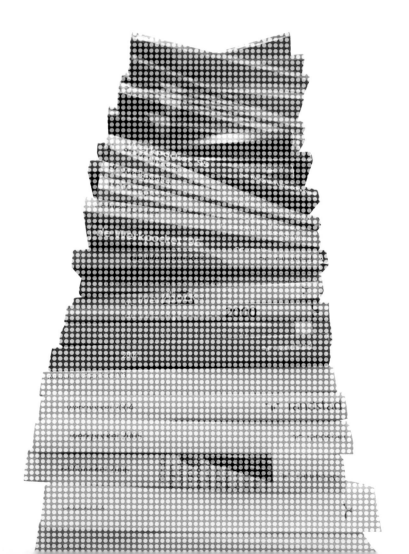

the success of the Workpocket

In 1978, Randstad came under attack from trade unions and the government. It was claimed that flexworkers were making a living at the expense of other people's salaries, and occupying jobs that ought to be filled by permanent staff. Rob Overwater, who was head of advertising at the time, took this unjust criticism very seriously. In order to prevent misunderstandings and untruths, Randstad would have to beat the drum a little harder, and in order to demonstrate its expertise on the labor market it would have to become a real authority. Overwater decided to publish a 'Workpocket', a paperback book in which labor legislation was explained in layman's terms. The first edition was published in 1978 and distributed free of charge to employers, trade unions, flexworkers and staff.

Thirty-two years later, the Workpocket is still one of the cornerstones of that great authority on the labor market: Randstad. Henk Janssen had the following to say about it: "I recently attended a meeting of the SEU, the Dutch foundation for staffing industry examinations. A board member of the NBBU, an employers' trade union and rival of ABU, the Dutch association of temporary work agencies, said to me 'Why should I spend time updating my knowledge? All I have to do is get a copy of the new Randstad Workpocket once a year, read it through a couple of times and I'm fully informed. I can recommend it to everyone!' Now who could ask for better proof that Randstad really is a great authority on the labor market?"

Henk Janssen – Former director of personnel at Tempo-Team; he also held various positions at Randstad (including Randstad Holding and director of Randstad Portugal), the Netherlands

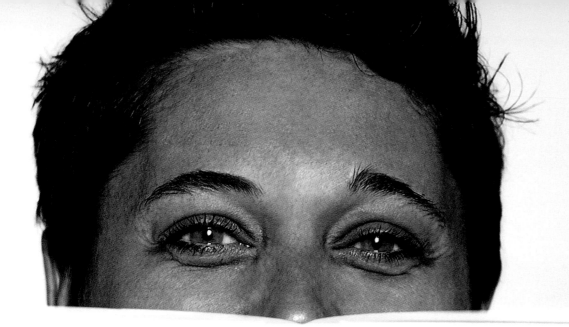

werkpocket
2010

FanZone BERN
FanZone BERN
CURIA CONFOEDERATIO
HOLLAND
FRANCE

Randstad. What else?

Switzerland is the home base of food giant Nestlé. Hundreds of Randstad temporary workers produce Cailler chocolate and trendy Nespresso capsules on a daily basis. Daniel Aumer describes how the paths of the two companies intersected.

"Orange is the national color of the Netherlands, and while the entire city of Bern was slowly turning orange due to the European soccer championships, the Swiss staffing industry was turning just as bright a shade of the color. Together with Vedior, Randstad became the second-largest staffing company in Switzerland and also a stronger business for its major clients. Having worked with Adecco for many years, Nestlé was looking for a new HR partner, and that is how the opportunity came knocking on our door. An excellent reference from Philip Morris, for whom we had achieved great success using our inhouse concept, pulled them over. Obviously, we were really pleased to have a client like Nestlé and we have since become experts in the field of chocolate and espresso! Nowadays, whenever I see George Clooney on television I think 'Randstad. What else?'"

Daniel Aumer – Process and ICT manager Randstad, Switzerland

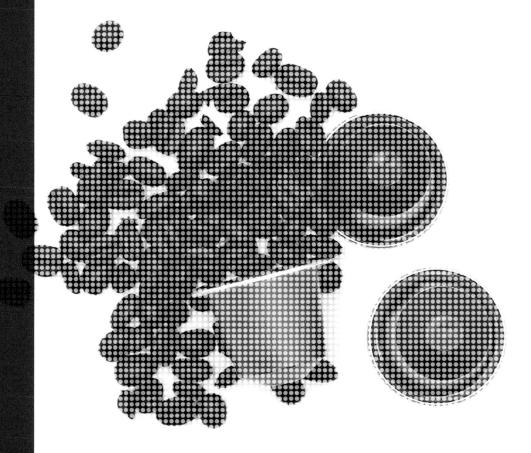

that's what I call freedom

the calling

It would make a lot of people nervous, but flexworker Alain Hus never knows what kind of goods he will be transporting until the Monday of any particular week. He doesn't mind. In fact, he made a conscious choice to work on a flexible basis. Freedom has always been more important to him than security. Hus started doing temporary work in France when it was still a relatively unknown. He always worked as a truck driver around Paris; now he gets weekly contracts through Randstad, and every week is different. Clients approach him for a wide variety of trips and freights, so his work is never dull. That's just how he likes it. In that respect, he considers flexible work to be 'a calling'. That may sound a little pompous, but he means it most sincerely.

As a family man, his weekends are sacrosanct; Randstad knows that, and Hus is never called for work in the weekend. "That is what I call freedom," Hus smiles. "And there is another benefit to being a flexworker. Clients are more likely to provide their permanent staff with relatively poor materials than they would an external worker. If they did that, they'd know they should expect an angry phone call from Randstad."

Alain Hus (not in image) – Flexworker Randstad, France

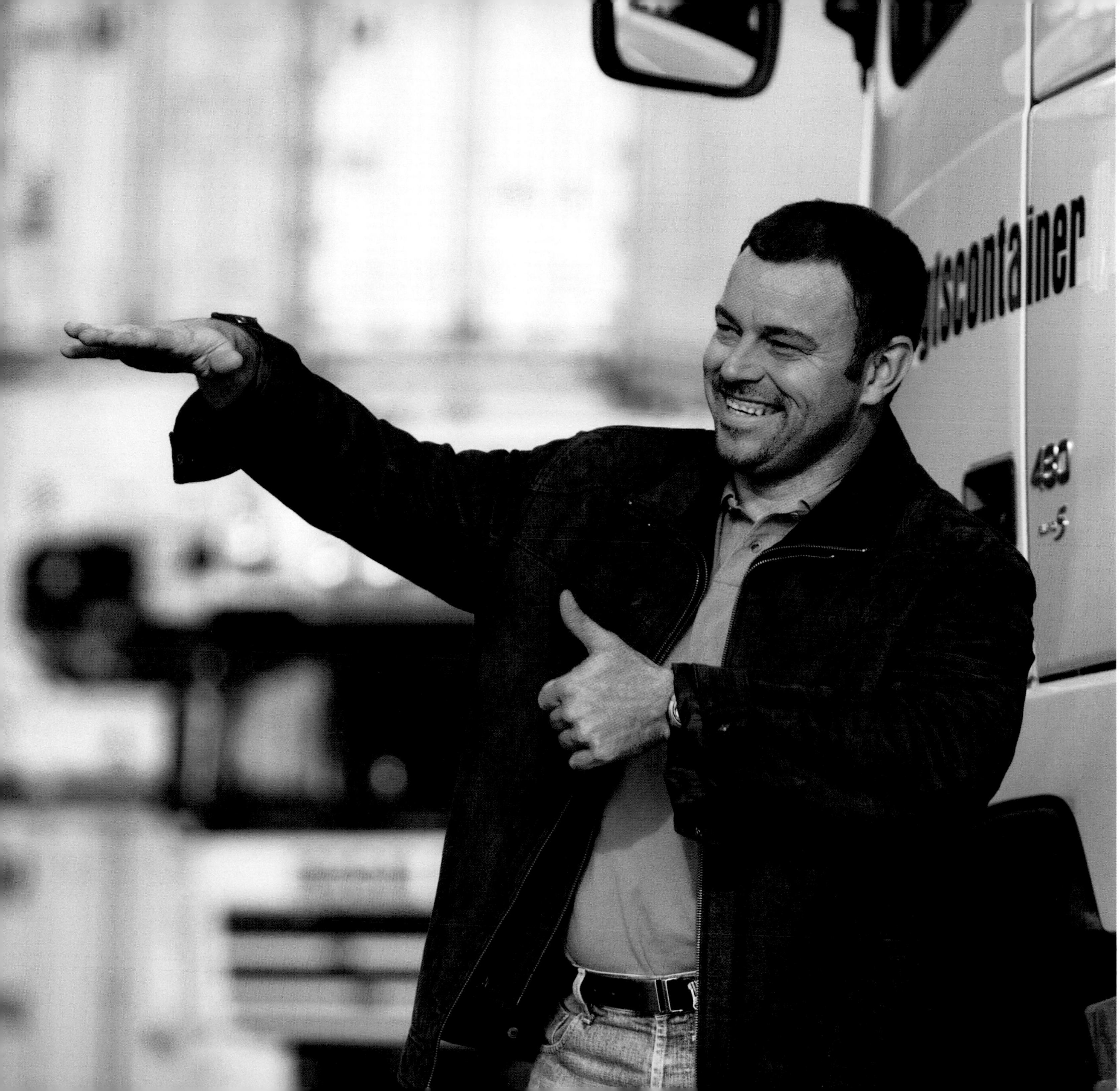

04

discovery expedition

On the 8th of April 2009, the Clipper Stad Amsterdam was anchored for a few days below the impressive skyscrapers on Rowe's Wharf in Boston. Visitors on board included an enthusiastic group of YMCA multicultural teen achievers, who had been invited by Randstad. Eileen Habelow, Randstad USA's specialist for organizational development, welcomed the young people on board.

"They knew there would be career activities on board, but they were mightily surprised to find out that the boat they'd visit would be such a magnificent Victorian-era clipper. After arriving on board they followed training sessions about resumé writing, networking, and business etiquette. After an exquisite lunch, captain Cosmo Wassenaar gave them a tour of the ship, and the Clipper proved itself again as excellent publicity for Randstad: these talented young people are not likely to forget the name of our company any time soon!"

Eileen Habelow (far right) – Senior vice president of organizational development Randstad, USA

I was welcomed with open arms

the tree and the ballerina

What's in a name? Tugba, staffing consultant in Utrecht, told us: "My name is Turkish for 'a tree in heaven'. It's also how I see myself, as a tree that people can lean on, whom they can trust." Tugba specializes in catering. "The work is just perfect for students and people who to want to work part-time. They begin late, around half past ten in the morning, and finish early in the afternoon, after lunch. Take Fleur, for instance. Fleur has not been with us for long, but you could place her anywhere; she has such a pleasant manner!"

Fleur is a ballerina, but having completed a costly dance training program on Broadway, her funds were exhausted. She has already found a job, but it will not start for a couple of months. Fleur told us: "I needed something to bridge the gap, so I went to Randstad. Tugba welcomed me with open arms and was able to find something for me straight away. Catering is flexible work that can sometimes take a turn for the unexpected… Some time ago, I was serving coffee to a couple of men in smart suits. They asked me what I did and I told them I was a dancer. As it turned out, one of the men knew Joop van den Ende's stage manager and he suggested I send them my CV. Guess what? I've got an audition coming up for the musical *Tarzan!*"

Tugba (left) – Staffing consultant Randstad, the Netherlands
Fleur – Flexworker Randstad, the Netherlands

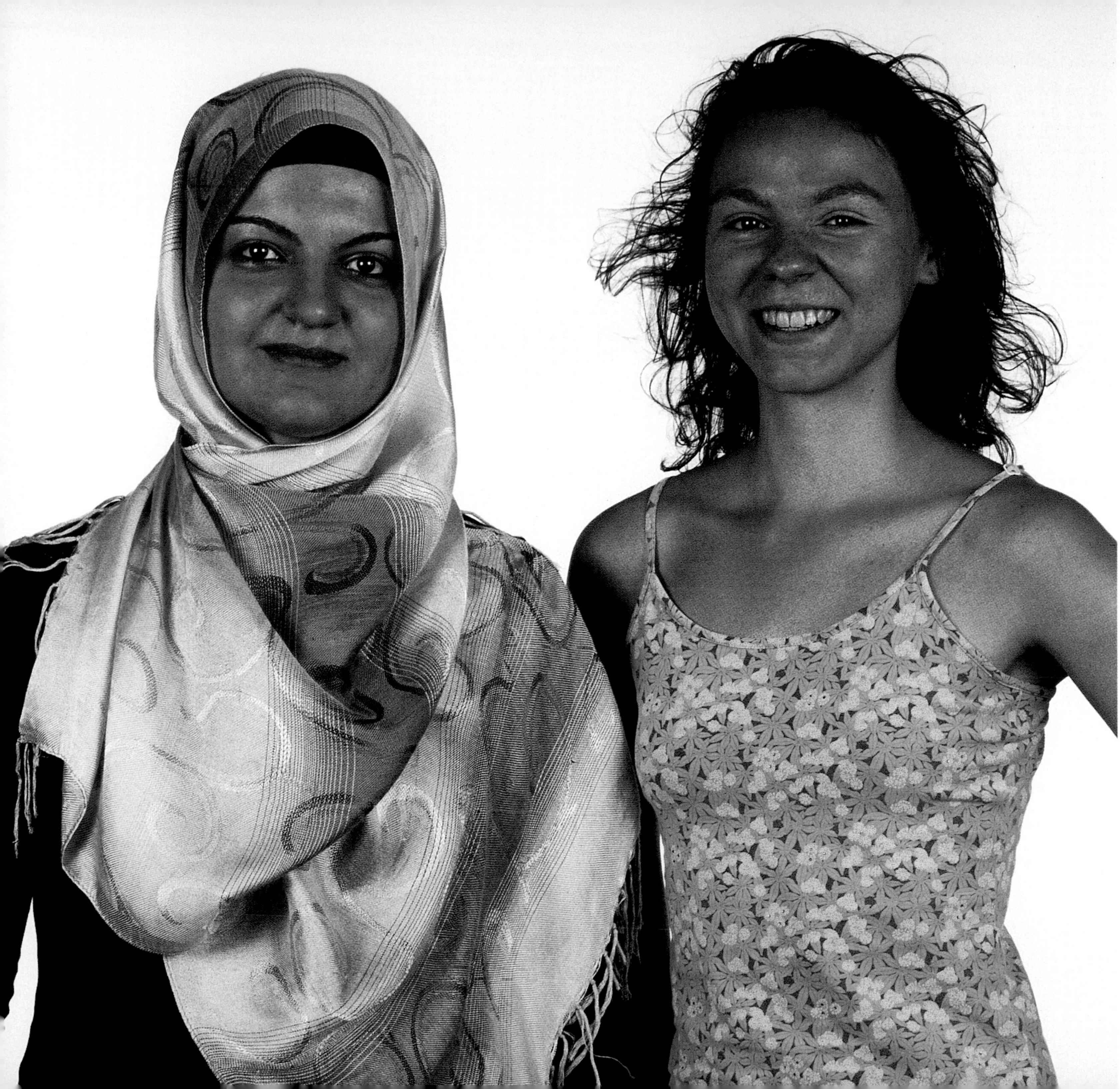

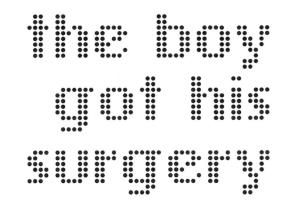

the boy got his surgery

happy Easter

"Randstad is not just any old staffing agency that happens to have an office in Swindon. We are deeply rooted in the local community," says Gemma Parry. "A few years ago I read in the local paper about a fundraiser for a child with a severe disease. If he did not get surgery by a specialist in the US, he was certain to die. The boy's parents could not afford that kind of surgery, though. So we, as an office, decided to participate in the fundraiser. It was around Easter, so we set up an Easter egg hunt. Our clients donated significant amounts and nice lottery prizes, and on the day of the egg hunt, children searched the meadows around Swindon for Easter eggs, while their parents participated in the raffle. All together we collected more than 10,000 pounds (11,500 euros) that day. With Randstad's help, the boy got his surgery – truly a happy Easter!"

Gemma Parry (left) – Branch manager Randstad Staffing Solutions, United Kingdom

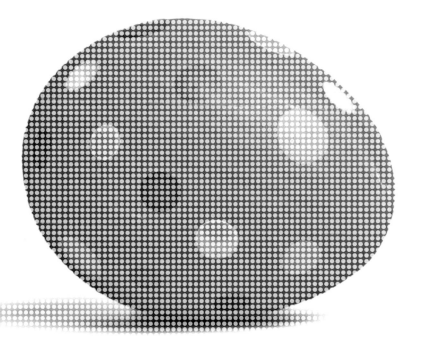

dedication to clients and flexworkers

87

wanted: m/f speaking Czech, Dutch, and English

Lucie Bláhová is a staffing consultant at a branch in downtown Prague. Shortly after the merger of Randstad with Vedior, she was approached by the Dutch embassy in the Czech Republic with what might have been an impossible assignment: "Find us candidates who speak Dutch and English, as well as Czech."

"This is a rare language combination; there are only few people who speak all these languages. But I took the rarity of the request as a challenge. I used all possible channels to find candidates: ads, networks, and international associations. And what did I find? That the ties between the Czech and the Dutch people have existed for centuries, and that quite a few Czechs have studied the Dutch language. Some of these people responded to the ad. But then, not speaking a word of Dutch myself, I had to test whether their Dutch skills were sufficient. I decided to use an article of which I had a Czech as well as a Dutch version. With my Czech version in hand, I gave the candidates questions about the Dutch text. This worked very well, The candidates that I sent to the embassy are still working there today."

Lucie Bláhová – Staffing consultant Randstad, Czech Republic

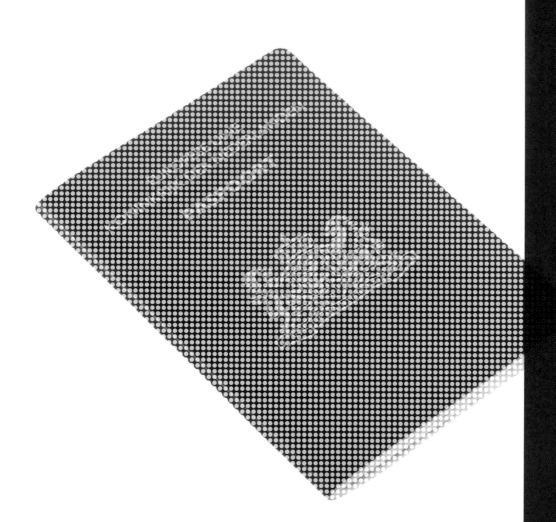

a life-changing experience

In 2006, Meghan Faith had just started working for Randstad when she heard of its partnership with Voluntary Service Overseas (VSO). Faith, who loves to travel and experience other cultures, was immediately enthusiastic and wanted to have a life-changing experience. "Getting accepted was not that easy. First, Randstad recommended me to VSO, and then there was an assessment followed by various interviews."

Faith was found suitable and was offered a place in Phnom Penh, Cambodia. "From March to August 2009, I worked as a marketing consultant for a healthcare training magazine. The knowledge and experience I had gained at Randstad were extremely useful to the organization. I built a database for them and improved their capital and client marketing strategy. I think I can safely say that the project was a success. Before I started they could only fund one magazine in advance – by the time I left they could fund four!"

"There are enormous differences between Cambodia and the United States of America. Compared with Americans, the Cambodians are immensely happy and hospitable people, even though they have practically nothing. They just love life, and take time to enjoy food, family and the simple pleasures life has to offer. This made me understand how incredibly important the balance between work and leisure is, and that sometimes you just have to get back to basics and take a good look at the way you live your life."

Meghan Faith (middle) – Staffing consultant Randstad, USA

they love life as it comes

a triple win!

time is money

"I am always on the lookout for things that might improve the production process of our client Mars. We have a branch at the Mars chocolate factory where we are optimally positioned to monitor the process. This sometimes allows us to contribute to its improvement."

"An example: a Mars technician used to have to come down to the production line about once every hour to replace a roll of adhesive tape. Flexworkers were not allowed to do that themselves. There had to be a different way of handling that! We made arrangements with Mars that allowed our workers to replace the wheel themselves. Instead of two minutes of waiting time plus one minute of roll replacement time, the employees could now do it themselves. Production was now halted for one minute only. The technician saved 24 working minutes per day, and moreover, the employee was paid for the wheel replacement. Production interruption was reduced from 24 minutes daily to just eight. It was a triple win for the client. This improvement contributed significantly to a total saving of 4% of the turnover!"

Laurent Herzog – Process manager Randstad Inhouse Services, France

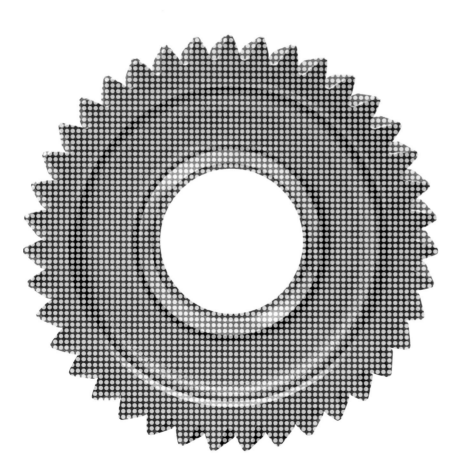

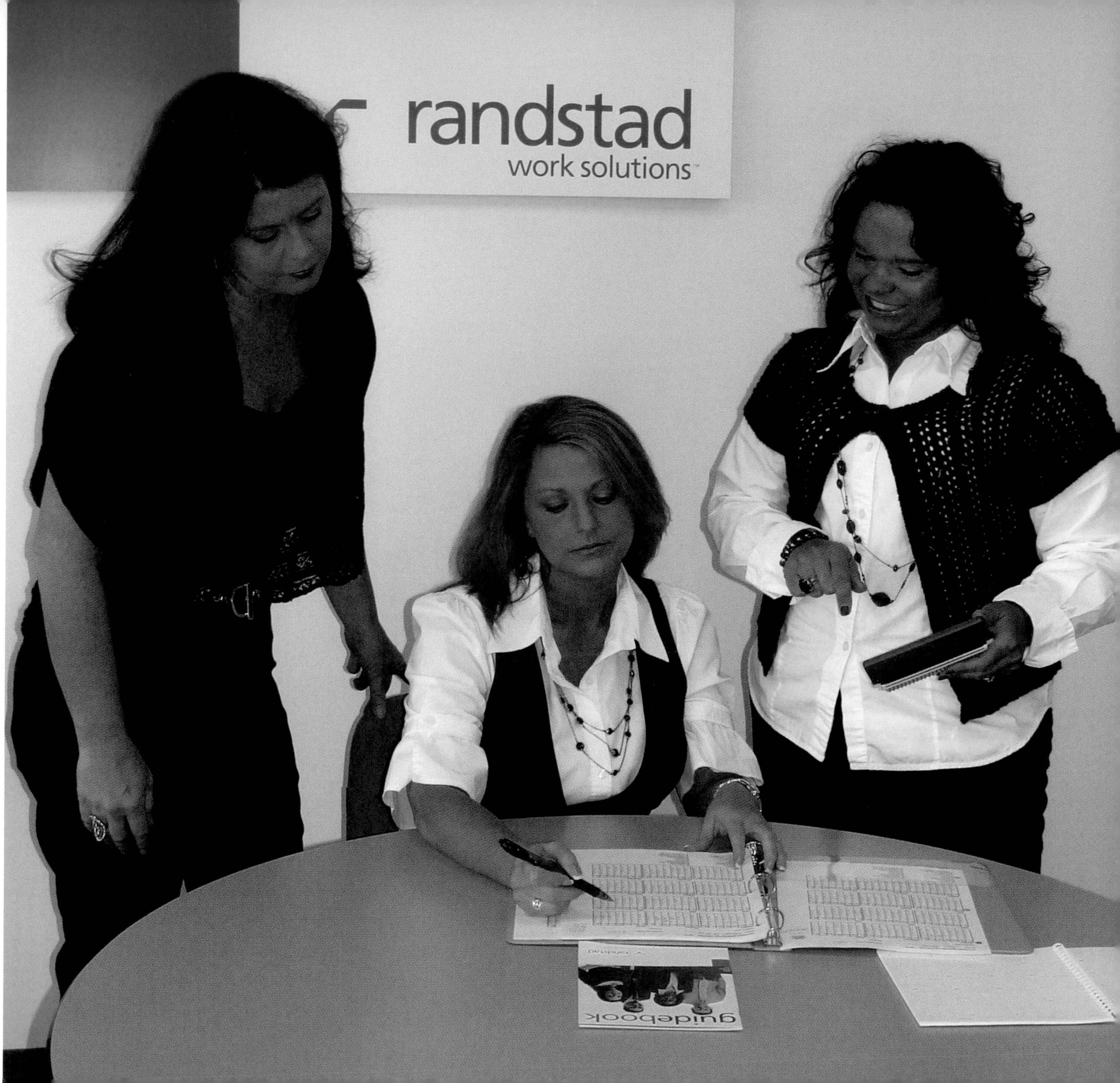
randstad
work solutions
guidebook

10

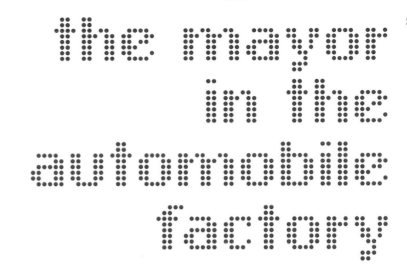

solidarity

Everyone thought that General Motors, the largest car producer in the world, was too big to fail. And yet, the unthinkable happened. In the summer of 2009, General Motors went bankrupt. Since then, a leaner version of the company has been kept alive by the US government. One of GM's production plants was in Spring Hill, Tennessee, population 23,000. At the last moment, Tracy Robinson, branch manager of Randstad Spring Hill, placed a very special flex worker at the production plant.

"When our mayor Michael Dinwiddie heard that this plant was to be closed as well, he signed up as a flex worker with Randstad. He wanted to save whatever could be saved for the three thousand Spring Hill citizens employed by the plant. Dinwiddie said that if the plant was to go down, they'd all go down together, and he joined his fellow citizens as they assembled three hundred final Chevrolet Traverse car doors."

"It was a noble gesture of solidarity with his fellow citizens, but to no avail: the plant was closed in spite of everything. However, signals have been received that the Spring Hill plant might become operational again!"

Tracy Robinson (right) – Senior branch manager Randstad, USA

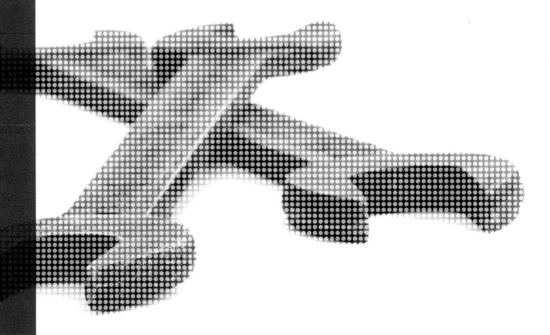

striving
for recognition

In the nineteen-seventies, there was strong resistance to the phenomenon of temporary employment. In the Netherlands, Randstad took the challenge head-on, and struggled tirelessly for recognition. Publicity was sought in order to refute the criticism of temporary employment. The company was inspired to develop a corporate philosophy which took into account all members of society: 'to know, to serve, to trust', simultaneous management of interests, and the striving for perfection.

the bank

The impressive entrance of the AMRO Bank in Amsterdam.

One Friday afternoon in early 1970, Goldschmeding reluctantly made his way towards the imposing AMRO Bank office building on Amsterdam's Herengracht. The closer he got, the more he noticed how austere the building's architecture was. The high windows, dark brick walls and heavy doors were obviously intended to overwhelm. As he reached the marble entrance, he hesitated. He had an appointment with a certain Mr. Vogelenzang, the youngest member of the bank's Board of Directors. Randstad's growth between 1966 and 1970 resulted in their bank balance now being significantly in the red. Herman Kolk, who had been Randstad's financial person since 1965, calculated that the company needed no less than EUR 1 million of credit in order to keep growing. The decision to lend such a phenomenal amount required the approval of a board member.

Goldschmeding was escorted into a large room in which the three bankers were sitting at an enormous conference table. Vogelenzang, as well as the head of the bank's Credit Department and Randstad's general contact person. Positioned in the center of the table was an unsigned contract. Vogelenzang spoke first, "Mr. Goldschmeding, I have received a number of documents from you and I understand what it is that you require. Your plans are impressive, but we do not wish to cooperate in your venture." Goldschmeding remained calm and said, "Let me tell you about our business." He proceeded to tell them how diligently their

The two directors of Randstad in the beginning of the nineteen-seventies: Frits Goldschmeding (left) and Ger Daleboudt (right).

staffing consultants worked to make the right match between clients and staffing employees, and how much money was involved in the process. He also emphasized the fact that the company had always managed to meet every requirement and that great opportunities now lay ahead of them. The bank manager was so impressed with his client's enthusiastic account that he finally said, "Mr. Goldschmeding, I am prepared to give you the credit you have asked for, but only on the condition that you achieve a 2% higher gross margin, otherwise you will be unable to repay the credit in time."

With that, Vogelenzang signed the contract and wished Goldschmeding good-day. The Credit Department supervisor muttered something about an audit having to be conducted and the whole thing being highly unorthodox, but the bank manager paid no attention. Randstad had always been a good customer *and* one that had doubled its sales since it began. And after such an inspiring story he had every confidence that it would continue doing so... Goldschmeding left the building with a sigh of relief, knowing that with this new line of credit, the company could now continue to grow.

The first computer used by Randstad.

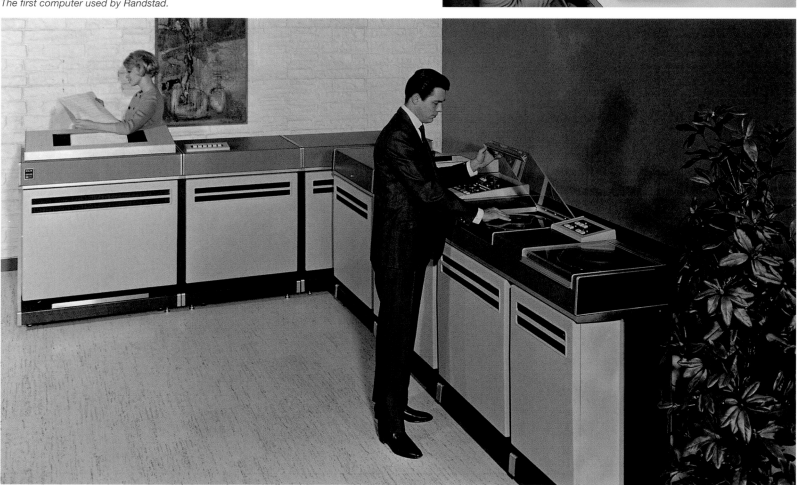

water and fire

A.B. Raven (left), Director for Employment Relations at the Dutch Ministry of Social Affairs, made life difficult for Randstad and other staffing agencies in the 1970s with a string of restrictive regulations. On the right of Raven is Minister Veldkamp of Social Affairs.

This financial leeway also made it possible for the company to move into a new head office on A.J. Ernststraat in Amsterdam in 1970. Time sheets from every branch came rolling in every week. The first real computer, which took up as much space as a large conference room, was installed to process the financial data. Internally, everything was running smoothly. It was the outside world that now demanded attention.

In the 1970s, employment agencies such as Randstad, ASB, Manpower, Evro and Tempo-Team fulfilled a growing need in the Dutch market, but not everyone was happy with the situation. Employment agencies still suffered from a poor image, one that was unlikely to change in the foreseeable future. Unions and left-wing political parties thought that the government should play a commanding role in the labor market, and that included labor mediation. The unions were of the opinion that agency-supplied workers were not entitled to any rights, and they were afraid that temporary employees would end up earning more than permanent staff. Moreover, they worried that employers would start taking on temporary rather than permanent staff. Randstad, on the other hand, believed they were helping people find work, people who would otherwise be unemployed. In other words, employment agencies were actually helping to create extra jobs.

The Dutch unions maintained the view that labor mediation for profit had to be abolished. This vision, however was, entirely at odds with the essence of employment agencies. Another problem of the unions was the perception that employment agencies only

1978 *After two years of discussions and an exploratory visit to Paris and London, Randstad decided on a different recruitment model. 'The nostalgic girl', which is what this poster was called, connected with young fashionable women in the bigger cities. Her clothes and appearance are reminiscent of the nineteen-twenties. This poster earned Randstad's US advertising agency, J. Walter Thompson, a first prize in the Netherlands, and later even a worldwide prize.*

The 'Staffing Complaints Agency' warns employees not to fall for the temptations of working with staffing agencies. According to critics of the staffing agency employment model, an employee would not be 'free as a bird', but unprotected. Posters like these are indicative of the stormy waters which Randstad had to navigate in the nineteen-seventies.

recruited young and other 'readily placeable' workers. Furthermore, it was assumed that agency-supplied workers were always given dirty, boring or heavy, assembly-line jobs. The unions regarded employment agencies as an alternative for overly naïve job-seekers, and an employment agency helpdesk was even set up for staffing employees with problems or questions.

The Dutch Ministry of Social Affairs also had great difficulty in accepting the concept of employment agencies. This hard-line stance was personified in labor relations manager and lawyer A.B. Raven, who was responsible for implementing and sanctioning regulations. Raven believed unconditionally that society could be engineered using regulations as a tool. The ministry therefore attempted to nip the growth of temporary employment in the bud by introducing a strict licensing system that would prohibit the further growth of employment agencies. Employment agencies were kept under scrutiny by being required to provide the ministry with regular details about their work activities. For every agency-supplied worker who was to be employed for over three months, agencies were required to report to the ministry, after which permission to continue was sometimes given – and sometimes not. The same procedure applied in order to extend a working period for up to six months. Moreover, temporary employees were not allowed to earn more than permanent staff at the client company. An unintentional effect of these low fees was that the demand for temporary employees subsequently soared.

Randstad was required to comply with the system, but tried every way it could to get out of it. With the help of the ABU (the Dutch association of temporary work agencies), a total of 22 cases relating to the license regulations were taken to court. Led by 'temp lawyer' Maarten van der Woude, some cases were even brought before the Council of State (an advisory body to the Government and Parliament on legislation as well as the highest administrative court in The Netherlands). The opposition efforts against the licensing were successful and the challenged ban on growth was lifted. In its place, Raven introduced conditions regarding the maximum permissible staffing period: staff had to report back after three months, upon which permission would be granted for an extension until further notice, up to a maximum of six months. The maximum period would later be (further) reduced to three months, with even periods as short as six weeks being considered. The fight against Raven and the policy he represented was regarded within Randstad as a fight for its very survival, and it resulted in an unprecedented feeling of solidarity both internally and externally.

the **tide** turns

Goldschmeding was not the kind of man to sit back and watch Randstad be driven into a corner. He developed a carefully crafted strategy based around a simple card index. Every contact, valuable or otherwise, had its own index card, and the first card under the letter 'R' was…. Raven!

The card index started to fill up quickly. Now and again, Goldschmeding would sift through the cards for his adversaries: the Dutch trade union federation FNV, various gangmasters, the Dutch young catholic workers' association KWJ, the Ministry of Social Affairs and Employment, the socialist and radical parties (PSP and PPR respectively), the Dutch Labor Party (PvdA), Raven himself, various unions… After every conversation Goldschmeding made a note of what had been discussed and what had been said. If, for example, someone told him about their son who had broken a leg while skiing, Goldschmeding would note this on the card. The next time they met, he would sympathetically inquire about their son's injury. The card index was more than just a collection of personal anecdotes, of course. Goldschmeding knew precisely who held a grudge against whom, and who thought what about various politicians. If he then happened to meet the person in question, he would ask, "Did you hear what so-and-so said about such-and-such?" Goldschmeding was becoming a true strategist.

Behind the cards for opponents were the cards for Randstad's many supporters. One of these cards he had marked with a star, that of the association of temporary work agencies ABU, of which Randstad had been a member for several years. This trade association was a true band of brothers with whom Randstad was putting up a fight against Raven, the unions and other adversaries. The Board of Directors consisted of Chairman Wim Ruggenberg, a strong character who would not be pushed around, Vice Chairman Frits Goldschmeding himself, and the pragmatist Bert Beugelsdijk. They were assisted by General Secretary and true intellectual Wim Garritsen, and a shrewd legal adviser, Maarten van der Woude. Under Ruggenberg's supervision, the ABU launched a fervent and lasting campaign to create a better image for reputable employment agencies. Goldschmeding also played an important role within the ABU as its Vice Chairman and as representative of one of the largest employment agencies in the Netherlands. In 1971, he and Van der Woude began negotiations with the Christian administrative staff unions HBV and BVA, and with Mercurius, a trade union affiliated with the Dutch Association of Trade Unions (NVV).

Now that the unions had strength in numbers, they were determined to use this collective position to their best advantage. They demanded that a collective employment agreement be introduced for all temporary administrative sector employees, and that temporary workers would no longer be required to sign a non-competition clause in employment contracts, making it easier for an employee to leave one company and start working for another. Goldschmeding and Van der Woude were surprised at these demands; the rate of unionization among agency-supplied employees was just 0.1 to 0.5 percent, quite low considering the demands being made. A collective bargaining agreement, however, would give employment agencies the opportunity to enhance their

met
randstad
in zee

circa 1970 *'Dive into a Randstad opportunity', is the inviting tone of this poster. Rippling waves adorn the display window with a maritime appearance, meant to attract potential employees who might sign up as staffers. Like the 'nest egg' poster, 'Dive into a Randstad opportunity' was another example of the high quality design of the Randstad posters.*

Towards the end of the nineteen-seventies, Frits Goldschmeding and Wim Ruggenberg (ABU) hosted Chris van Veen, the chairman of the VNO, the Dutch entrepreneurs association. He is often considered the founder of the Dutch polder model, the form of cooperation between workers unions and employers which would eventually lead to the Flex Agreement.

image and the public's perception of them. So, after careful consideration, they decided to accept the demands, much to the surprise of the trade unions, who had not expected them to be so reasonable and obliging. Van der Woude worked through the night, and the following day, on December 1, 1971, the very first collective labor agreement for the staffing sector was ready for use. The ice was beginning to break on the trade union front, and in early 1972, they signed the agreement. Even the Ministry of Social Affairs and Employment was beginning to accept the idea of employment agencies. A year later, the ministry reluctantly declared the 1973 collective labor agreement applicable throughout the entire staffing sector. It was the first step towards recognition.

These developments were not unique to the Netherlands. The staffing sector was also surrounded by suspicion and rejection in other countries in which Randstad operated. For this reason, reputable agencies had joined forces in 1967 and formed the CIETT, an international trade organization promoting and representing the joint interests of employment agencies worldwide. Slowly but surely, society began to see employment agencies in a different light. In 1972 in France, for example, the first regulations were written that would put an end to the tinge of illicitness associated with temporary employment. The first branch opened by Randstad in France in 1973 was fully legal in every way.

That same year in Belgium, the government still considered temporary work to be a form of labor mediation and therefore wanted it prohibited. The government collapsed, however, before it was able to pass legislation. The subsequent government had less radical ideas about temporary employment, and in 1976, a provisional law was adopted in which it was assumed that the employment agencies would gradually be replaced by public agencies. In 1978, despite having gained a combined market share of 24.1 percent in Belgium, the future of Randstad and Interlabor was still uncertain. Fortunately, things are often not as bad as they seem. Initially, the share of temporary employment, which at the time was affiliated with public labor mediation, grew steadily and reached a maximum market share of thirty percent of public and private agencies by the mid-eighties. This share, however, dropped quickly due to complaints from private employment agencies about the government's bias in favor of their own public placement agencies.

In Germany, general opinion on temporary work remained unfavorable. The unions were also negative – outright hostile, in fact – and governments expected that employment agencies like Randstad would play no more than a minor role in the future. The situation in England was entirely different. Permanent employment was not held in high esteem as much as it was on the continent, and flexible contracts were therefore perceived quite differently. This did not mean, however, that Randstad had an easy time in England. The country was known at the time as 'The Sick Man of Europe', paralyzed as it was by massive strikes and its outdated, costly industries. Randstad described the English market simply as 'difficult'.

the in-house **psychologist**

One late afternoon, a middle-aged man walked along the deserted Oranje Nassaulaan in Amsterdam. Every time he approached what he thought was a business located in one of the elegant houses, he pulled a leaflet from his bag and put it in the mailbox. When he reached number 7, he hesitated; a sleek BMW and a Jaguar were parked right outside. "They must be doing well" the man observed with a smile and pushed one of his leaflets through the mailbox. He continued doing this until he reached the end of the street and disappeared around the corner.

The man was a Mr. Hammelburg, a psychologist who was using the leaflets to promote his corporate psychology practice. It had been a remarkable career switch for a man who had trained to be a rabbi and devoted his youth to the Torah and Talmud. But his calling turned out to be elsewhere, and when his faith began to dwindle, Hammelburg turned his attention to psychology. He became an occupational psychologist more or less by accident; he had planned to go into child psychology. He did not consider himself robust enough to be an occupational psychologist. In his view, most of them were "con men who drove Maseratis". Hammelburg had opened his first practice in 1948 in Hilversum before moving to Amsterdam three years later.

Perhaps it was due to the similarity between Hammelburg's tactics and the way Goldschmeding and Daleboudt had first advertised their services that made them decide to call the number on that leaflet. When Hammelburg answered, Daleboudt explained that he wanted a number of candidates to undergo psychological tests to see if they would make suitable employees.

Randstad now wanted to be certain of the quality of their staff, as did all good service providers, so Daleboudt carried out an experiment. He sent the occupational psychologist five consultants who were already employed by Randstad; two of whom performed well, one who was average, and two whose work was below par. Hammelburg tested the candidates and indicated the two who would be suitable for Randstad; the very two who were already performing well. When Daleboudt admitted that the test had been rigged, the psychologist calmly replied, "no problem, I am confident in my work." Randstad needed no further persuading, and Mr. Hammelburg was informally appointed as its in-house psychologist.

"The leaflet worked", Hammelburg told his wife enthusiastically. It was 9 a.m. on a beautiful spring morning as he sat in his office on Amsterdam's Prinsengracht Canal. Two candidates would be arriving shortly from his new client, Randstad Uitzendbureau. His wife, also a qualified psychologist, was downstairs in the kitchen making coffee. Her job was to gain a first impression of each candidate as she let them in, carefully noting whether they were polite, condescending, nervous, etc. The session was to begin from the very moment they stepped over the threshold, and at nine o' clock exactly, his wife showed the first candidate in. "A bright young man", Hammelburg noted in his report. "Good morning and welcome", he began. He sized up the candidate

je zit goed bij randstad

uitzendkrachten hebben rechten
vraag de CAO of arbeidsvoorwaarden–regeling

19 77 *There are very few situations that are as cozy as a purring cat curled up on her favorite chair. That was what Ben Bos thought when he designed this poster. This poster expresses nicely how well flex workers are treated by Randstad: nice jobs, good pay, and social security too. If you're treated that well as a flex worker, why leave? The cat knows the answer: she stays where she is.*

gentlemen together

as he filled his pipe. Three minutes passed without a single word being exchanged. Hammelburg tried, in vain, to light his pipe upon which his guest offered him a match. "Thank you" Hammelburg said, blue smoke curling lazily from his pipe. He leaned back contentedly and asked "So you'd like to work for Randstad, would you?" The candidate's face lit up, "Yes, I'd love to." Hammelburg continued: "let us take a look at your credentials and your résumé, always assuming you have not left them at home in your parent's safe." "No, I have them here in my briefcase. Here is my college diploma…"

Hammelburg went on to discuss the candidate's career, asking questions, listening carefully to the answers, and now and then looking deep into this eyes. Finally, he brought out the traditional Rorschach test, a psychological personality test in which subjects are asked to describe what they see in haphazard ink blots. The test is based on the principle that what individuals see represents their psychological state of mind. It didn't, however, reveal much about this candidate; he saw a butterfly in every ink blot. Hammelburg wrote, "honest young man, probably a little naïve, cooperative. Test outcome: positive."

Randstad had opted for a psychologist who used unorthodox methods. The merits of the Rorschach test, for example, were much disputed among psychologists. As far as Randstad was concerned, however, Hammelburg's methods worked just fine. Every time Goldschmeding had doubts about a candidate, Hammelburg's analysis proved to be correct; the candidate was indeed unsuitable for Randstad. With his accurate analyses, the occupational psychologist achieved a position of great authority within the company. He assessed every new employee to see if they possessed the required combination of a service-oriented character and a commercial approach. In fact, Hammelburg had created a blueprint for the ideal Randstad personality.

It was time that Hammelburg put his methods to the test where higher management positions were concerned. One of the first people to be interviewed was Frits Drost, who applied for a position in 1970. He was a lawyer but also worked as management assistant for a publishing company. Now he was looking for something new. A newspaper advertisement for the position of personnel manager at Randstad Uitzendbureau had caught his eye. "An employment agency…hmm." Drost had some doubts but decided to apply nevertheless; a company with such a professional marketing presence couldn't be all bad.

He was accepted for the position on the premise that 'a good lawyer will always be handy to have around.' Drost was soon given an important task. A portion of the profits that Randstad made in the year 1971 was reserved for attracting new

*Frits Drost was involved with policy-
making at the Randstad Group for three
decades, during which he occupied
various management positions.*

management staff. This was part of a plan to open new branches throughout the Netherlands, and in so doing, approach sales in a more structured fashion. Until then, with the exception of branch supervisors, Goldschmeding had been juggling all of Randstad's management plates single-handedly. So far, branches had been opened in the urbanized Randstad area itself, in Belgium, Germany, and the United Kingdom. In order to set up branches in the south, east and north of the Netherlands, Randstad would need to find fifteen new managers with excellent pioneering qualities.

Drost was assigned the task of finding them, and Hammelburg would subsequently test them. Randstad placed an advertisement in all the national newspapers; it read, 'wanted: regional or branch managers to supervise three to five offices'. Drost got to work immediately. In the period between 1971 and 1973, fourteen new managers started their career with Randstad: Eef Puyk, Rob Schlichter, Coen Hommel, David van Gelder, Fred Farber, Wil Kitslaar, Jan Bosch, Peter Remmelts, Henk Verbeek, Jan de Wit, Gerard Groeneveld, Jos Ottes, Rob Overwater and Cees Schildkamp. The new managers initially worked under the supervision of district managers Gerard Bloos, Fons Roebroek and Walter de Hart, but as time progressed, the workload became too heavy for them and the managers were instructed to report back to Frits Drost, who was now director of operations. When the workload became unmanageable for him too, he received backup from David van Gelder, Peter Remmelts, and Gerard Groeneveld.

The new management team helped make Randstad's position in the Netherlands stronger. Supported in an unprecedented fashion by Hammelburg, Drost had set an example for the way in which the highly people-oriented Randstad company would select its managers for many years to come. Sensitivity, emotion, empathy, social intelligence and the ability to supervise – at that time – mainly women were the essential qualities required of every Randstad manager.

The company was resolute in its commitment to becoming market leader in the Netherlands, but as the years went by, the ambitions held by Goldschmeding and those of director Ger Daleboudt began to differ. Daleboudt derived little pleasure from the rapidly-growing world of Randstad and after much deliberation he decided that his future lay elsewhere. Supported by fourteen very promising managers, Goldschmeding set out on a new phase in the life of the company. Over the years many of these managers became the mainstays of the future organization. Cleem Farla, for example, became CEO of Randstad Holding, having held several management positions beforehand, and David van Gelder played key roles in Randstad Nederland, Tempo-Team, and in starting up operations in Spain, Italy, Hungary and Turkey. Wil Kitslaar became supervisor of the administrative shared service centre E-Bridge, Fred Farber was HR manager of Randstad Nederland for many years, and Jan de Wit, after having fulfilled various positions, is now active within Group Control.

voilà: the staffing consultant

The fourteen managers started their careers as branch office managers in places such as Den Bosch, Arnhem, Utrecht, Apeldoorn, Groningen, and Nijmegen, where they came into contact with the company's very foundation, the branch staff, responsible for both clients and staffing employees. Until 1970, the responsibilities of acquisition and client management, and of the recruitment and placing of staffing employees had been carried out by different members of staff. The two job descriptions gradually started to overlap until the decision was taken to integrate them into a single position. This unusual concept of employee acquisition/matching and sales being carried out by one person was fairly unique within the staffing industry at the time and distinguished Randstad from the other employment agencies.

A suitable job title, however, had yet to be found. The employees who first held these positions, most of whom were women, were known as 'vassis', short for 'VestigingsASSIStent', Dutch for 'branch assistant'. They were also known as 'temporary employment assistants', but district managers did not consider either job title adequate to describe the work. The title was too limited, it didn't describe the true nature of the job. District Manager Walter de Hart: "I'd been saying for some time that we had to do something about it. 'Yes, yes of course,' everyone would say, but as so often is the case, nothing happened. I decided to approach the subject at a regional meeting, and before long we had a long list of the most amazing job titles."

Mentrix, for example, and midu, interfemme, incotrice, informatrice, mediatrice – all combinations of Dutch and French words associated with the staffing services business. The ideas were as numerous as they were diverse, until De Hart decided to consult a French-to-Dutch dictionary, and under 'i', he found the word 'intercéder', meaning 'to mediate'. The word described perfectly the position of an employee whose job it was to mediate between a client and a temporary worker. De Hart changed the suffix to make the word sound suitably Dutch and ended up with 'intercedent'. *Et voilà*: a new word and a new job had been created! The word became widely accepted and was later added to the highly authoritative Van Dale Dictionary of the Dutch Language.

Both clients and temporary workers had a common aim, which was that they were both searching for something: one for temporary employees, the other for temporary work, and without any help they were unlikely to find each other. An 'intercedente', or staffing consultant, works like a spider who keeps a close watch over every thread in its web, determining whether there are enough experienced workers for a new client, whether a new client is satisfied with an assigned temporary worker, whether or not the worker is happy with the position, and whether that new company around the corner might be interested in the agency's services. These are the kind of issues that staffing consultants dealt with all day long. Randstad then considered women generally making the best consultants with their ability to play a multifaceted role that included carefully assessing various situations and making intuitive decisions.

Randstad had style, and this included a dress code and well-grounded manner. The consultants learned the dos and don'ts of their job as they went along. Within their first hour they learned never to let the telephone ring more than three times before answering it, and that wearing jeans was out of the question

in the Randstad corporate culture. They soon learned that 'the card index is to the staffing consultant what the toolbox is to the carpenter.' The index contained all they needed to know about any particular client or staffing employee. Each temporary worker had a card with a short description of their personality, a photograph and a list of the clients for whom they had worked. Once they had completed several assignments, a new card was stapled to the original. This was a useful way of finding an experienced temporary worker since thicker cards were easier to pick out from the card index. In other words, the thicker the card, the better the staffing employee. Moreover, the cards were arranged in a range of soft colors (to prevent the eyes from becoming tired): yellow cards for clients, and gray cards for temporary employees except for those who were suitable for industrial (blue cards) and healthcare (green cards) jobs. Finally, white cards represented workers who could provide holiday cover. This meant that the consultants had all the information they needed at their fingertips.

The consultants worked in pairs with their desks facing each other and the card index placed exactly in the middle for easy access when either of them had someone on the phone; each was allocated approximately forty to fifty temporary employees. Together, every two consultants formed a single unit, a unit that Randstad regarded as being optimal for this type of work. The workers in every unit kept each other informed about their clients and temporary workers so that if one staffing consultant was occupied or visiting a client, the other could always fill in.

de Werkkrant

**belasting-special
toelichting t-biljet**

de Werkkrant

met gratis
belasting tips

**19
76** *In this year, the first issue of the Werkkrant bulletin was published, in which Randstad addresses its staffers. The idea was to provide staffers with information about salaries, tax issues, and social security. The promotional brochures by Wim Verboven are based on the old Dutch bank notes of 5 and 25 guilders.*

the crown
jewels

Friday afternoon is when wages were paid at the Randstad branches. The flex workers turned this into a fun event every week.

Friday was the most important day of the week for every branch. At the end of the afternoon, all the staffing employees would gather at their particular branches where they would receive their week's wages. They were paid in cash in those days, which was a risky business for the consultants since it sometimes meant carrying around tens of thousands of Dutch guilders. It was an incredibly busy afternoon for many branches but also the perfect opportunity to provide the staffing employees with a little extra attention in the form of drinks, snacks and cigarettes. The 'Friday get-together' served as an opportunity to maintain contact with the temporary workers in an informal atmosphere. The younger workers in particular tended to stay longer and the consultants often went out together afterwards as a way of starting off the weekend.

Friday was also the day on which the time sheets used to record the number of hours worked were turned in to the head office in Amsterdam. Every week, Goldschmeding's secretary, Hielkje Beetsma, carefully noted down the number of time sheets submitted from each branch in *Het Groene Boek* ('The Green Book') that Goldschmeding had introduced. The endless flow of time sheets provided a wealth of information on which he partly based his company policy. The consultants were more than happy to submit the time sheets and admired the charisma of the man who founded the company they worked for. He was, after all, the man who had taken an idea for a thesis and in less than fifteen years turned it into the largest and most important staffing service in the Netherlands. The consultants, generally

19 or 20 year old women (Randstad began to appoint more mature consultants – 22 to 23 years olds – some years later), were very happy to be part of this successful story. Goldschmeding made regular visits to the various branches, emphasizing to the delight of the consultants that they were the 'crown jewels' of the company. Goldschmeding was of the opinion that the 'ideal consultants' were shopkeepers' daughters. He believed that retailers' children grew up in environments in which the customer was still 'always right'. He was convinced that this mentality was Randstad's true source of capital.

The consultants fulfilled a growing need by constantly matching the supply of and demand for temporary work. Randstad was the go-to address for any company that wanted to temporarily increase its production capacity, or indeed maintain production its when large numbers of permanent staff were on annual vacation. Public labor exchange services simply could simply not deal with the high demand, and the only other alternative, which was to employ more permanent staff, was not practical. Moreover, companies like Randstad offered people who did not wish to be tied to a single employer, those who were between jobs, or others who were only able to work on a temporary basis the ideal opportunity to earn some money *and* stay in touch with the labor market.

thinking
big

Initially, Randstad consultants focused primarily on providing temporary office workers such as typists, punch card operators, bookkeepers, administrative assistants and secretaries. In the early 1970s, however, many companies decided to spread their risk by expanding and diversifying their products and services, and Randstad was no exception. In 1973, the consultants had to focus not only on office staff but on all types of personnel, from medical to industrial. Randstad even set up a subsidiary company, Capac, which concentrated on the large-scale dispatch of staff to companies in the industrial sector. At the head office, plans were also developed for new activities in sectors such as cleaning, security and catering, in the hope that Randstad would become an interesting employer that could offer people lifelong career opportunities. It was important that consultants and managers in the employment and recruitment sector were young, as a large share of the people they dealt with were also young, although cleaning and security work involved staff of all ages.

The first step towards diversification in Germany was made in 1974. Werner Then, director of Randstad Zeit-Arbeit, had heard from his district manager that a steel factory in the city of Moers was on the verge of bankruptcy. Randstad rented a large area of the factory's space and started to train and retrain technical staff. Werner Then, an eternal optimist, regarded this as a singular opportunity; not only was he in a position to purchase a training center for technical staffing employees, he would be able to provide 150 technically trained staff to companies that needed them. Moreover, Werner Then firmly believed that having a

The rapid growth of the seventies led to the need for a new head office. Randstad decided on the suburb of Diemen as a suitable location. Many companies moved their headquarters to this area in the late seventies and early eighties. The photo shows the laying of the cornerstone in 1977.

19 74 *In the mid nineteen-seventies, Randstad started to diversify its activities. If in 1960 the focus had been on office work, after 1974 Randstad started placing medical, technical and industrial staffers. In order to make clear what kind of people a branch was recruiting, Total Design developed some pictorial icons for Randstad. The colorful symbols were posted on the fronts of buildings, allowing visitors to see at a glance whether they had arrived at the right address.*

The bolt stands for industrial and technically skilled workers, the paperclip represents office workers, the cross symbolizes medical staff, the person with the book represents student jobs, and the punch card stands for IT workers.

From 1977 to 1990, Randstad's head office was located on Wildenborch Street in Diemen.

dedicated technical subsidiary would also enhance Randstad's credibility.

After a long day of meetings, Then and his district manager managed to persuade the Randstad head office that this was a golden opportunity. Without further ado, and for the grand sum of only one German mark, Randstad was now the proud owner of a steel factory. The reality turned out to be less than ideal, however, and the factory proved a serious drain on their financial resources. Former Dutch Naval Officer Jan Herlaar, who had been appointed Venture and Diversification Manager on July 1, 1975, and who was nearly the oldest employee, was left with the dubious task of sorting things out. The factory was floundering and Then saw no option other than to close it down as quickly as possible. The golden opportunity they had bought for one German mark was sold at a considerable loss. The experience had taught Randstad some lessons that were as hard as steel. First, never embark on a venture that, sooner or later, will involve a large capital investment. Second, never venture into sectors which do not complement the core activity: providing commercial services. In other words, stick to what you are good at.

Herlaar therefore advised Randstad to diversify by exploring the cleaning sector. Branches in Belgium and Germany had done so too, and were now experiencing growth, albeit modest. Randstad Belgium had taken over Belglas NV in 1975 and two companies in Frankfurt and Hamburg in 1974. Herlaar received the management's blessing to take over the small but reputable

Korrekt company, a Utrecht-based cleaning and catering company with revenue in the range of EUR 2.7 million. New branches were opened immediately following the takeover and within two years, Korrekt had expanded from one to ten branches throughout the Netherlands.

Since recruitment and selection were no longer Randstad's only activities, the company's management decided to reorganize the company to better suit the new situation. Randstad Holding was established in 1978. Each of the holding company's activities became part of a separate division. Recruitment and selection were a single division, as was cleaning. A few years later, Randstad set up the security service, Randon, also a separate division within the holding company. Jan Herlaar was responsible for all of Randstad's non-recruitment activities, stamping his own unique hallmark on this part of the company for many years (until 1994).

more than just **profit**

Randstad had had head offices on Sloterkade, Koninginneweg, Oranje Nassaulaan, and A.J. Ernststraat, but constant growth meant that they needed a new office again. In 1977, construction work began on a new office building in Diemen, a small town near Amsterdam. The new head office in the Wildenborch commercial district was to house the company's management team. While Randstad's sales had exceeded approximately EUR 22.7 million in 1970, seven years later it had grown by a factor of six to EUR 136.4 million. The Netherlands, Belgium and France accounted for the most significant part of this growth, and the number of branches increased from 25 to over a hundred, spread across the Netherlands, Belgium, Germany, the United Kingdom and France. In 1977, Randstad Nederland provided almost 50,000 of the 300,000 staffing employees provided by all the employment agencies in the Netherlands, and in 1979, the number of agency-supplied workers provided by all of Randstad's branches combined was approximately 93,000. Randstad's company profile had changed over time. Apart from married women, Randstad's rolls now included students, unemployed people, people trying to fill the time gap between school and military service, and mothers. The range of personnel they could provide had also increased to include not only office staff but also medical, technical and industrial workers. Moreover, the range of services that Randstad could provide now included cleaning and security.

Pure entrepreneurship had strengthened and broadened the structure of the company, but while it was the recruitment sector that had been frowned upon originally, in the 1970s it was entrepreneurship. At the time, the Netherlands was primarily left-leaning. From 1973 to 1977, Prime Minister Joop Den Uyl led a cabinet that strongly believed in the beneficial effects of its government. They believed that entrepreneurs were not to be trusted, a sentiment made blindingly clear by Den Uyl during a lecture for an employers' organization held in 1974. Profit-making was regarded with suspicion, particularly when it involved staffing companies: they were regarded as organizations that made profit at the expense of other people's jobs.

Goldschmeding was highly indignant at the suggestion, especially since this was totally unrelated to the way in which Randstad operated. The way Goldschmeding saw it, Randstad was forming cooperative alliances with various groups such as employees, customers, suppliers, temporary workers, governments, fellow agencies and social partners. He felt a responsibility towards each and every one of these groups and tried to take their individual interests into account when doing business. In 1968, Randstad set up a pension fund for its employees, a highly progressive move for such a young company. Goldschmeding repudiated the idea that a company might only exist in order to make a profit. To him, profit was simply "a sign that the product was satisfying the needs of the consumer". In fact, profit was nothing more than an administrative error; profit just happened. A business was a dynamic entity grouping together staff, clients and suppliers; an entity as complex as any human society. Goldschmeding wondered how he could make this clear to others. This was essentially a problem regarding the identity of the company, a problem he had been wrestling with for four years already. He did not have the time, however, to sit down and find a solution, since the growth of the company and new initiatives were taking up all the time he had.

Late 1977, Frits Goldschmeding began spending more and more of his evenings putting various ideas down on paper. At home in his study, he spent hours puzzling over the identity of Randstad. The following day at the office he would dictate the ideas to Hielkje, whose notes helped put his ideas into some semblance of order. He would pace the room with his hands on his back, dictating and correcting. Sometimes he would be struck by a flash of inspiration. At other times the paper went straight from the typewriter into the wastepaper basket. These jumbles of words and ideas would be polished and refined until it was just right and he could continue to think, dictate, correct and so on. It soon became clear that he needed a new sparring partner, now that he was running the company on his own. Then he remembered the controller he had employed a year earlier, Ed Bolk – someone who seemed to have a philosophical bent.

randstad
uitzendbureau

(para-)medisch
personeel

19 78 *The placement of medical and paramedical personnel was one of the new activities started by Randstad in the nineteen-seventies.*

1978

19 78 *In the 1978 annual report, the company's corporate philosophy was published for the first time. Concepts such as 'to know, to serve, to trust' and 'simultaneous promotion of interests' were introduced. Bees building honeycombs or beavers building dams illustrate that an enterprise is a form of cooperation.*

simultaneous promotion of
interests

Bolk was flattered by Goldschmeding's invitation to assist him in thinking about Randstad's corporate culture. Every evening, the two men carried on Socratic dialogues in which they exchanged ideas with the aim of defining the Randstad corporate culture so that it could be incorporated into the 1977 annual report. Goldschmeding and Bolk bombarded each other with texts that they each then duly returned to the other with countless comments and suggestions added. When the final version was included in the annual report, they were still not satisfied. In retrospect, Bolk realized that too many compromises had been made, which resulted in an esoteric text that was virtually incomprehensible to the reader. It included sentences such as "a technically and mechanically oriented interpretation was initially adhered to, which henceforth evolved into a philosophy in which the enterprise was regarded as an economic abstraction" and "a bureaucratic structure id est a cluster of groups, and sociological aspects of which were hence made consummate."

Goldschmeding and Bolk decided to take a different approach with the next annual report. They took a very large sheet of paper and drew a chart on it that included a series of squares, each square representing an interested party in Randstad – a Randstad stakeholder. These included clients, suppliers, staff, governments and unions. In each square they defined what the company meant to that party, and what they meant to Randstad. This created a structured overview of each and every party involved with Randstad, and it clarified the company's objective, which was to maintain continuity and "facilitate growth where

necessary, whether it be in the general interest of the company or for the benefit of interested parties." Goldschmeding and Bolk were finally satisfied. They nevertheless decided to submit their latest version to economics professor Van der Kooy in order to confirm their vision. The professor was impressed with the stakeholders' concept, but felt that subjects such as continuity and growth and the proviso on profit should be emphasized more clearly. The phrase "to achieve a satisfactory profit that will provide security for all interested parties" was therefore included.

The subsequent annual report for 1978 was clear and concise, thanks to their resourceful chart. The design further enhanced the text – bees in a honeycomb and beavers on a dam represented the central theme of the company as a collaboration of individuals. The metaphor of bees working together in a honeycomb was both elegant and simple, representing the mutual interests of the bees taking precedence over those of any individual bee. Randstad also saw the company in wider terms than the interests of its director and staff. Clients, suppliers, bankers, governments, fellow agencies and social partners played an equally important role in the company's existence. The annual report described the way in which Randstad wanted to be regarded by society: "It is our duty to pursue the interests of our interested parties, both direct and indirect, in every aspect; in other words, to operate in such a way that the interests of the various groups involved are protected". Randstad's unique doctrine of protecting the mutual interests of all parties concerned had been established.

corporate
identity

Randstad's 'in-house philosophers' Goldschmeding and Bolk began once more to spend much of their time working on the annual report for 1979. The result was a well-formulated document which clearly defined the abstract concept of individual interested parties helping to protect mutual interests. In 1978 and 1979, the house style that had been developed in 1967 was brought in line with the newly established company philosophy. Goldschmeding wrote, "our group's work ethic, our 'corporate identity', must serve as a set of criteria against which everyone involved in the company can measure his or her performance and assess whether or not their behavior complies with a system 'dos and don'ts' which is only partially documented, but overall intuitively well-understood."

So what did this mean the various stakeholders? According to the Randstad corporate culture, employees were entitled to careful selection and adequate premises in which to work where they would feel safe and well. The government could expect its regulations to be adhered to not only to the letter, but also in their broader, social sense. Membership of professional groups such as the ABU association of employment agencies should not only serve to protect one's own interests but also offers the opportunity of making a constructive contribution to society. Clients could expect good fees that also provided Randstad with reasonable remuneration for its efforts. Values such as mutual trust and consistency in behavior had to become an integral part

of the company culture, and Randstad was to strive for perfection in all areas of its performance.The combination of house style and corporate identity formed a powerful whole. Slowly but surely, this total philosophy was incorporated into every fiber of the company. Branches in Amsterdam were similar to branches in Maastricht, Brussels, Paris, or Frankfurt. Every client was treated with the same pleasant hospitality, every temporary worker with the same dedication and every supplier received the same degree of respect. Randstad had become a pioneer in total identity and sustainable *corporate vision*.

The streamlined interior of a Randstad branch office.

to know, serve and trust

A corporate philosophy was further developed in 1984, this time with the help of former marketing manager Koos Teule. The philosophy was phrased as follows: "We regard our company as an integral part of society (…). It is therefore our duty to operate in such a way that the interests of our interested parties, both direct and indirect, are protected. Since Randstad is likewise reliant upon the community, it also has a duty to recognize the responsibility that others have towards the company. This means that the company must *know* the groups. It must also have *trust* in these groups and organizations, while achieving and maintaining their trust in return. Furthermore, the company must be committed to *serve* the interests of others while bearing in mind an obligation to also serve its own interests."

To know, serve and trust. These principles summarize the Randstad culture succinctly, consistently, and optimally. Together with the protection of mutual interests and the quest for perfection, these three principles form the structure of the company. Randstad had grown up, and recognition was just around the corner.

In the nineteen-seventies, Randstad made extensive use of photography in personnel magazines. Images were placed for their beauty; not necessarily also because of any specific meaning. This particular image, however, most definitely conveyed a meaning: trust is all about the ability to look someone into the eyes.

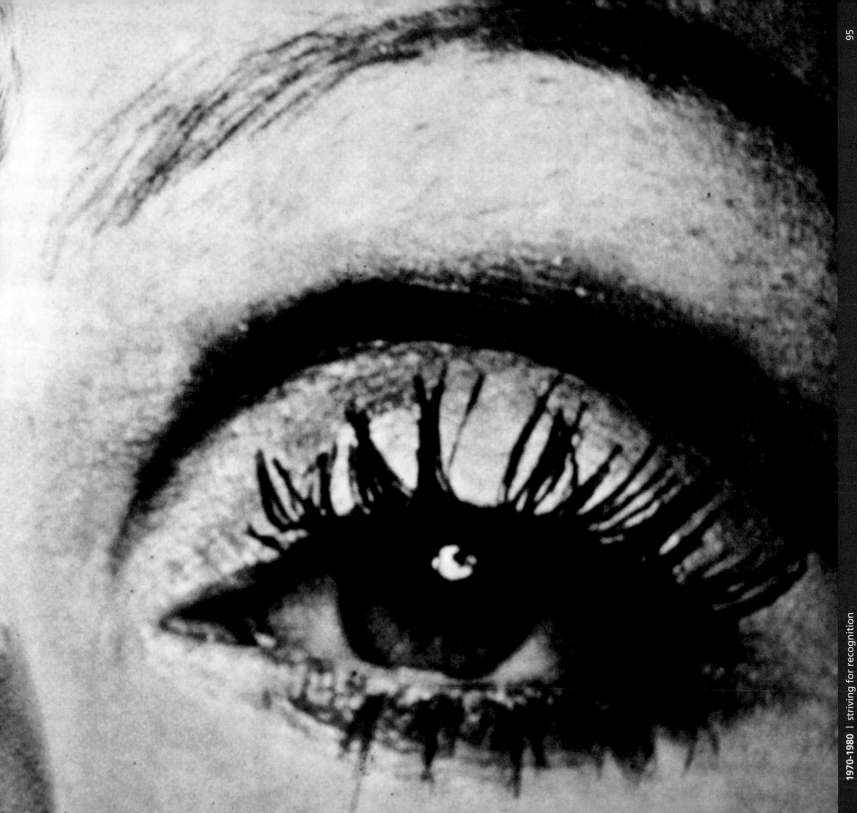

Randstad stories

n, Sébastien Boileau-Picard
and trust, Germaine Visser
Passos 14 happy birthday,
first name terms, Andrea
s, Brien Keegan 17 going,
bella 18 captain Randstad,
vide 19 the perfect match,
20 hanami, Marcel Wiggers

11

we've got the power

uncle Sébastien

"I was welcomed into the Canadian Randstad family as a young man in 2004. I joined the staff association immediately, and as luck would have it, the very first activity was the annual River Rafting trip. One thing is certain: there is no faster way to get to know your colleagues than by hurtling over wild water in a rubber raft. Our team became closer with every crashing wave!"

Six years later, Boileau-Picard can genuinely be described as a bearer of culture. "I am no longer the new kid on the block, but rather the friendly uncle of the 'family', teaching people the ins and outs of Randstad's culture and treating them to a healthy dose of humor to boot. Taking pleasure in one's work is all-important. At last year's Christmas party I did a sketch that included making fun of our managers' names; not exactly difficult with a CEO called Terry Power. My tongue-in-cheek play on words was 'Randstad Canada can take on the world, 'cause we've got the **Power**!'"

Sébastien Boileau-Picard – Market development manager Randstad, Canada

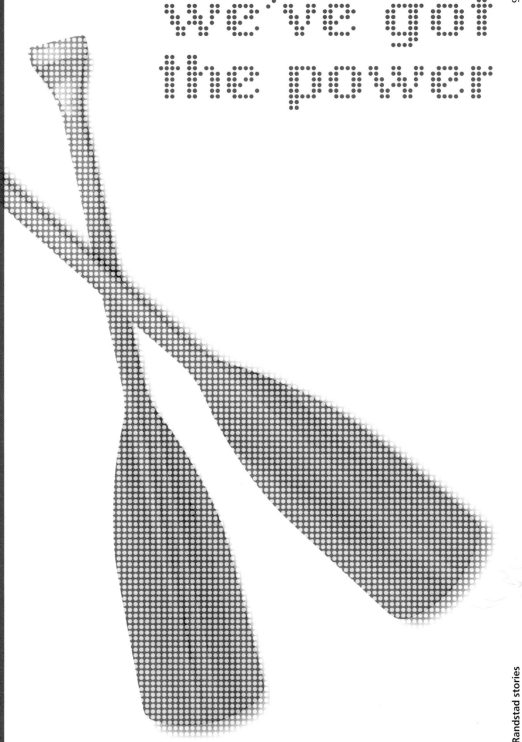

I trust their opinions, and they trust me

to know, serve and trust

Germaine Visser is a flexworker for Randstad and is working for Rabobank on a temporary basis. She is very positive about Randstad: "The staffing consultants always show an interest in me. If I haven't been in touch for a while, they always call me or send me an email asking how I am doing. I think that's very thoughtful."

Her husband's experience is similar. He used to be a cameraman, but it was heavy work, and he had to stop when he became ill. He contacted Randstad in search of alternative work and told them about his illness. According to Ms. Visser, "Randstad said to my husband: 'We never look back, we always look towards the future.' He got a job and since then they call him every once in a while to ask how he is getting on. Isn't that great?"

When we asked Ms. Visser to tell us what Randstad's motto 'to know, serve and trust' meant to her as a flexworker, she said: "Actually, I think it has everything to do with taking an interest, with understanding, seeing and knowing what you are doing. The first thing I was told during my interview was that 'if we take you on, it will be for Rabobank. ING or ABN would not suit you.' They know the companies that they are sending people to. I have confidence in their judgment, they have confidence in me and my work, and my husband has regained his faith in the future."

Germaine Visser – Flexworker Randstad, Netherlands

13

going grey

It happens frequently in the labor market: some companies are reluctant to hire people over fifty years old, because they are relatively expensive. The result is that many people in this age group are sitting at home despite being able and willing to do the work.

Randstad Germany felt particularly strongly about this group, and accepted an invitation from the Social Affairs department in the state of Hessen to take part in a project to help people in their fifties or even sixties to re-establish themselves in paid employment. Maxi Passos is responsible for the project within the Randstad Foundation. Helping reintegrating people in this age group is not easy. Project participants first spend twelve months working in a public institution such as a school, society or foundation in order to get back into the rhythm of working, after which a facilitator helps the candidate find regular paid work. However, they are often so happy with their initial work that they do not want to take this next step. Moreover, the business community is less than welcoming when it comes to employing people from this group.

Governments should recognize the need to keep the employment market participation as wide as possible. This kind of support is exactly what Passos wants. Until that time arrives, however, she will continue to do everything in her power to allow people in their fifties and sixties to continue playing a valuable role in the workplace. This will be crucial in the future, as the country attempts to increase labor force participation.

Maxi Passos *(right) – Projectmanager corporate affairs*
Randstad Germany

so good to know you

happy birthday

International organizations are like talent magnets, and Fortune 500 companies may be among the creators of the strongest force fields. This list ranks the 500 largest companies in the world by annual revenue. Randstad's inclusion in this list was certainly the deciding factor for Delphine Su when it came to choosing a company to work for; Chinese employers didn't stand a chance.

"Randstad is international in every way and obviously good at what it does. Working for an organization like that gives me the opportunity to experience different cultures; its staff are true professionals and there are countless opportunities for me to further my career."

"What's more, Randstad is very different from Chinese companies. The corporate culture at Randstad is much warmer and more personal. On your birthday you get a card from the entire team including the manager – *so good to know you!* That would never happen with a Chinese company, even if you had been working there for years. You'd be lucky if they remembered your name, let alone your birthday!"

Delphine Su – *Sales manager Randstad, China*

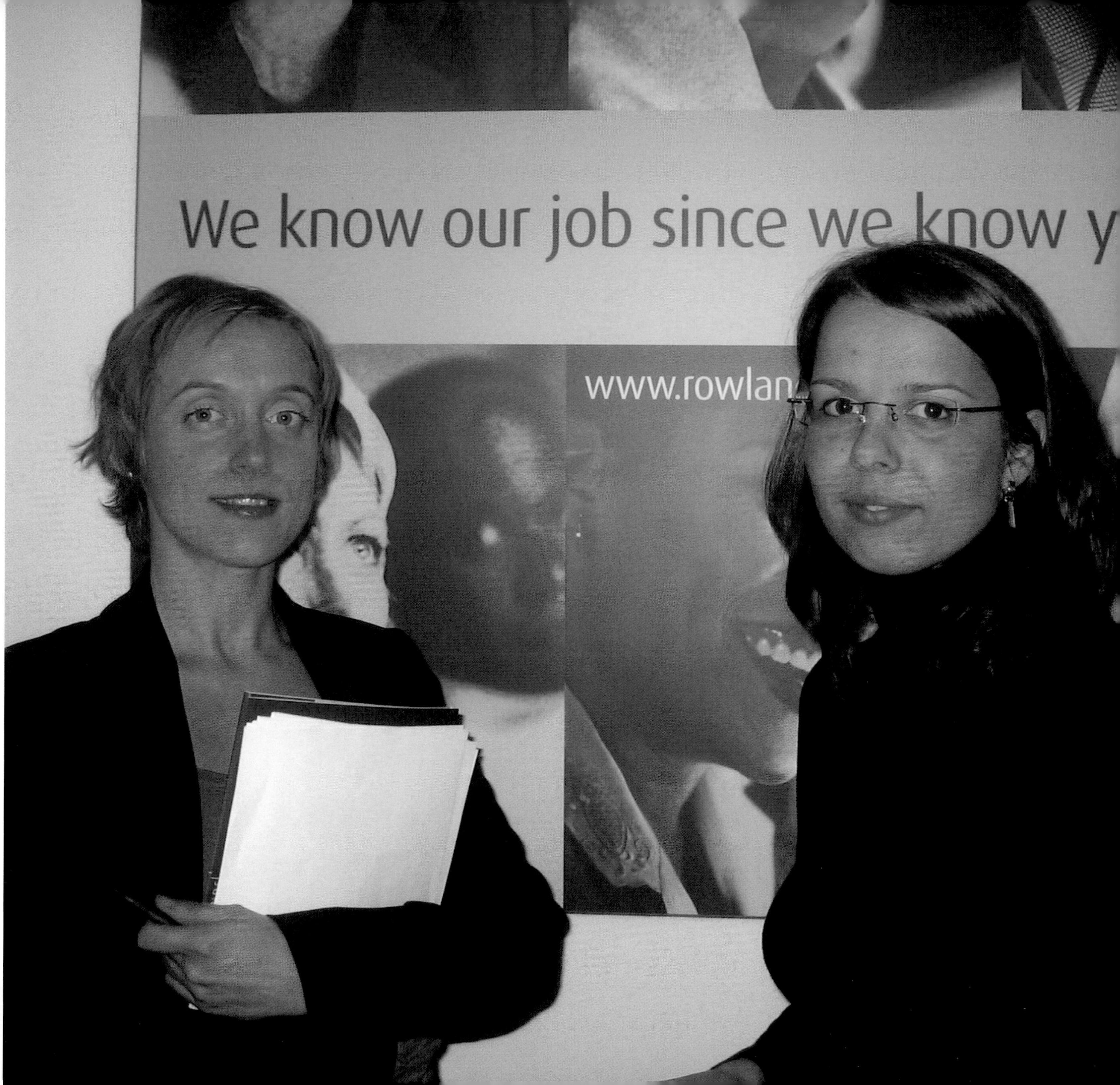
We know our job since we know y
www.rowlan

15

first name terms

"Through recruitment and selection, we look for highly qualified professionals to fill management positions. Our clients with different cultural backgrounds are primarily active in the financial sector, which is very large in Luxembourg. We take great care and effort to seek out the right candidates matching our clients' growth strategy; after all, we are judged by the quality of the service we provide to both clients and candidates."

"I once had a potential German client who was very reluctant to work with a recruitment company, as he had a bad experience with a competitor. He was actually forced to approach us, as we had provided his head office with a very good service in the past, and they insisted on working with us."

"At the beginning the process was very difficult. The client was not convinced that our recruitment strategy was suitable to his needs. As the process went on, however, he could see that I was doing my very best for him and that Randstad was a reliable service provider. I am proud to say that, in our final meeting, he acknowledged that the quality of our service changed his resistance to working with us and that he now considers us as his partner for any future collaboration. He even insisted that I call him by his first name and address him using 'du', which is the familiar form of you in German and normally only used among family and friends. This was definitively a very strong sign of confidence."

Andrea Tiefenbacher (left) – Senior recruitment consultant, Tempo-Team Search and Selection, Luxembourg

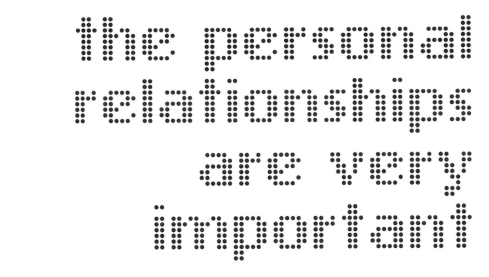

the personal relationships are very important

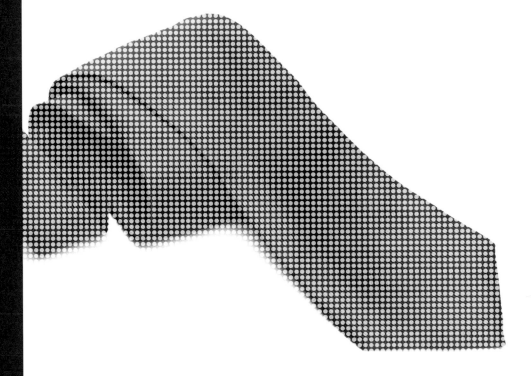

it is all about teamwork

16

Kiwis

The international scope of Randstad implies that the company must interact with many countries and cultures. According to Brien Keegan: "Our New Zealand business is built on forging strong relationships with our clients, candidates, and staff. New Zealand is a small country in size and population, but we consistently perform above expectations on a global stage."

"The business culture of Kiwis, as we proudly call ourselves, can be summed up well by the national sport, rugby union. Before a game, our national team performs a haka, a traditional Maori dance. The team unites to defeat its opponents. Similarly, when doing business in New Zealand, it is important to work collaboratively and come together as a team with common goals, strong relationships, to involve the community and then work together to grow our business."

Brien Keegan – Regional manager accounting, procurement, banking & finance Randstad, New Zealand

Randstad has been present in New Zealand since its merger with Vedior. Activities focus primarily on staffing and recruiting, selection and placement of professionals.

17

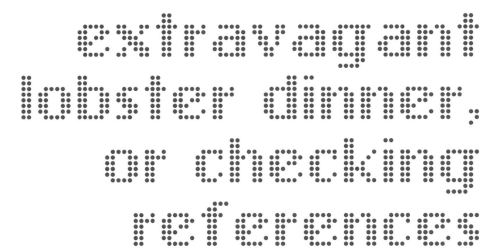

extravagant lobster dinner, or checking references

going, going, gone...

You wouldn't immediately think that about someone who specializes in the placement of IT professionals, but once a year, Sapphire Canada holds a charity auction. Something that makes this auction stand out is that the 'suppliers' as well as the buyers of the goods come from within Sapphire itself. Employees offer babysitting services, a gift certificate for a fancy lobster dinner or a sports magazine autographed by a celebrity athlete, and then their colleagues bid on those prizes.

"A particularly popular item is the promise to check a number of references for free. This is not exactly the favorite job for the average recruiter," laughs David Colella, a resourcing manager with Sapphire.

David is passionate about the volunteer work of his employees. For a long time, the auction has no longer been a trivial event. It appeals to the core, to the understanding that the company is there to do good in the world. "Randstad's slogan is *Shaping the world of work*. I would like to see that from a wider perspective. Our responsibility is 'Shaping the world.' Mind you, in 2008 we were able to collect 270,000 dollars for charity. For a large multinational that may not be much, but we did this with a group of three hundred employees who contributed everything by themselves. That says something about the special spirit of this company."

David Colella – Manager resourcing Sapphire Technologies, Canada

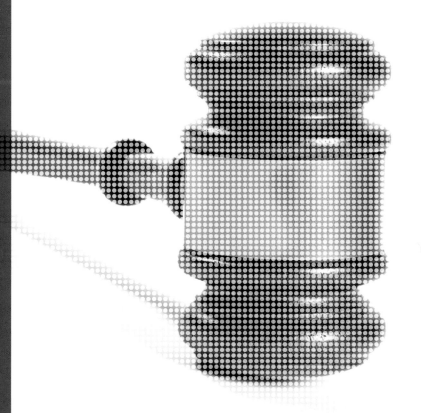

on board the big ship

captain Randstad

"What a sight it was. Slowly, the Clipper sailed up the Rio de la Plata. High masts, wide sails, a tangle of ropes: one doesn't get to see that very often. The Clipper was a real hit in Buenos Aires. In less than four days, thousands of people visited the ship. TV stations talked about it non-stop. What a way to establish the Randstad brand in Argentina!"

Alejandro Servide, regional manager in Buenos Aires, was talking about how his home city was visited by the Clipper Stad Amsterdam in October 2009: "During its visit here, the ship hosted the thirtieth anniversary party for Sesa Select. In the evening we gave a grand party for all the employees, and during the day clients were invited to sail the Rio de la Plata with us. Many leading managers and the director of Sesa were on board, as well as Greg Netland, and even founder Frits Goldschmeding. Their presence helped the company reach an agreement that very day with a prospect with whom we had wanted to cooperate for many years. It feels good to be part of Randstad. Indeed, it feels a bit like being on a journey around the world on board of Captain Randstad's ship!"

Alejandro Servide – Regional manager Sesa Select, Argentina

Sesa Select was established in 1979 as a staffing agency for temporary personnel in the administrative and industrial sectors. After having been purchased by Vedior in 2000, Sesa was merged with Select Executives, which focused on recruitment and selection of professionals. Sesa Select has been a Randstad company since 2008.

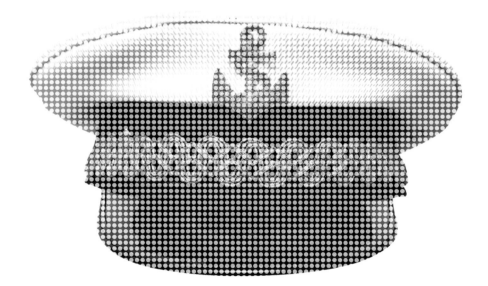

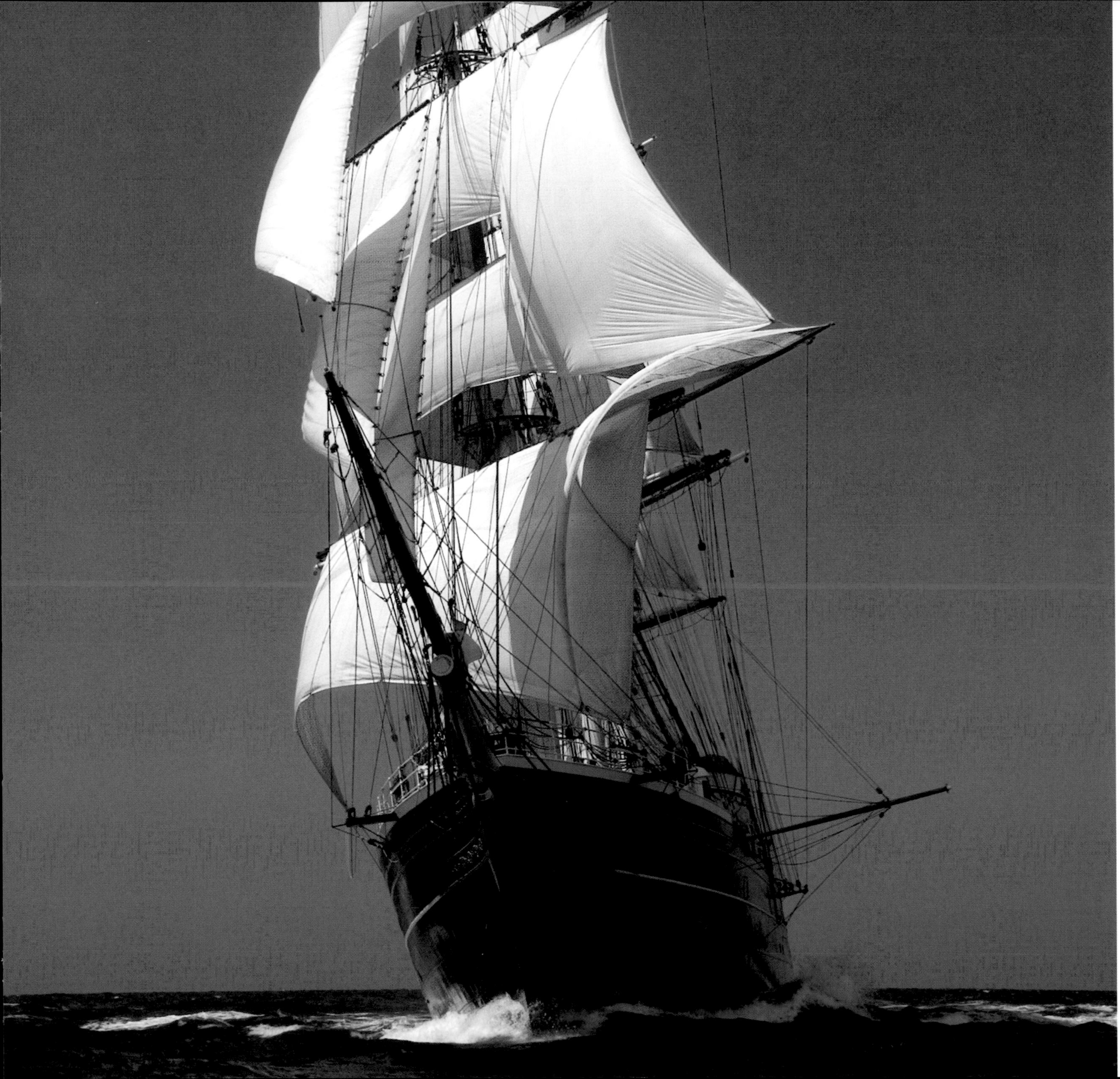

St Estèphe
St Emilion
Pauillac
Pauillac
CHATEAU
HAUT-BAGES-LIBERAL
PAUILLAC
CHASSE-S
CRU EXCEPT
HAUT BEYCHEVELLE GLORIA
ST JULIEN
PROMO
CHATEAU
HAUT BEYCHEVELLE GLORIA
SAINT-JULIEN
Château
12 Btles
PAUILL
CORDE
Cordeilhan Bo

19

the perfect match

"What gives me the most job satisfaction is finding the ideal job for a flexworker. I once received a request from a wine merchant for a secretary. He was a somewhat eccentric man, maybe forty years old, and although his office was very small, it contained a very large desk around which four people were expected to work. We sent him various candidates, but none of them were interested. 'Their bathroom facilities date all the way back to the 1960s!' one of the candidates told us."

"Some time later, a young woman came into our office. She was of upper-class origin and had been brought up at her family's castle in France; her family was very much into wine. She accepted the job and turned out to be the perfect match! It was a meeting of old-style values and upbringings. Initially you think you'll never fill a vacancy like that, and then suddenly everything changes."

Fabienne Fobe – Senior staffing consultant Randstad, Belgium

they have a restroom from the sixties!

we're here to stay!

hanami

Whenever the warm southern wind starts blowing in April, Japan comes out of hibernation. Cherry blossoms gradually color the country pink, and weathermen guess when the blossoms will reach Tokyo. And when the moment arrives, the festival of the cherry blossom is celebrated, the *hanami matsuri*. "Randstad Japan is obviously part of it", says Marcel Wiggers. "According to tradition, one celebrates *hanami* with one's employer. When the blossoms arrive, the youngest employee goes with blankets to one of Tokyo's parks, and tries to get a good location, which he then guards until the older colleagues arrive in the evening. Then it is time for drinking and eating, laughter and dance."

"Since 2006, Randstad has been following a strategy in Japan of having its own operating company, apart from having a significant percentage (20 percent) in the sixth-largest staffing company on the Japanese market, Fujistaff. This way we are on a stable path towards building up our position in the second-largest economy of the world. Randstad has been approaching the Japanese market since 2006 much like the way cherry blossoms cover the island: gradually, but inevitably. The big difference is that the cherry blossoms disappear, but we're here to stay!"

Marcel Wiggers – Regional managing director Randstad, China, Hong Kong, Japan en Inhouse Services Australia

building a
reputation

The long struggle for recognition eventually led to a more open-minded approach to temporary employment by the authorities in the eighties. The results were spectacular. Randstad grew as never before. From 1983 to 1985, sales grew from EUR 204 million to EUR 545 million. Randstad crowned its excellent results with an IPO at the beginning of the following decade.

stormy weather

The early 1980s were a stormy time for the world economic climate. The recession began with a second oil crisis in 1979. One of the first sectors to feel the pinch was the staffing industry. Temporary jobs are always the first to go when sales decline and, as a result, Randstad put increasingly fewer people to work throughout the second half of 1980. In 1981, Randstad, now one of the largest temporary employment agencies in both the Netherlands and Belgium with market shares of 20% and 22.7% respectively, saw its sales plummet from EUR 245 million to EUR 198 million within just one year. The prospects were even bleaker, given

Occasionally, in the nineteen-eighties, Frits Goldschmeding had to deliver tough messages, like here, during the 1986 'Quality Day' event. After a decline of sales in the first half of the decade, Randstad had to deal with growing pains. These peaks and valleys sometimes gave employees the feeling that the company had lost contact with its roots.

the fact that the company had fore-casted it would achieve sales of EUR 168.2 million by 1982. Randstad felt that it had no choice but to close a number of branches in the Netherlands and, regretfully, the company's management was forced to let 160 people go. Some branches were closed, and the smallest of the remaining ones were staffed by just one employee.

It was a traumatic event for Randstad; laying people off was entirely at odds with its philosophy of continuity. The agency did everything in its power to help those who were laid off. Thanks to the nature of their work and their close contact with clients, most staffing consultants were able to find alternate work. Within one month, 130 of them had found employment. It took the remaining 30 a little longer to find new jobs, but ultimately no one had to be laid off without the prospect of a new job. It was a solution that matched the philosophy of the company. Business was also declining inter-nationally, with all branches in England closing and Randstad Ltd. facing an indetermin°ate period of near-dormancy. Germany and France had incurred losses too, and Interlabor and Randstad Belgium were barely managing to keep their heads above water.

Not surprisingly, the economic malaise topped the agenda for the company's senior management in 1981 and 1982. Randstad's top management at the time formed two coordination teams, the Groeps Coördinatieoverleg (GCO), which coordinated the entire Randstad group, and the Randstad Coördinatieoverleg (RCO), which focused primarily on the Dutch market. The GCO consisted of Frits Goldschmeding (chair), Ed Bolk

(marketing), Herman Kolk (finance), Frits Drost (staffing services abroad), Jan Herlaar (cleaning and security diversification programs) and Hielkje Beetsma (secretary). The RCO consisted of Frits Goldschmeding (chair), Fred van Haasteren (personnel and organization), David van Gelder (operations) and Ed Bolk (finance and marketing).

As the principal operating company, Randstad Uitzendbureau had the majority vote within the GCO, a privilege that was justified by its revenues. In 1980, Randstad Uitzendbureau accounted for EUR 156 of the EUR 245 million in sales, the German subsidiary Randstad Zeit-Arbeit followed at a sizeable distance with EUR 27.7 million. The relatively good results achieved by the Dutch agency were the reason

that the group as a whole still managed to make a slight profit, despite the recession. In order to improve the results, a campaign was launched called Operatie Stofkam (or in English, 'Operation Fine-Toothed Comb'). The entire company economized on things like coffee, paper, pens, staples, flowers and so on. But Goldschmeding had another idea which, though less obvious, ultimately had a far greater effect.

The oil crises resulted in massive fuel shortages. Inventive solutions were tried out in Germany, like here, where a horse was hitched onto the front of a Volkswagen bus. The oil crisis also led to an economic crisis, which led to massive youth unemployment. On the adjoining photo we see unemployed young people signing up at the labor office.

19 80 *The turn of a decade is always a special event. Randstad asked Total Design to design a poster to welcome the nineteen-eighties: 'In the eighties too, you will be able to rely on Randstad'.*

The Randstad branch on Dam Square in Amsterdam.

the 'Classic Campaign'

During his branch visits, Goldschmeding had noticed that many staffing consultants and branch managers were careless when carrying out basic tasks, such as making phone calls to clients, greeting applicants, handing out pencils and notepads and maintaining directories – in short, traditional branch tasks. None of these tasks were carried out with the level of care and efficiency that he considered essential. He had practically invented the profession of staffing consultant and was therefore in a position to understand the importance of such attention to detail.

As 1982 progressed, Goldschmeding saw from the financial figures that the economy might soon take a turn for the better. The decision was therefore made to start recruiting new employees in order to re-staff the branches. Two months later, however, no new employees had been recruited. Goldschmeding decided, in consultation with David van Gelder, to visit a number of branches in person and see if he could persuade the branch managers and consultants to take some firm steps towards acquiring new employees. He also seized this opportunity to explain to the consultants the finer points of their profession, hoping that his description of the model staffing consultant would bring about a sense of urgency within the organization. His theory was that more staff would mean more clients.

The branches in Apeldoorn and Zwolle were selected for the so-called Classic Campaign. During his visits, the director provided the branch staff with graphs which clearly indicated that even though the economy was already suffering, it would soon begin to recover. He emphasized that in addition to economizing, they should now also focus on visiting as many clients as possible. This was the ideal time to get one step ahead of their competitors. Randstad had telephone stickers, memo pads and notepads made with its logo and phone number printed on them, in order to gain and maintain 'top of mind' awareness. The campaign worked fabulously, and sales at the branches in Apeldoorn and Zwolle went up

tijdelijk werk voor industriepersoneel

tijdelijk werk voor data- en tekstverwerkend personeel

tijdelijk werk voor gezondheidszorg-personeel

19 84 *After the 'Chinese Girl' (1975), the 'Nostalgic Girl' (1978), the 'critical generation' (1980), and the 'Utrecht girl' (1982), it was time for a new model, and in 1984, Jane made her appearance: a confident 24 year old young woman would be the face of all of Randstad's promotional campaigns for the next 4 years.*

At the branch shown here, the 'Classic Campaign' clearly had not been implemented yet, as evidenced by the messy interior. On the right in the foreground is the card file, which for years was the staffing consultants' most important tool.

immediately. There was, however, some criticism from within the Randstad organization itself. Goldschmeding himself had been successful in using his tactics to raise profits, but would he be able to get the branch managers to do the same?

The management took on the challenge with enthusiasm and vigor. 'Super-consultant' Goldschmeding chose the failing Sittard branch to be the first to benefit from the new campaign. Goldschmeding visited the branch and asked regional manager Leo Lindelauf what advertising materials were available and whether the address database was up to date. He then took Lindelauf by the arm and said, "Come and take a look at this." They walked over to the corner of the office. "You see? If you enter the office through the same door every day, you'll see the same things every day. You become blind to things that aren't quite right. Stand in a

corner to get a different perspective and you'll notice lots of different things". Lindelauf looked and nodded. On the left he saw a pile of reports, in full view of visitors to the office, which, needless to say, were not where they belonged. A desk that was damaged on one side was in full view to the right, and at the back of the room there was plenty of room for another desk at which two additional consultants could sit. Lindelauf clearly understood the message behind the Classic Campaign: success can only be achieved through perfect service and absolute dedication to the client! The next day, he started visiting branches throughout the southern province of Limburg and inspiring workers in Classic Campaign style, and it worked: performance started improving immediately, proving that branch managers could indeed achieve the same degree of success through the campaign. The Classic Campaign could now be rolled out to all of the remaining branches.

The campaign message filtered through the entire organization to the company's divisions, subsidiaries, regions, districts, territories, branches and finally the units. Randstad would now start to focus on

growth rather than cost – a surprising choice at a time when its competitors were still licking their financial wounds. The number of commercial accounts was increased by way of conventional methods such as telephone calls, client visits, and the updating of the database. Moreover, individual branches were given greater responsibility and the freedom to allocate their budgets as they deemed necessary.

Many staff and managers had spent several years inside the Randstad corporate culture. Almost eighty percent of the managers had come from within the organization, and they were quite enthusiastic. Everyone made sure that the telephone lists were regularly updated, that promotional material was distributed consistently, that each branch looked meticulous, that budgets were strictly adhered to, and that regular contact was maintained with potential and existing clients. Everyone pulled their weight, and within just a few months, revenue and market share began rising again at many branches. The campaign had been a success due to the commitment shown by everyone within the organization.

eat or be eaten

Randstad was one of the few staffing firms that managed to keep so many branches open during the economic downturn; in fact, it even managed to make a modest profit. Larger companies like Randstad were able to survive due to their size, whereas smaller companies survived due to their specialization in markets for which the demand remained reasonably stable. Average-sized companies, however, enjoyed neither of these benefits. Fellow agencies such as Tempo-Team, Content and Vedior were forced to close a large number of branches in 1981 and 1982 in order to cut costs. Competitor ASB had to close almost half of its branches and in doing so it lost its strong second position in the Dutch market. Randstad Nederland, which, under the direction of Frits Drost, had come through the crisis with its head held high, and was able to maintain its position as market leader.

Ironically, the crisis resulted in an increased focus on the staffing market. Legendary Dutch entrepreneur Anton Dreesmann, director and owner of the Vroom & Dreesmann department store chain (later Vendex), took over the temporary employment agencies Vedior and Dactylo in 1979, but he wanted

more. Dreesmann reasoned that since business enterprises, and temporary employment agencies in particular, were facing such hard times, they would, in theory, be up for grabs. "Wouldn't it be wonderful if he could add Randstad, which had recently become the largest player in the market, to his empire," he thought.

'Nothing ventured, nothing gained' was Dreesmann's philosophy as he instructed his chauffeur to take him to Randstad's Diemen office. When he arrived at the reception desk he announced that he wanted to speak to Randstad's director, and that no, he did not have an appointment. Somewhat taken aback, Goldschmeding ushered him into his office, shook his hand and asked, "What brings you here?" Not one to beat around the bush, Dreesmann answered resolutely, "I want to buy Randstad." Goldschmeding looked the entrepreneur calmly in the eyes and said: "then you had better turn around and leave, immediately. A sale is out of the question."

Randstad had an alternative strategy in mind. It worked on the assumption of autonomous growth, which the

company directors considered the best and most stable way to expand. The spectacular growth seen over the last twenty years had not been achieved through acquisition upon acquisition, but by expanding the network of branches according to the lily pad principle. In other words, by first creating a stable foundation in one city before pursuing the next.

In the summer of 1982, Randstad's economic barometer began to look more favorable. For over ten years, their 'barometer' had been calibrated using financial data based primarily on the weekly time sheets. This data was processed into logarithmic graphs which provided the company's management with strategically useful information and indications for future market developments. Competitors sometimes wondered how Randstad managed to anticipate economic changes so well. Figures showed that temporary workers were changing jobs more frequently and that clients were once again starting to place long-term orders. Randstad realized that this would be an ideal time to make investments, and in September 1982, the opportunity arose to do so.

Randstad houdt niet van half werk

19 88 *Four years later, Joanna succeeded Jane as face of Randstad. As of 1988, Joanna occupied center stage in the Dutch 'She sought, I found' campaign. Joanne, a staffing consultant, finds a perfect match for every client, because she does not like jobs half done. The campaign took place on radio and TV, and of course by way of posters in the streets.*

In 1989, Randstad rented a billboard in the Amsterdam Zoo. A variation of the 'She sought, I found' campaign was designed specifically for that location. The result was the famous lions poster.

Rival agency Tempo-Team had incurred significant losses as a result of the economic crisis and could only finance ten more days of pay. Frits Hünd, interim manager at Tempo-Team, was under enormous pressure from the owner, Mutator, to make the company profitable again. Mutator was owned by the successor to Marinus Spruijtenburg, who had founded Tempo-Team. When it became clear that profitability was not feasible forTempo-Team, Hünd was assigned the task of asset liquidation.

In 1982, the industry association CIETT organized an international congress in Washington, D.C. Representatives from

A Tempo-Team staffing consultant.

every internationally significant agency were present. It was the ideal place for him to approach potential buyers, including the director of Randstad, about a takeover bid for Mutator, which also owned UB2000. Goldschmeding listened with interest, while keeping in mind the approaching upturn in the temporary employment market; the takeover could further strengthen Randstad's position as market leader. Hünd emphasized the fact that they wanted matters finalized as quickly as possible, and they were. The takeover was completed in 1983 for the sum of EUR 125,000 and included the obligation to settle the company's significant debts. The new subsidiary was integrated with Capac, which had been

established in 1973 and focused on providing temporary industrial workers under the name of Tempo-Team. For a relatively modest sum of money, Randstad was now the owner of a second market brand. Tempo-Team had thirty branches and a force of approximately 1,100 working temporary employees a week.

After the takeover, David van Gelder, who had started as a manager in 1972 and worked his way up to become Randstad Uitzendbureau's director of operations, devoted all his time and effort to restarting and creating a profile for the new subsidiary. It was essential that Tempo-Team exuded an entirely different image than that of Randstad

so that the very real danger of corporate cannibalization could be averted. Van Gelder therefore opted for a different type of consultant. Instead of employing fresh college graduates, he appointed people with specific recruitment and selection skills. Branch policy was also different: instead of a network of smaller branches, Tempo-Team established one large branch per city. Tempo-Team also chose to keep orange as its house color, in order to further emphasize the difference. The color was changed to red in 1987, while Randstad's color remained blue. Variety was, after all, the spice of life.

Frits Hünd was made director of Randstad Uitzendbureau, but he did not hold the position for long. A couple of years later, his financial policies were found to be inadequate; he was asked to leave, and Frits Goldschmeding took over his duties. Frits Drost had already been appointed director of operations in Belgium, Germany and France. Werner Then, director of Randstad Zeit-Arbeit, reported to him as did Marc Sidler on behalf of Randstad France and Dutch-Belgian Wim Bakker for Interlabor. Under Drost's direction, Interlabor became a disciplined, profitable organization, taking over market leadership from rival Gregg Interim (later to become Vedior Interim) in the late 1980s. The concept of temporary work was becoming more accepted in Belgium, as it was in the Netherlands. The economic crisis of the early 1980s had proved to be a tough but effective lesson. The industry had suffered greatly and had become more prudent when it came to fixed contracts. It realized that a flexible work force made companies

less vulnerable in times of economic hardship, and Interlabor and Randstad were therefore in a position to provide industrial companies in Belgium with increasing numbers of temporary workers. The rapidly growing areas in the Belgian employment agency sector were health care, which accounted for twelve percent of the temporary workers employed, and technical companies, which hired eight to ten percent of the temporary workers available. The development of a 'flexible layer' around companies could also be seen in the other Randstad countries. In the Netherlands, Randstad was focusing primarily on administrative staff for the service sector as well as hiring out medical and industrial workers.

In 1981, the ABU organized a demonstration in The Hague against dropping the limit on staffing work from six to three months.

a new direction

In addition to the Tempo-Team takeover, the crisis of the early 1980s provided Randstad with another positive opportunity. The two traditional adversaries to the concept of temporary employment, the unions and the government, had decided to try a different approach. Since 1977, the largest labor union in the Netherlands, FNV, had refused to negotiate with temporary employment agencies, although the smaller unions CNV and De Unie had left discussions open. The FNV, however, was well aware of the fact that companies everywhere had resorted to a plethora of flexible labor contracts in order to get through the recession; the companies had arranged a multitude of temporary contracts such as zero-hour contracts, minimum and maximum contracts, and evening and weekend contracts. In an independent survey on flexible contracts, the FNV came to the conclusion that the temporary employment contracts were at least preferable to many of the unorthodox contracts currently being used.

The FNV therefore decided in 1985 to resume talks with the staffing industry. Seasoned unionist Guus van Betten was put forward as the union's negotiator. Wim Ruggenberg, illustrious chairman of the ABU, subsequently took him to meet their key members and provide him with an initial impression of the temporary employment world. In turn, Van Betten provided him with a comprehensive description of the FNV's latest perspectives. The union appreciated that there was a strong demand among workers for flexible labor and that flexible work could indeed create employment opportunities. They also saw that it would help employers by fulfilling the need for flexible labor during peak periods or staff shortages. Moreover, temporary employment was often the first step towards a permanent job for many people. The FNV, however, was clear on the subject of social security

Unemployed signing up
at the labor office.

Wil Albeda, Dutch Minister of Social Affairs, addresses hundreds of demonstrating staffing consultants from various agencies on 20 January 1981, as they assembled at the Binnenhof Court in The Hague, the political heart of the Netherlands.

and hard-won rights, stating in no uncertain terms that the union would not accept any compromise in these areas. The negotiations resulted in a collective labor agreement for permanent employees in 1986, and in another collective agreement for all temporary workers in 1987.

The government initially opted to continue with its policy on limiting temporary work. The Ministry of Social Affairs and Employment was still convinced that temporary workers were taking jobs that could be filled by per-manent staff. The government con-sidered this an unacceptable situation, given the rapidly deteriorating economy. In 1981, the Ministry decided to further reduce the maximum allowable staffing term from six to three months. Needless to say, this touched a raw nerve with employment agencies. The ABU decided to take the drastic measure of organi-zing a demonstration to take place in The Hague on January 20, 1981. Most

employment agencies attended the rally, and around 3,000 demonstrators traveled to The Hague in approximately 60 buses to show their support. The throngs gathered at the Binnenhof, the political heart of the Netherlands, where they shouted so loudly that Minister Albeda of Social Affairs had no choice but to go outside and face them. He accepted their petition, and Randstad's management, which would not have missed the demonstration for the world, acknowledged to its great satisfaction that the ABU was now a serious item on the political agenda.

The formation of a new cabinet in 1982 meant a fresh start on the government's stance on temporary employment. Ruud Lubbers' no-nonsense Christian Democratic (CDA) and Liberal (VVD) coalition government wanted to put an end to the ongoing bickering between the Ministry of Social Affairs and the staffing industry. Prime Minister Lubbers carefully weighed the pros and cons, asking himself what staffing services were really all about. He reasoned that since they were putting people into the labor market, and since unemployment was widespread, he did, in fact, need them. Following diligent lobbying by the ABU, a short yet ground-breaking sentence was incorporated into the coalition agreement of 1982: "A more liberal policy on temporary staffing

must be adopted." In other words, the government was planning to slacken the reins on current regulations. In 1985, the maximum legally allowable staffing term was once again extended from three to six months. The minimum age for temporary workers was reduced from eighteen to sixteen, and cross-border staffing was no longer prohibited.

The development of the new company Start was also a sign that the government no longer categorically ruled out temporary staffing. This temporary employment agency was established in 1977 by the Regional Labor Office (GAB) and the Ministry of Social Affairs. Start's management committee was a tripartite committee comprised of government, unions and employers who shared the responsibilities equally. Their joint objective was to reach out to those in the labor market who had little or no prospects, such as the long-term unemployed, and offer them a better chance of finding a permanent position via a temporary employment agency. In the 1980s, however, Start, which was partially financed by public funding, became a formidable competitor for commercial employment agencies; by increasingly supplying regular temporary workers. There was little difference between public and commercial agencies in practice. Start, however, benefited financially from its links with labor exchanges and did not pay corporate tax. Randstad and the other ABU agencies regarded this as unfair competition and had no qualms about publicizing this fact, and their opinion about it.

Je volgende baan begint bij Vedior.

VEDIOR. ALS JE VERDER WILT KOMEN.

VEDIOR UITZEND- EN PERSONEELADVIESBUREAUX

Waardering voor je werk begint bij Vedior.

VEDIOR. ALS JE VERDER WILT KOMEN.
VEDIOR UITZEND- EN PERSONEELADVIESBUREAUX

Na school aan de slag begint bij Vedior.

VEDIOR. ALS JE VERDER WILT KOMEN.
VEDIOR UITZEND- EN PERSONEELADVIESBUREAUX

19 86
'Vedior. If you want to go forward'. Used this slogan, Randstad's then-competitor would recruit potential staffers. This advertising campaign from 1986 focused on high school graduates and on people with technical and medical skills. Emphasis was also placed on personal development. 'Discovering your potential starts with Vedior', 'Appreciation for your work starts with Vedior', and, perhaps most important of all, 'Your next job starts with Vedior'.

"A more liberal policy on temporary staffing must be adopted". It was just a short sentence in the coalition agreement, but for Randstad it was a landslide. The company no longer felt that it was part of a problem, but rather, part of the solution. Flexible labor was now seen as a potential solution for unemployment.

In 1983, this recognition and the quickly recovering economy allowed Randstad to flourish. The acquisition of Tempo-Team and the fact it had been able to keep so many branches open gave the agency the capacity to meet the rapidly growing demand for temporary workers. Sales soared from EUR 204 million in 1983 to almost EUR 518 million in 1985. Randstad Uitzendbureau (The Netherlands) was primarily responsible for this huge increase. The Dutch employment agency sector as a whole benefited from the recovering economy and between 1985 and 1990, the number of temporary jobs increased from 72,000 to 120,000 in total. As a result, competitor ASB celebrated its 40th anniversary in grand style with a four-day trip to Israel for 900 staff members and other guests. Tempo-Team traveled to Paris by train and Vedior used its profits to expand its international activities in the United Kingdom, France and Germany. Randstad and its subsidiaries, however, experienced by far the fastest growth in the Dutch market. Its market share increased from nineteen to twenty percent in 1980 to approximately 30 percent in 1990. In order to serve its clients even better, Randstad set up a training center, the *Randstad Opleidingscentrum*, in 1985 in Diemen.

The center offered staff training in subjects that included computers, word processing, and telephone skills. This initiative was so successful that a second training center was opened in Rotterdam that same year. The centers also trained temporary workers for the tasks they would be carrying out for clients.

Randstad's 25th anniversary, in 1985, was celebrated with a sense of achievement and peace of mind. That year, the market leader organized various lectures on flexible labor in the economy and society, as well as a special anniversary symposium in the Dutch resort town of Noordwijkerhout. Jan de Koning, minister of Social Affairs, who attended the occasion, had agreed to make a speech. He opened with a short introduction but soon digressed from the proposed theme of 'Flexibility works, provided it is used sensibly.' Without unnecessary fuss and formality, he came straight to the point, announcing in a stately voice, "It has pleased Her Majesty…"

Goldschmeding looked around in surprise. What was happening? Was he the only one who knew nothing about this? The minister continued, "….to appoint Mr. F.J.D. Goldschmeding Officer in the Order of Orange-Nassau". Thunderous applause resounded before the minister could continue. "Mr. Goldschmeding, you have played a fundamental role in the development of the concept of temporary employment in general and of the Randstad organization in particular. You have achieved something very special. Thanks to you, employment agencies have become a valued part of society." With these words, he pinned the ribbon on Goldschmeding's lapel. In the auditorium, Goldschmeding's colleagues were visibly moved by the event.

The ribbon was more than just a personal honor. The royal gesture was nothing less than the ultimate recognition after years of opposition. Wim Riggenberg, figurehead of the trade association ABU, sat in his chair beaming. The royal insignia was a pivotal moment for the entire industry. It was the ultimate triumph over the perception of temporary employment agencies as rogue traders. The honor was a recognition of everyone's efforts over the previous twenty-five years. That day was not simply a silver jubilee; it was a jubilee cast in gold.

Maar worden mijn vakantiedagen wel doorbetaald?

de Werkpocket

haal 'm binnen

10e HERZIENE
DRUK
5,75
NIEUWE
CIJFERS

randstad uitzendbureau

Alles wat iedereen zou moeten weten over werk.

Heb je de blauwe werkpocket al?

19 81 *Since 1978, Randstad has been publishing an annual 'Workpocket'. This convenient booklet tells staffers, clients, and students everything they need to know about legislation, studies, training, vacation, holiday, and social benefits. This so-called 'Cloudpocket' was published in 1981, and its existence is advertised on posters.*

Randstad does not like half work

Frits Goldschmeding is applauded by his employees after his speech at the so-called 'Quality Day' of 1 November 1986.

The company's growth, changes in management, confusion following Hünd's departure, and the royal honor made many employees feel they were suddenly riding a proverbial roller coaster. The company was growing rapidly and that old, familiar Randstad feeling was getting lost somewhere along the way. That sentiment was confirmed when staff members were asked to fill out a questionnaire designed by the management team in which many complained about the high staff turnover. The complaints were not unfounded: as a result of the sixty-percent growth between 1983 and 1985 and of the fast increase in the number of new and inexperienced staff, just seven percent of the staff now had more than two years of practical experience. The company's management expected that turnover would stabilize in 1987, and that the problem would then sort itself out. Moreover, the only alternative was

The Lange Viestraat branch in the Dutch city of Utrecht, wrapped in a life-sized advertising poster of Jane.

for growth to stop, and that was not a good option.

Another complaint from staff was the centralized manner in which the company was organized. Branch workers were frustrated that huge sums in revenue were generated, while the purchase of a new office chair still required permission from almost half the organization. The management's main concern, however, was the complaint that the Randstad culture -- the culture in which every employee was aware that he or she was part of a team whose members needed each other, a culture based on sharing for mutual benefit -- was gradually breaking down. A weakening of this culture meant that employees would start pointing fingers when things went wrong and that consultants would selfishly start 'time sheet hunting.'

On November 1, 1986, in a packed pavilion in Diemen, Goldschmeding spoke to Randstad employees. "We have spent the last few years building a much

bigger 'Randstad House' together. Some construction faults have crept in here and there, a window that won't close, a wall that's a little crooked, a leaky roof, but let's remember one thing: the foundations are strong." It was cold and wet outside that Saturday, but the atmosphere inside was warm. Many people had given up a free day to attend the talk, but it was quite a sight to see practically every Randstad employee from all over the country gathered together under one roof.

The director continued, "In our corporate culture there has always been, and hopefully there still is, a feeling of pride among employees, pride in Randstad. And we want you all to show and feel that pride, because we want the best 'house style' there is. In fact, we have it. And we are also proud because we have the best and most stylish branch offices and head office designed by the best architects, because we have the best promotional items, because we have the best copywriters, and because we want the best terms of employment

The riddle as to why every branch had to hand in a puzzle piece led to the new slogan: 'Randstad does not like half work'.

and better salaries than are paid on average in the staffing industry in the Netherlands. In short, we are proud because we all work together to show the world that we are the best temporary employment agency: youthful, progressive, dynamic and modern!"

There was a large board behind the speaker on which Randstad employees from all over the country had hung jigsaw pieces upon their arrival. It was not clear what it was all about until, after exactly an hour, Goldschmeding closed his speech with the words, "Randstad does not like half work." Suddenly, the lights went out. When they came back on a couple of seconds later, the board had been turned around and displayed the slogan for a new advertising campaign: 'Randstad does not like half work'.

Goldschmeding asked the audience what they thought of it. They almost raised the roof with their enthusiasm for the new slogan and five minutes later the applause had still not subsided. It was an outpouring of emotions after a year's hard grind. But there was still more to come. Ed Bolk, who had organized the whole event together with Cleem Farla, had also arranged for every staff member to be treated to an exquisite meal. Furthermore, everyone was handed a check as they left for 111.86 Dutch guilders (EUR 50.85), an amount that represented the date, January 11, 1986. The publication *Memorandstad* later reported that, "A sense of togetherness, of everyone 'pulling their combined weight' was felt by all that day." From that moment on, the corporate culture of Randstad became stronger again, due also to the excellent results achieved by the

company year after year. Personnel knew once again that they were working for a company with a strong corporate culture which produced excellent results. The company's new spirit was summed up succinctly by 'Randstad does not like half work'.

12
randstad
houdt niet van
half werk

**randstad
houdt niet van
half werk**

**19
88** *The slogan 'Randstad does not like half work' was adopted internationally. The subsidiaries in Germany, Belgium and France adopted the slogan as: 'Randstad macht keine halbe Sachen' and 'Randstad ne fait jamais les choses à moitié'.*

the Quist quest

With the company's dramatic growth, there came a point when Randstad's head office began to burst at the seams. If in 1982 the Diemen Wildenborch office building had still been half empty, now there was hardly any space left. The management team planned to build a new head office in another part of Diemen, at the exact spot where the pavilion had stood on November 1, 1986. Randstad was, of course, looking to find the very best architect to design the new building, and after careful selection, Wim Quist was chosen to design the new head office. Quist was an experienced architect with an impressive list of prize-winning buildings to his name, such as the NedLloyd office building in Rotterdam. Between 1975 and 1979, he had been government architect for the Netherlands, a prestigious position involving the responsibility for maintaining and improving the quality and appearance of government buildings. His architectural style was that of the *Gesamtkunstwerk*, an art form that strives to embrace and combine many different forms. In other words,

he was an architect with a passion for perfection and quality.

Before he had time to put pen to paper, Quist was inundated with a huge number of reports from various Randstad managers stating what he could and could not do. He wasted no time in approaching Goldschmeding about the matter. "Listen, this isn't going to work. What I want is a single sheet of paper summarizing what is important to the company."

It was a little more than a single sheet of paper in the end, but the message was loud and clear: "Randstad serves to protect the interests of everyone involved in the organization, whether they be clients, staff, suppliers, or other stakeholders. Moreover, the internal organization promotes a high degree of mutual openness. We want to recognize that protection of interests and openness in the building's details, the choice of materials, the light and the proportions; everything about the building has to be just right". This was

just the beginning of Quist's quest: to represent this 'promotion of interests and openness' in steel, stone and glass. That quest was made even harder by the fact that Quist was given strict instructions to remain within the given budget. He made some quick calculations and came to the conclusion that he could build a head office in the style that Randstad wanted for a maximum of EUR 41 million. That sum included every detail down to the air-conditioning system, the hand rails and the bricks. Nothing had escaped the attention of the architect and his client.

From the very beginning, Quist and Goldschmeding got along well, They had similar interests. Quist got to know Goldschmeding as an old-fashioned property developer who wanted to be involved in every aspect of the design, right down to the last detail. The

Consultations between Wim Quist (left) and employees over construction plans for the new head office.

elevators were a good example. The specifications indicated that the building needed high-quality elevators, although these were slightly slower than other versions. Goldschmeding, however, wanted faster elevators. The designer advised against this, as it would be very expensive, but after some hesitation, Randstad's director replied, "What are the benefits of investing in a more expensive and faster elevator? Apart from the fact that they are more attractive, they save time. The question is, how much?" Goldschmeding compared the volume of work carried out by an employee against the time that would be lost through using a slower elevator and came to the conclusion that the less time a member of staff spent in the elevator, the less it would cost the organization.

In 1989, after the drawings were approved and the specifications completed, staff members gathered to see the first stone laid for the new head office. Over the next few months, the steel grey building, 177 feet high and 328 feet long, gradually began to take shape. The building's exterior was striking in its modern design and the entire structure blended seamlessly into the surroundings with its sloping sidewalls. Inside, it was the attention to detail that caught the eye. The window ledges were set at a slant so they would not become cluttered; clutter would be incongruous with the design. Every door reached to the

ceiling, a typical feature of a genuine 'Quist'. The corridor walls were tiled by the best masons, who also laid the natural stone floors that gave the building its calm atmosphere. The walls were pointed meticulously and the curved, steel handrails on the staircases were welded with a precision only found among builders of luxury yachts. The entire interior breathed an air of calm and would allow the employees themselves to give the building its internal color. Quist's quest was complete. His creation was perfectly constructed, completed within the given budget and, above all, it expressed the concepts of 'promotion of interests and openness' in steel, stone and glass.

The grand opening of the head office, on April 6, 1990, was arranged by none other than Johan Stekelenburg, chairman of the largest Dutch trade union, the FNV, and Onno Ruding, chairman of the Dutch Union of Christian Employers and former Minister of Finance. The presence of these two prominent representatives of the so-called 'polder model' – the unique and internationally acclaimed consensus policy used by Dutch government, employers and unions in order to carry out major projects through close mutual cooperation and consultation – was another important step towards recognition of both Randstad and of the concept of temporary employment.

the next step
Beursplein 5

The IPO was celebrated at a party at the Amsterdam stock exchange, at 5 Beursplein Square.

To make it possible for Randstad employees to share in the company's successes was a wish that Frits Goldschmeding had long cherished. Staff already received a competitive salary, dividends and a good pension, but he wanted to go one step further. Randstad was convinced that employees who had felt a financial and emotional commitment to the company for many years would be wholly prepared to dedicate themselves to the common interest of the company: its continuity. Goldschmeding pledged 25% of his shares in order to finance the plan; it was a unique step. The Randstad options fund was established in 1988. Every employee who had worked for Randstad for at least twenty hours a week for two years or more was allowed to participate in the fund. The number of options an employee was entitled to was proportional to the size of his or her salary. Interest in the options was limited at first and the fiscal arrangements at the time were not exactly favorable. Employees who purchased the options had to pay seven percent tax. Some

years later, when this policy changed, the enthusiasm for Randstad options began to soar.

Establishment of the Randstad options fund foundation coincided with the important decision to prepare the company for a public stock offering via the Amsterdam stock exchange. There were various reasons for this decision. First of all, the future stock market price would benefit and further build Randstad's reputation. Moreover, the stock price would serve as a standard for the Randstad staff stock options. Another reason was that it was becoming increasingly important to find good managers who were also suited to the scope of the company. An initial public offer would strengthen Randstad's image by making it more attractive to new, talented staff members. It would also provide Randstad with immediate access to the capital market. Although Randstad's war chest was more than adequately filled with over EUR 91 million, it was probably still not sufficient to finance a significant

De flexibele manager blijft iedereen 'n stapje voor.

ᴕ randstad uitzendbureau
01620-2 92 80 kantoor-, industrie-, technisch en gezondheidszorgpersoneel.

De flexibele manager reageert op elke verandering.

ᴕ randstad uitzendbureau

19 88 *Every year, Randstad organizes New Year activities for its clients. Through the mailing of New Year cards and job offers, end-of-the-year meetings, and invitations to the head office, Randstad strengthens its bonds with its customers. 1988 was the year in which a theme was chosen for the first time. Work and art. In order to draw attention to this theme, special posters were distributed, specifically targeting managers hiring temporary staffers, because 'a flexible manager remains a step ahead'.*

takeover. Another important incentive for Randstad was the expansion of its international strategy. A stock market offering would accentuate the fact that the company was ready to take its next big step forward. Market leadership in the Netherlands was already a fact; internationally, however, Randstad held only fifth place after Manpower, Kelly Services, Adia and Ecco. There was still a long way to go before it reached the top.

In 1988, the long process of preparations began that was to end in a successful stock market offering for Randstad in 1990. Banks drew up extensive reports, accountants calculated share values, and AMRO Bank, which had been Randstad's 'house' bank since 1961, performed a due diligence analysis in which the entire company underwent meticulous scrutiny. Questions had to be answered: "How do you intend to achieve this?" "Is a high liquidity position necessary?" "Is Randstad dependent on large clients?" The consequences of the public offering became very clear at the presentation of the 1989 annual report, which for the first time in the company's history involved a large press conference. The marketing machine was cranking up. Good brand recognition was vital for Randstad's stock market success. Surveys showed that recognition in the Netherlands was no problem: no less than 99.5% of the respondents were familiar with the name Randstad Uitzendbureau. Countless interviews were published in newspapers and magazines, Randstad held roadshows at the old and the new head offices for institutional investors and financial journalists, and traveled the business circuit, introducing itself as a source of new stock on the market.

Meanwhile, an announcement regarding the introduction to the stock market was being prepared with the greatest care and attention. If it would impress potential investors, they would buy shares immediately. The registration period lasted for three tense days, from 10:00 a.m. on May 28, 1990, until May 31 at 3:00 p.m. Advertisements were placed in the newspapers that evening and again the next morning, and Randstad spent an exciting weekend waiting for the results. On Tuesday, June 5, 1990, a gong stroke would ring in the first day of Randstad's official listing on the Amsterdam Stock Exchange. The big day was drawing near.

One by one, Randstad employees closed their umbrellas. A decade that started with rainy weather ended with sunshine. Sales were up, the number of employees had grown, and the international market was tempting. The IPO crowned the achievements of the eighties.

21 a consummate p...
Arasappan 22 Gene...
Christmas in Porto, Pe...
Melissa Roberts 25 ...
and the beat goes on...
Deandra Drewke 28 mixe...
29 peace, love and i...
like in the...

good
to know
y

personal growth is best

a consummate professional

It sounds like a riddle... How do you work for three different employers without ever changing jobs? Muthokumaran Arasappan, also known as Kumar in the Randstad world, started in 2000 working with Select Appointments, which was taken over by Vedior and later by Randstad. Since the merger and integration, Kumar is now the Manager Contracting, Staffing.

"The way I started out here is quite ironic. I walked into Select Appointments to sign up as I had just graduated with a Bachelor's degree. My interview went so well that I was called two weeks later to work for Select Appointments. Since then, I've been sitting on the other side of the desk, interviewing and consulting candidates who want to sign up. In the ten years that I've been doing this, the stories about personal growth are still the ones I like best. I once had, for example, a very shy temporary worker, who only conversed in monosyllables: yes or no. I bumped into her two years after I had placed her with my client, whom she was still working for. Initially I did not recognize her. She approached me full of the self-confidence of a consumate professional. That's what motivates and gives me a sense of satisfaction."

Muthokumaran Arasappan (second of the right) – Manager contracting, staffing Randstad, Malaysia

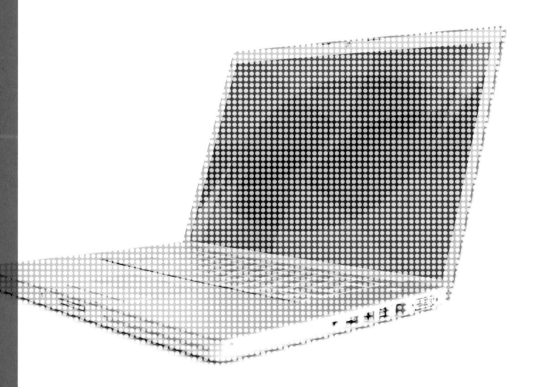

employees build their own world

22

Generation Y

Type the name Tina Thomsen into Google and a Randstad personality springs to life. Thomsen is an active member of *Facebook*, *Twitter* and *LinkedIn*, and even has her very own blog, but there's more to it than meets the eye, it would seem.

Thomsen: "A couple of years ago I earned a master's degree in Management Development which opened up a whole new world to me and showed me the importance of social media. I think it's important to keep up-to-date with the latest developments. The younger generation – Generation Y – integrates the Internet into their lives on a day-to-day basis. They prepare for interviews with me by reading my blog and tweets… this is how young employees develop their own worlds. It's fascinating!"

"Social media offer Randstad the opportunity to expand on the Good to know you theme. GTKY can be implemented on a wider scale than by just shaking hands and talking to one another. I know that my blog brings people closer together through the Internet, and I see social media as a great opportunity for Randstad to do the same."

Tina Thomsen – Director HR Randstad Denmark and Sweden

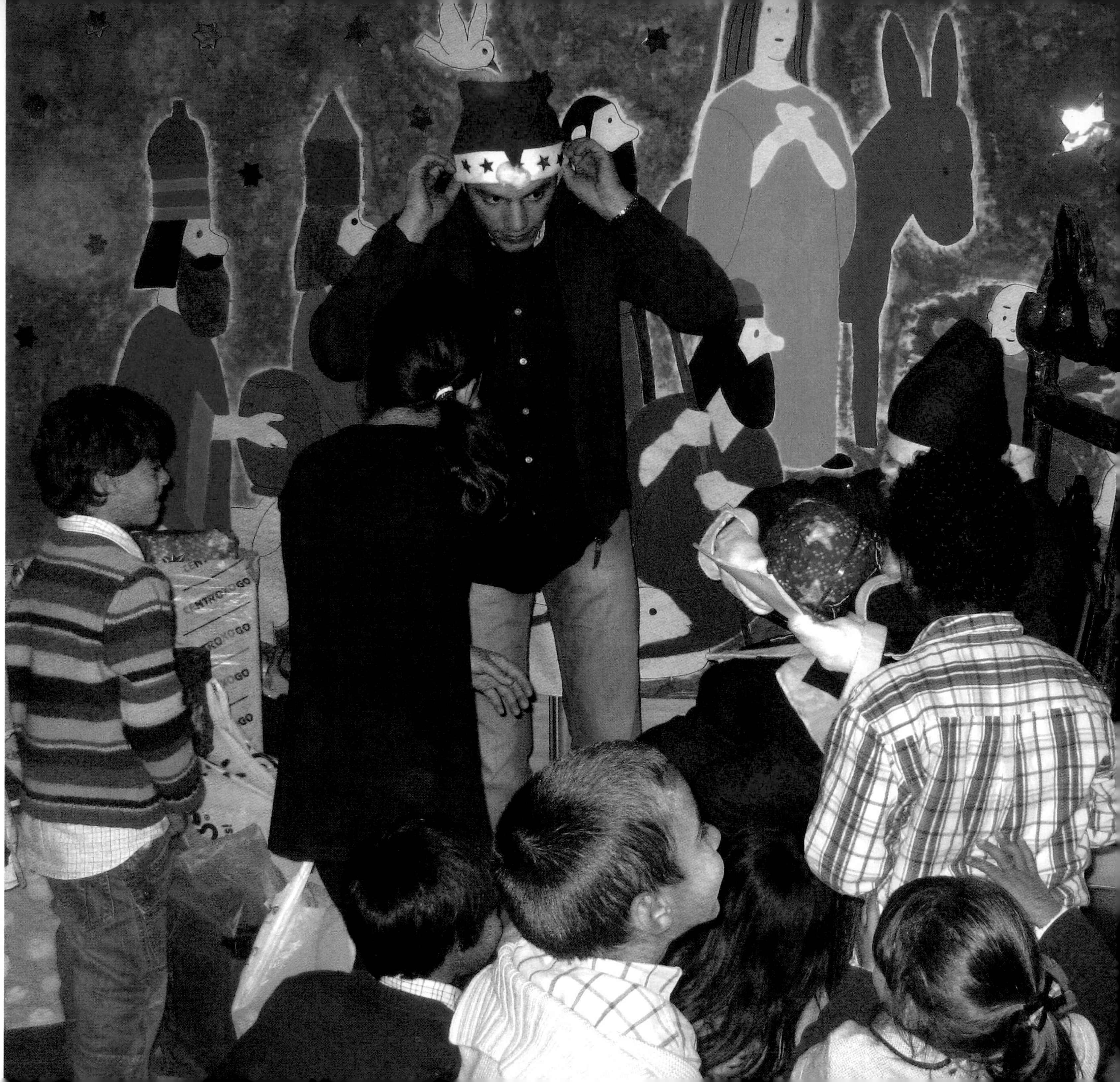
CENTROXOGO

23

Christmas in Porto

NBS is the market leader in Portugal when it comes to outsourcing, staffing, and the recruitment and selection of IT professionals. Pedro Mota is manager of a branch located right in the medieval center of Porto. "Even though we work in the IT sector with all its technology and computers, the quality of work carried out at NBS depends just as much on the ability to get on with people as it does anywhere else. It is important to like people and to have a feeling for personal relationships. This attitude goes deeper than simply being reflected in our working environment. NBS acknowledges its responsibility towards society. Last Christmas, our branch took the initiative to support the Associação Acreditar, a local organization that provides help for homeless children. We asked 52 children to write a letter to Father Christmas asking him for a gift. Their requests varied from footballs to trendy shoes to MP3 players and rucksacks. Our staff then bought the presents, which were then given to the children by Santa at Christmas. I have never seen such happy faces! It required only a small effort on the part of our branch, yet it provided us with the most wonderful reward imaginable."

Pedro Mota – Branch manager Randstad, Portugal

The name NBS (New Boston Select) originates from the time when the professionals company was still part of Vedior. The European Commission ruled that these names could not be changed immediately following the merger with Randstad. The company will be endorsed by Randstad as of August 2010.

client is king

24

one stop shop

Ten years ago, Melissa Roberts and four colleagues opened the first branch of Randstad Canada in Toronto. "In order to acquaint people with the Randstad brand, we made hundreds of phone calls. We had a lot to explain. When they heard the name Randstad, some people thought we were some sort of exclusive European jeweler!"

"People walked into our office and asked us what it was that we were doing. Actually, this still happens occasionally, which is why I always have my answer ready: 'Randstad helps clients find strong candidates for temporary or permanent vacancies, locally and nationally'. Isn't that a clear explanation?"

"With the introduction of the *capability line* – a list of services offered under the Randstad brand name – our story has become even clearer. We now offer our clients a one stop shop. Whichever type of staffing needs they have, they can find it through us. If, for instance, a client needs professionals as well as administrative or industrial flex workers, we can help. The coordination between the various services is done behind the scenes, as much as possible, so that the client does not have to deal with constantly new contact persons. We work together to provide the best possible service to the client."

Melissa Roberts – Senior market manager Randstad, Canada

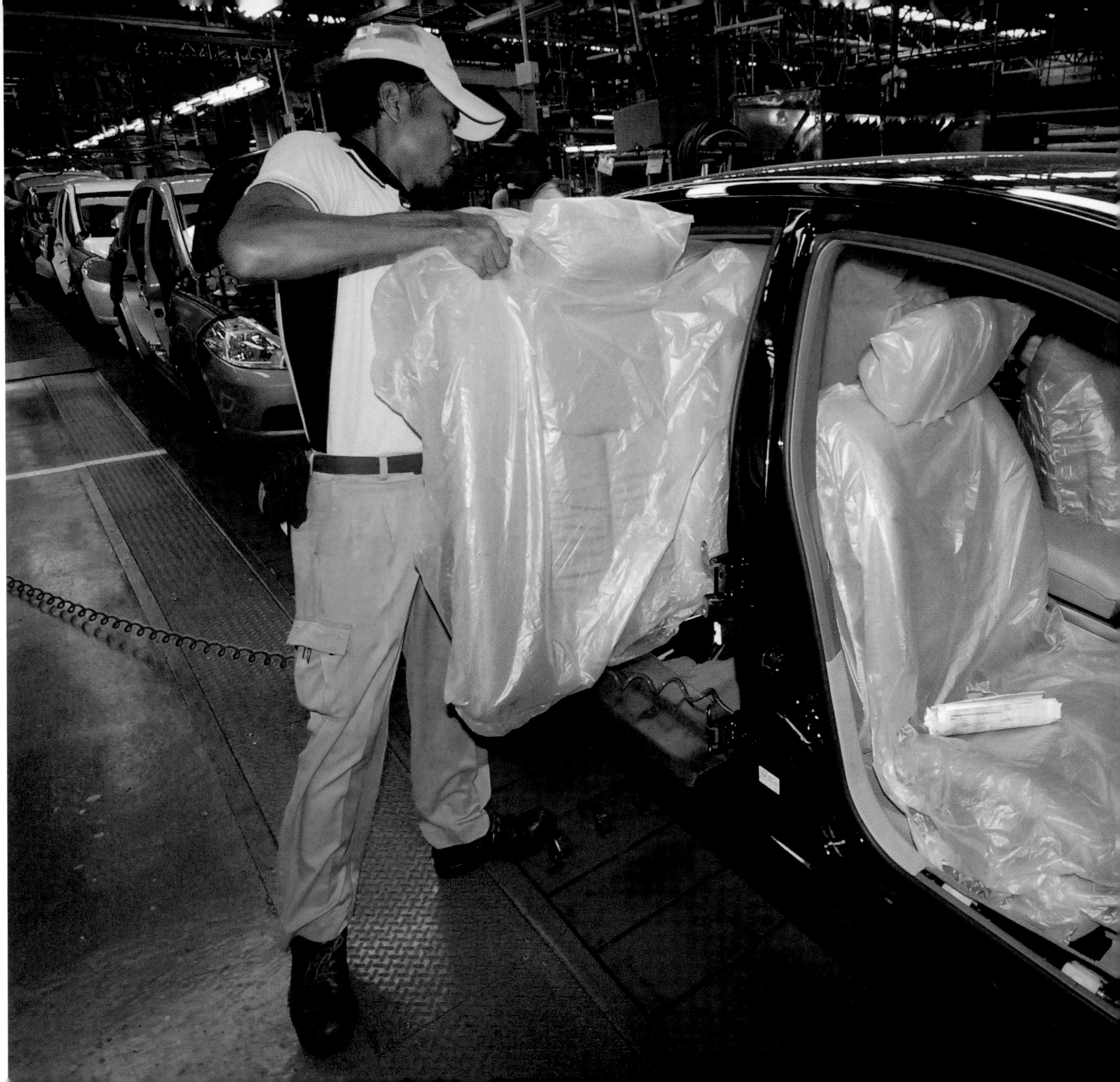

25

haute couture

Faurecia is a producer of car seats with a production and assembly site in Nogent sur Vernisson in France. Randstad Inhouse Services (RIS) specializes in providing large numbers of flex workers, and when it offered its services to Faurecia, it turned out that a competitor had been there first, and established an onsite branch for 'temporary and permanent workers'. However, RIS was given three months in order to prove that it could do better.

"I always say: 'Randstad is the grand couturier of the staffing business'. We create custom solutions, like Dior, Yves Saint-Laurent and Chanel. The secret of our custom work is our selection process. Every client is given a similar test, but the details are specific to the work for which flex workers are needed. We therefore send only the best flex workers to our clients. Our custom work produced good results to Faurecia too: thanks to the high quality of the flex workers, productivity went up immediately. Usually we assume a productivity of fifty percent on the first day, eighty on the second, and one hundred on the third day. Our flex workers already achieved eighty percent on their first day! This persuaded the client, and we were allowed to open a branch at their site!"

Ali Tifaou – Account manager Randstad Inhouse Services, France

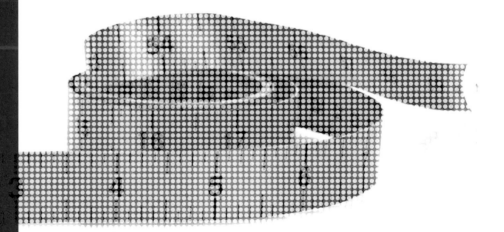

in no time we found one rhythm

26

and the beat goes on

Karin Clarke previously experienced an difficult merger of two of the recruitment industry's major players. It was for this reason that her attitude to the merger of Vedior and Randstad was cautious. This time, however, the integration process was strikingly different.

"Throughout 2009, I was involved in an integration program that from the outset motivated, engaged and inspired our people. Our local team dedicated to the merger organized a variety of themed events to build the Randstad spirit including 'blue days', for example. Everyone dressed in blue from head-to-toe and branch offices were painted almost completely blue. An internal marketing competition was also created, the *Randstad Rally*, the aim of which was to make Randstad the strongest brand, company and culture in Singapore. We're definitely seeing how working together can achieve great results. Because of that, 2009 was, despite the economic crisis, a good year for Randstad Singapore."

"The merger and the name change to Randstad was an event we celebrated with a launch party and drumming session that had everyone beating their drums in the same rhythm and tempo as a symbol of what we could achieve together. We were beating our drums simultaneously in no time." *And the beat goes on.*

Karin Clarke (right) – Regional director Randstad Singapore and Malaysia

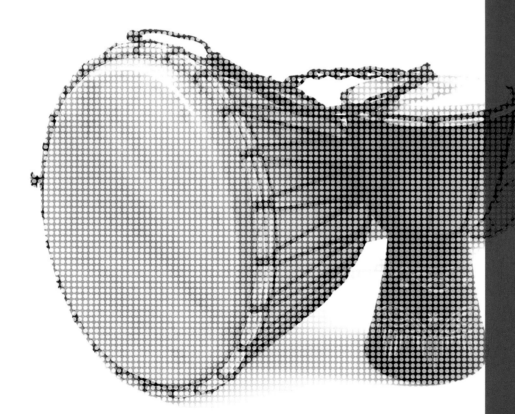

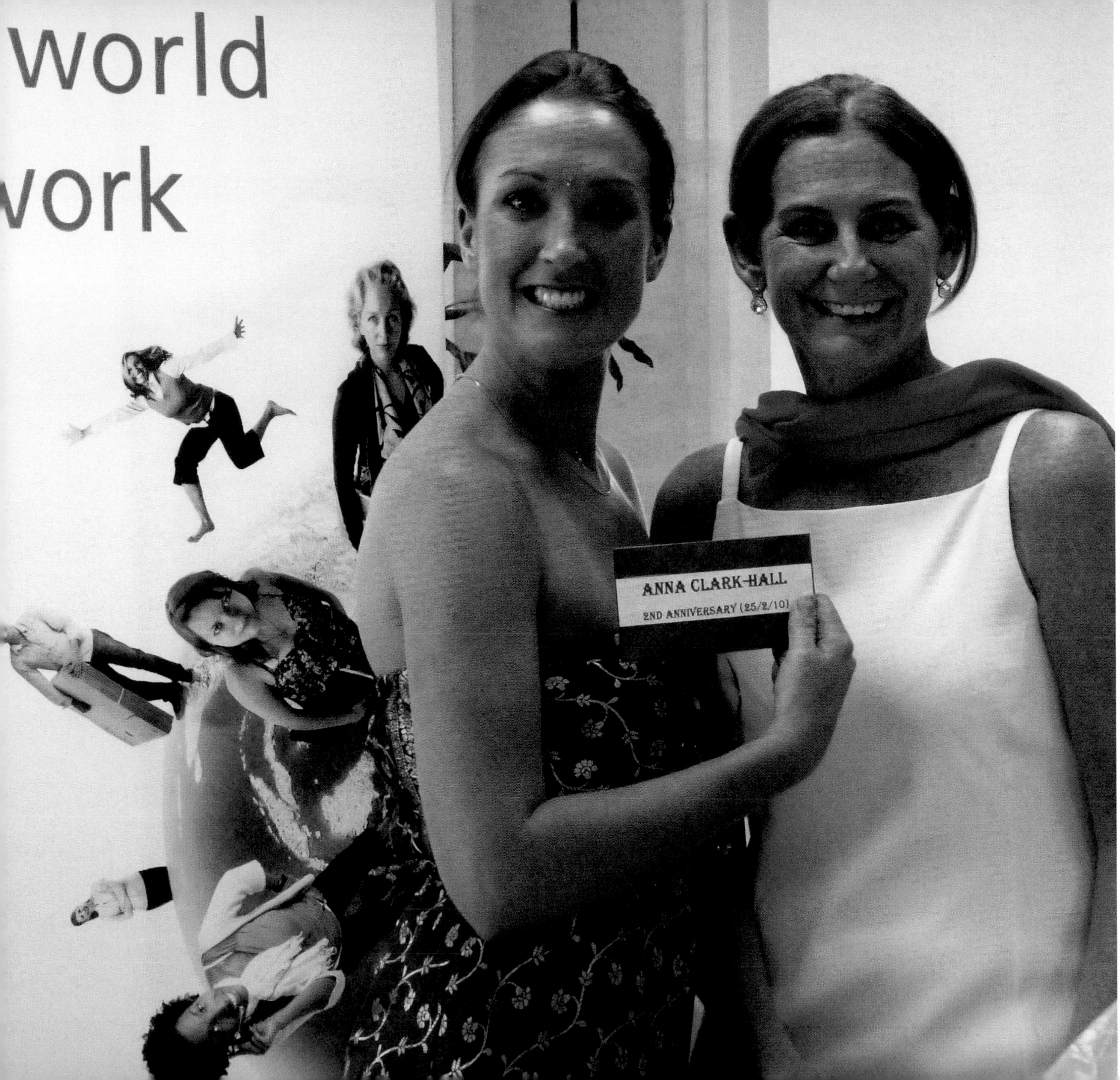
world
ANNA CLARK-HALL
2ND ANNIVERSARY (25/2/10)

27

high tech

The cream of the crop of technicians: that's what Randstad's subsidiary Yacht Teccon offers its clients. The company dispatches only highly qualified 'state of the art' engineers in the fields of aviation, IT and mechanical engineering. Teccon has been in business since 1975. Yacht is a bit younger: it started in Germany in 2001. In 2008, these two specialists merged into a single company with three thousand employees (regular as well as flexible), comprising branches in Germany and France.

Communication specialist Deandra Drewke: "We are the right address for clients with complicated technical projects. One project of which we are very proud is the Airbus A380. Two hundred of our project managers and aviation engineers participated in constructing the largest airplane in the world. In July 2008, the A380 flew to Hamburg in Germany. I was present at that high-profile media event, and later wrote an article about it for our in-house magazine."

"Yacht Teccon and Randstad cooperate closely with each other. Here in Stuhr we're even in the same building. It feels good to be able to tell our clients that we are part of a large international HR corporation."

Deandra Drewke – Communication specialist Yacht Teccon, Germany

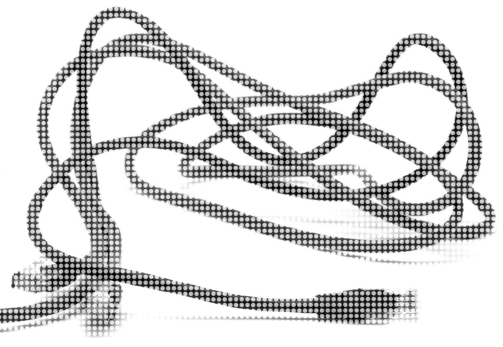

my heart is orange and blue

28

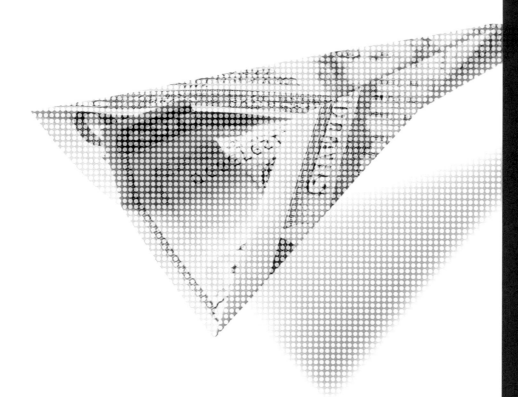

mixed feelings

According to Piethein Leune, Randstad is a fairly small company. It is all relative, of course. Leune was comparing Randstad to ING, a large Dutch bank with branches around the globe. Some years ago, Leune switched from one quality brand to another. As a management trainee in the late 1990s, he experienced a period of dynamic growth within Randstad during which the company made the decision to spread its wings overseas.

It was during that highly enterprising period, which included several takeovers, that he had first had the chance to develop direct business relations in corporate finance, first as a controller and later as investor relations manager. Banks were more than interested in his experience and network, but Leune held back until ING made him an offer he could not refuse. And no, it was not because of the money. "The bank made it possible for me to expand my financial expertise and also remain in contact with Randstad, by experiencing the company from the other side. ING hires flexworkers from Randstad. From that vantage point it is easier to see how unique their corporate culture is, as is the solidarity among Randstad workers. I think it comes from years of organic growth, and the fact that I have been part of that, albeit indirectly, is hugely valuable. Don't ask me to choose between Randstad and ING; my heart is blue and orange."

Piethein Leune – Account manager, ING Commercial Banking, Netherlands

29

peace, love, and ice cream

In the late 1990s, Nienke Mulder was working as a Randstad staffing consultant in a Dutch provincial town during the last year of her university studies. Now, eleven years later, she is HR director for the 'Go to Market' organization of Unilever Australia and New Zealand. Nienke Mulder is on the other side now, as Unilever is one of Randstad's clients. They continue their relationship with some new and exciting business opportunities launched recently by Unilever, such as the opening of the first Ben & Jerry's store in Australia.

"Randstad helped us form the team for our shop at Manly Beach in Sydney. Jointly we were able to work through the work force composition: should we use temporary workers, part-timers or a mix of both? Randstad made sure that the people they employed were at the same level of expertise with regard to various issues, such as workplace safety, as the rest of our Ben & Jerry's team. The shop was a great success right from the start. On a typical sunny day we serve approximately one thousand scoops of our super premium ice cream!"

Nienke Mulder (not in image) – HR director at Unilever Australia and New Zealand

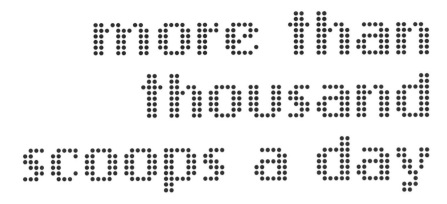

more than thousand scoops a day

the movie game clarifies a mission

like in the movies

Different generations or different groups with conflicting ideas on how to run the family business, and a clashing of cultures in a multinational organization: situations like these can be a major impediment to the growth of a company. Randstad Italy has a specialized training team led by Daniela Ferdeghini, and one of the areas that it focuses on is internal relationships and communication within companies.

"Our team is very resourceful when it comes to helping clients. One example is the movie game, a new way to improve communication and cooperation. The game also helps to improve team spirit within a company, but it can also help staff to accurately visualize a mission or objective. Employees are divided into groups and might, for example, be given the assignment to make a film about internal client friendliness. They then have to create an entire script complete with role assignments, plot, and text, and allocate team members to their roles as director and actors. The purpose of the task is to use the film in order to illustrate what employees consider to be a friendly way of approaching internal clients. The films are edited and shown to the other course participants. They should clearly illustrate how each group of employees would like to approach clients, the idea being, of course, that clients should be approached in the same way in the future. Just like in the movies!"

Daniela Ferdeghini – Training coordinator HR Solutions Randstad, Italy

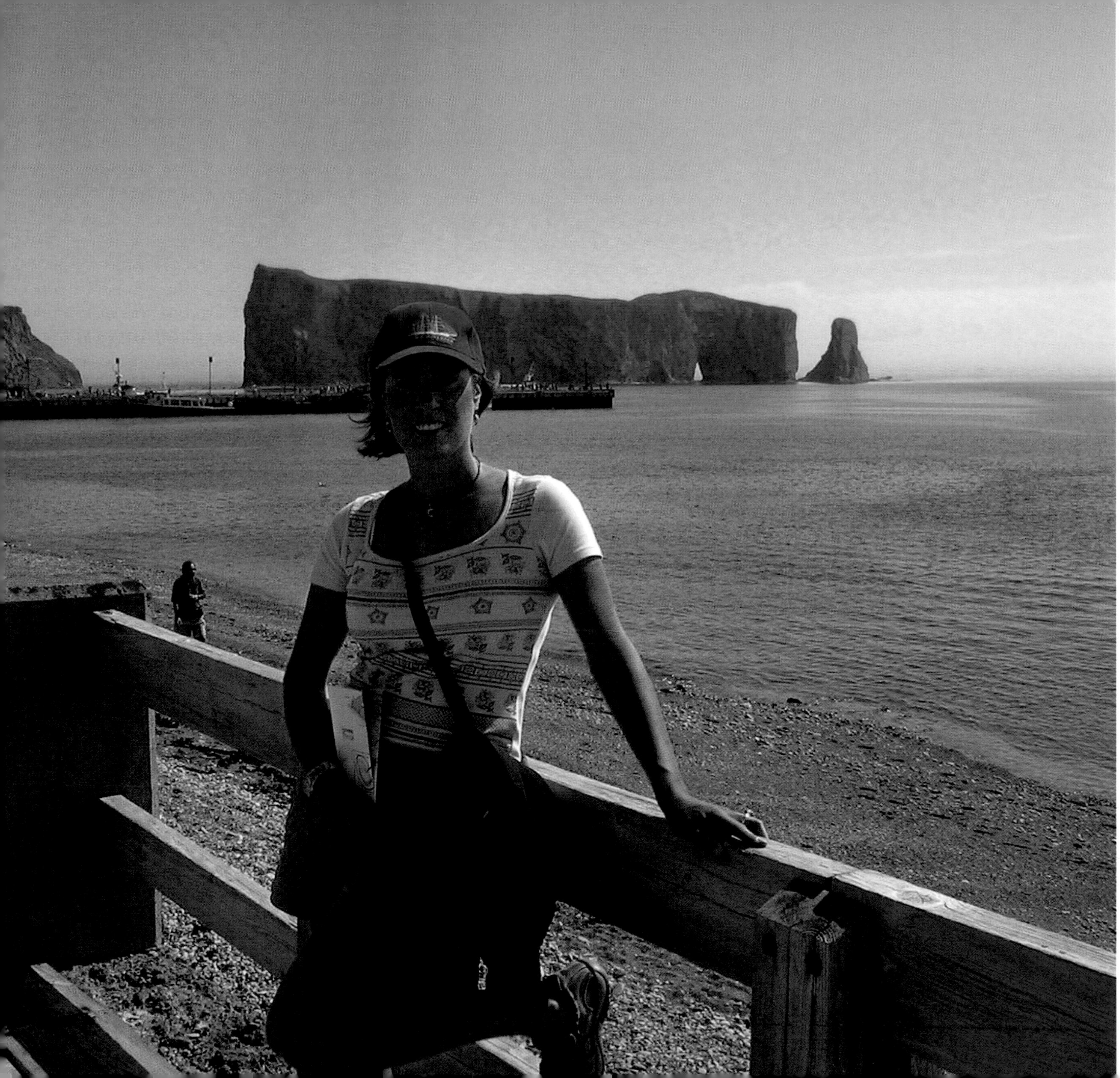

internatio-nalization
as a challenge

The sound of the bell at the Amsterdam Stock Exchange marked the beginning of the trade in Randstad shares. That bell also rang in a process of globalization. The borders between national employment markets became vaguer, and the phenomenon of staffing spread to an increasing number of countries. The company established new stepping stones at a high speed. America was waiting for Randstad to plant its flag there, too.

dealings
and doings

*Frits Goldschmeding (right)
at the Amsterdam Stock
Exchange on Damrak Street,
surrounded by traders*

The Amsterdam Stock Exchange opened for business on June 5, 1990, with the stroke of a gong. It was the first day of trading for the newly listed Randstad shares, and traders were keeping a close watch on the electronic board that hung above the trading floor. At zero hour, the introductory price for Randstad shares appeared: 48.00 Dutch guilders (EUR 21.78). Once the gong had officially sounded, countless balloons were let loose and the guests raised their glasses. Planes flew advertising banners over Amsterdam to mark this milestone in the history of Randstad.

The financial world, however, followed the stock exchange introduction with some skepticism. The introduction was supervised by AMRO Bank, which had achieved little success with previous share introductions of Air Holland and Pirelli. The opening price turned out to be too high, and the bank was left with approximately 2,000,000 of the 4,320,000 shares available, rendering the stock exchange introduction a failure, despite the careful and comprehensive preparation that had taken place. Randstad was bitterly disappointed; how could this have happened? For many days following the stock exchange introduction, newspapers and magazines were crammed with analyses. The issue price of 48 Dutch guilders had been too high, they wrote, especially since share prices and the economy were experiencing difficult times. The result was that a significant group of institutional investors, including managers of professional share portfolios and pension funds, declined to invest. The reason was that the name Randstad meant nothing to institutional investors. Name recognition may have been very high among consumers, but it was a different story where the financial market was concerned, and in that respect, Randstad was going to have to build its reputation and brand recognition from scratch.

Less than a week after their Stock Exchange disappointment, the management board wrote a report entitled "The Stock Exchange Introduction: What Went Wrong?" The board took part of the blame upon itself. The directors wrote that an introductory price of forty Dutch guilders per share had in fact been considered in 1990, but that "Somehow, sometime in the course of April 1990, we must have had an aberration and we even thought of the price of 52 guilders." AMRO bank was also apportioned some of the blame; according to Randstad, the bank's sales channels had failed in their mission. It came to light that some of the bank's branches had probably advised their clients against the purchase of Randstad shares and some had even failed to inform clients of the share offering. The board was dissatisfied, in retrospect, with the quality of the road shows in which Randstad and AMRO Bank had presented the stock, and thought there had been insufficient focus on institutional investors, both at home and abroad. The analysis concluded by stating that timing had been the main problem; the period between two Dutch national holidays, Ascension Day and Whitsun, was not the time to introduce new stock.

The opening price of 48 Dutch guilders gradually dropped to 41.30 guilders by February 14, 1991, but the company remained calm. Randstad's sales were still growing faster than those of its competitors. That calm attitude turned out to be justified; 1990 was a good year for Randstad, with the company making a profit of EUR 42.16 million and registering sales of over EUR 1.15 billion. These figures were a breakthrough for Randstad's stock. The sale of shares had originally been dependent on private investors, but all that changed after the presentation of the company's annual report. Institutional investors were now interested in participating and were soon making their way to AMRO bank. No fewer than 2 million shares were re-issued to institutional investors such as Aegon and DeltaLloyd. For the first time since the introduction, all the shares had now been placed. By mid-March 1991 the share price reached a preliminary record high of 49.70 Dutch guilders, and financial analysts all agreed that Randstad Holding's stock was off to a new start.

In 1993, Randstad introduced *falcons*, Randstad share options that had a three-year life and were freely marketable. They were introduced in order to promote Randstad shares, and the issue price was very attractive. Moreover, the share price increased throughout the three-year term, making them an excellent investment.

The hall of the Amsterdam Stock Exchange.

the world is expanding

A Randstad Holding board meeting in 1994, with (from left to right): Cleem Farla, Erik Vonk, Theo Pruntel, Frits Goldschmeding, Fred van Haasteren, Frits Drost, and David van Gelder.

The Randstad governing structure was adjusted following its public stock offer. The management board became known as Randstad Holding Beraad (RHB), and in 1991 it comprised Frits Goldschmeding (chairman), Dick Beutick (controller), Cleem Farla (international staffing services), Fred van Haasteren (corporate affairs), Jan Herlaar (cleaning and security) and Herman Kolk (financial affairs). The RHB was expanded later in 1991 to include Frits Drost (director of Randstad Uitzendbureau), David van Gelder (Tempo-Team director and later international staffing services) and Erik Vonk (USA staffing, from 1992). Herman Kolk, who had been Frits

Goldschmeding's financial right-hand man since 1965, left the RHB in 1993 upon reaching retirement age. Theo Pruntel was his successor. David van Gelder's position at Tempo-Team was taken over in 1994 by Leo Lindelauf, who had started as a branch manager at Randstad Uitzendbureau and gradually worked his way up through the organization. Lindelauf would eventually be appointed a member of the Executive Board in 2001.

The RHB focused on the further internationalization of the company. Until then, Randstad had primarily been a Dutch company with branches in Belgium, Germany, France and

England. The Dutch operating companies for staffing, cleaning, security and training formed the backbone of the Randstad Group, and in 1991 they were responsible for EUR 864 million, out of the company's total sales of EUR 1.2 billion. The remaining EUR 318 million, less than a quarter, were achieved through international activities.

An important step in Randstad's internationalization was the decision

to promote its stock internationally. In 1991, investment bank Goldman Sachs brought the stock to the attention of investors in Britain and in the United States. That same year, the RHB began working on a new, more internationally oriented strategy for Randstad. The branches in Belgium were doing extremely well at that time. Interlabor, established in 1965 and therefore the oldest foreign branch of Randstad, was a stable market leader. Randstad Interim, the company's second brand, which was introduced to the Belgian market in 1970, was also doing well, albeit on a more modest scale.

The German market, however, was an entirely different story. The percentage of so-called flexworkers remained low at just 0.3%, with stringent regulations and a licensing system that created the greatest barrier to further growth. The Bundesagentur für Arbeit, the German federal employment agency, ensured that the act introduced in 1972 to regulate temporary staffing was observed, with permanent employment serving as its basic

principle. A temporary worker was considered a permanent employee of Randstad Zeit-Arbeit, and dismissals were subject to stringent restrictions. The employment agency was required to continue paying a salary when the employee was sick or had no work. Moreover, the temporary worker had to be recruited for more than just one company, since otherwise the agreement would be regarded as labor mediation, and that was strictly prohibited. Temporary workers were not allowed to work for a client for more than three months. Randstad Zeit-Arbeit always had to have new positions with different clients at the ready for its temporary workers. Powerful trade unions such as IG Metall, which emphasized its strong demands with countless strikes, served to reinforce this image of a 'difficult' market.

Randstad was a relatively small player in France, a country in which the temporary employment market was more developed than anywhere else in Europe. In the early 1990s, 1.2 percent of the working population

were temporary workers. Three main players dominated the French market: Manpower, Ecco, and BIS, the oldest employment agency, which had been established by Laurent Negro in 1954. Although the French market was not yet a top priority with regard to Randstad's foreign strategy, France was an important potential growth market for the future. Randstad also played a limited role in England. In 1989, the company entered the British market for a second time, this time under the name of Randstad Employment Bureau. Although its competitors placed permanent as well as temporary staff, Randstad made a conscious decision not to do so as it specialized in the placement of temporary staff.

In January 1992, the RHB approved a report entitled *Strategic Planning Randstad Group*, which referred once again to the company's three fundamental principles of continuity, growth and profitability. The RHB subsequently introduced its ambitious plans for the future based on these three principles. Randstad planned to do business in every remaining Western-European country and in the United States. The target was to obtain 25% of its sales in the Benelux countries, 25% in the rest of Europe, 25% outside of Europe, and 25% from activities other than recruitment and selection.

working
on your
experience?

randstad makes it possible

Urlaubs-
kasse
auffüllen?

Fragen Sie Randstad Zeit-Arbeit

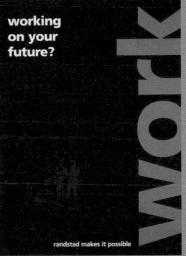

working
on your
future?

randstad makes it possible

**early
1990** *The internationalization of
the company led to posters and
publications in many languages.
Most prominent were classical
subjects such as temp-working
during one's holiday, or building
one's resume through acquiring
practical experience – 'Randstad
makes it possible'.*

flex (ibility)

A Randstad branch in Düsseldorf, the city where the first German branch was opened in 1968.

Randstad's corporate philosophy had always been based on autonomous growth, but where the new challenge of internationalization was concerned, the RHB was intent on keeping its options open for growth through takeovers. In the spring of 1992, an excellent takeover opportunity presented itself: Flex Holding was up for sale. Flex was the brainchild of Eddy de Vries, who had been successful in expanding Vedior Holding's staffing brands Vedior Uitzendbureaux, ASB, and Dactylo. As a result of a conflict with the senior management at Vedior's holding company Vendex, however, he decided to leave in 1988. This put an end to his ambitious plans to take Vedior Holding abroad. But De Vries was not a man to be put off easily, "If I can do it for Vedior, I can certainly do it for myself" was his philosophy. And so, together with Aat Schouwenaar, financial director at Vedior, De Vries established Flex Holding. Flex went European immediately with a starting capital of EUR 127 million gained from private equity funding. Flex took over employment agencies everywhere from one country to the next, creating, in De Vries' own words, "the first European employment agency".

The entire staffing industry, and therefore Flex, grew at a remarkable rate in the second half of the 1980s. Over a period of just three years, Flex's sales increased from zero to EUR 295 million. This fast growth, however, came to an abrupt end when Flex took over an employment agency in France whose branches were not financially viable. They were forced to invest millions in that company just to keep it afloat, and the economic downturn only made matters worse. Creditors had no faith in an economic

Randstad took over the Flex Group in 1992.

Adia and Ecco merge in the nineteen-nineties and continue as Adecco, the largest (international) competitor of Randstad.

turnaround and refused to lend Flex any more money. There was no option but to sell the company.

The sale of Flex coincided with further internationalization within the staffing industry. Large international clients were more inclined to do business with a single employment agency. If Adia, Ecco, Manpower or Randstad wanted international clients, they would have to become international staffing agencies. This was the start of a great battle between competitors to win clients, and Randstad was following every development in the Flex saga like a hawk. Alarm bells started ringing when Randstad learned that Ecco – the French employment agency that later merged with Swiss staffing service Adia to become Adecco – was planning to make a bid for the insolvent company. Ecco wanted to use the takeover to gain a firm footing in the Netherlands, where Randstad had been traditionally dominant. At that time, Flex had 200 branches (70 of which were in the Netherlands) plus several subsidiaries including Werknet, Werkpool, Technisch Bureau

Visser, Uitzendbureau Otter-Westelaken, and Flexmen.

Randstad was interested mainly in the Belgian and French branches, and it decided to stop Ecco in its tracks by making a bid for Flex. It was the start of an exhausting takeover dance at Randstad's head office. Among the players were representatives of investors from England and Switzerland, and representatives of Randstad and Flex from various other countries. Each party also brought along its own advisers and lawyers. They stayed there, on the same floor, for days and days, each party in its own room, with their fax machines doing overtime. The corridors became congested with people, making it increasingly difficult to tell who worked for whom. On the Randstad team, Frits Drost and Herman Kolk were starting to have doubts about the potential takeover. Frits Goldschmeding, however, was convinced of the benefits and was determined to see it through. Randstad's offer of EUR 6.8 million was finally accepted after ten days of scrutiny, meetings and negotiations.

On April 1, 1992, the takeover was an accomplished fact.

The company had done the same with this takeover as it had done with Tempo-Team in 1983, which was to invest during economic hard times, allowing it to expand its position greatly on both the Belgian and particularly the French market. In the Netherlands, the newly acquired Werknet merged with Tempo-Team in 1993. The integration was supervised by David van Gelder, Hans Hogeveen and the new manager Ben Noteboom, who had previously worked for Dow Chemical. With 7.5% of the market, Randstad now held second place in Europe after Manpower, and with that, an important international step had been taken.

Randstad sets the standard

Randstad Staffing Services office in Atlanta, Georgia.

In mid-1992, Erik Vonk joined RHB's Executive Board. He was appointed with a view to turning an old dream into reality: the dream of taking Randstad to America! Goldschmeding had already traveled to New York in 1969 to get a feel for the market, but Randstad was growing so fast in the Netherlands and Europe at the time that further expansion would be extremely difficult. Its 'American dream' never faded, however, and in 1992 the time was ripe to put plans into action. The 'war chest' was more than adequately filled with EUR 63.5 million, enough to warrant taking a chance in the market where temporary employment had practically been invented. Randstad was about to enter the lion's den; after all, this was the home market of staffing service giants Manpower and Kelly.

In late 1992, after an intensive introductory period in the Netherlands, where he learned all the finer points of being a staffing consultant, Vonk set out for Atlanta, Georgia. After having explored possibilities in Boston, Seattle, and Los Angeles, Randstad picked this Southern metropolis as launching point for its next big international move. It was a very deliberate choice: market research was indicating that the region was likely to be the first to recover from the recession that had

*Downtown Atlanta, where
Randstad started its
US adventure.*

been weighing down the economy for several years. Moreover, it was an economically strong and diverse region with a large high-quality service industry. Atlanta is home to one of the busiest airports in the world, a primary generator of employment opportunities.

Randstad was able to rent a small office at an Atlanta law firm. From this room, Vonk searched for a suitable take-over candidate, and in March 1993, Randstad had the opportunity to take over TempForce, an agency with 12 offices, 90 employees, and 22 million dollars in annual sales, for the grand sum of 10 million dollars. Vonk became chief executive officer

of the new employment agency, which was renamed Randstad Staffing Services (RSS).

The name change was not as simple a task as it might have seemed. Two leading advertising agencies had carried out surveys to find out how the name *Randstad* would be received in America, but their results contradicted each other. The New York agency thought that people would associate the name with a German steel factory. The agency in Chicago was more positive since they thought that people would associate the Dutch name with that of the Häagen-Dazs ice cream brand. Randstad USA noticed that the name

Randstad was a perfect anagram of the word 'standard'. An advertising agency used that beautiful link between the two words and came up with a powerful advertising slogan: Randstad, the New Standard in Staffing Services.

Randstad's tried and trusted method of growth, the water-lily method, was also applied in America. From Randstad's existing base in Atlanta, the number of branches increased, one by one. In December 1993, the company established itself in the neighboring state of Tennessee by

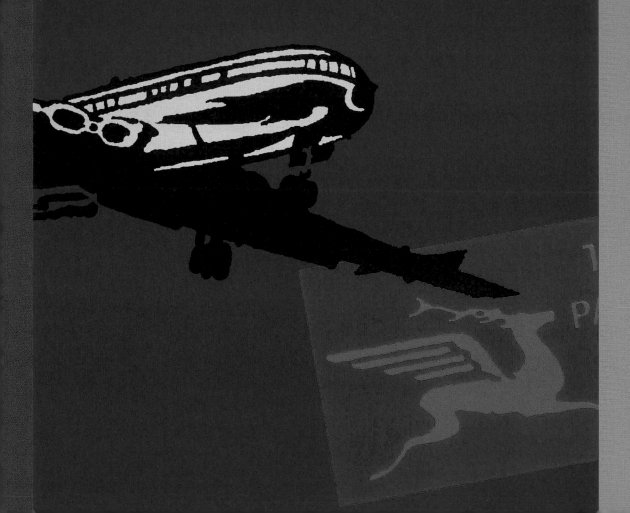

medical cover?

please come in and ask

holiday pay?
please come in and ask

19 94 *Staffing consultants specialize in many fields. They excel in acquisition and client management, and they can also answer staffer questions about legislation, wages, tax, and health insurance. This poster invited staffers to come in and ask their questions.*

The New Standard in Staffing Services

taking over Jane Jones Enterprises in Nashville. This growth meant that further professionalization was needed. Ben Bos, designer of the Randstad logo, was flown in from the Netherlands to introduce the company's house style to the various branches. The Dutch working methods, however, had to be adapted in certain areas. For example, filling in an employee's sex on an application form was strictly prohibited under American law. One typically Dutch element, however, was implemented: branch employee earnings were to consist of a fixed salary without sales commission. Randstad did, however, offer its American staff health insurance and some form of retirement plan.

By mid-1994, with 32 branches in the states of Georgia and Tennessee, Randstad Staffing Services achieved sales of 65.7 million dollars (EUR 46.93 million). Positions for approximately 5,500 temporary workers were found on a daily basis. Likewise, Randstad Nederland registered sales of EUR 909 million, Belgium EUR 238 million, France EUR 100 million and Germany EUR 70 million. At the time, these new branches at the center of the world's largest economy were still making only a modest contribution to the Randstad Group's total sales.

the spark

In 1994, Atlanta began to catch Olympic fever: the Olympic torch would be brought to the city in just two years' time. The Olympic Torch Relay would bring the flame to the Centennial Olympic Stadium, which was still under construction, to light the Olympic flame. The fire would be kept burning in Atlanta throughout the 100th Summer Olympics.

The Olympic Games are primarily a wonderful sporting event, but they are also a media spectacle, a gigantic logistical undertaking and an organizational challenge of the highest order, which also makes them highly attractive to businesses. Coca Cola, which has its head office in Atlanta, as well as McDonald's and IBM were involved from the very start, sponsoring the event both financially and in kind. They were not the only interested companies; Randstad too was lit by the Olympic spark.

During his monthly visits to the head office in Diemen, Erik Vonk (whose last name is the Dutch word for 'spark'), persuaded his initially hesitant fellow board members of the enormous benefits that could be gained through sponsoring the Olympic Games. Even more remarkable was the fact that it would be the first time ever that the

Olympic Games would be sponsored by a staffing agency. It would also be Randstad's first step in large-scale sports sponsoring. Randstad wanted to establish its brand in the United States, but it was also looking for worldwide recognition and the Olympic Games would serve as the perfect vehicle with which to achieve both of these aims. Randstad knew all there was to know about temporary work and how to deal with the supply and demand involved; it could therefore play a vital role in the largest temporary event in the world. Moreover, Atlanta was home to the head offices of many large companies. If Randstad could provide a staffing service to the Olympic Games in Atlanta, it could potentially gain immediate access to these large, prospective clients. The company's management duly gave the go-ahead and on September 7, 1994, Randstad signed a contract with the Atlanta Committee for the Olympic Games (ACOG). It was announced to the entire United States that it would be the first ever staffing services sponsor of the Olympic Games. One of the reasons for ACOG's decision was the promise Randstad made to help the temporary workers find new positions once the Olympic Games were over, but its international character also appealed to the committee.

the torch

A month before the Olympic Games started, Frits Goldschmeding was visiting Randstad branches in the USA. He was interested in finding out how the preparations were going, and he also wanted to visit a couple of clients while he was there. His American colleagues, however, had other plans in store for him. During a visit to the Nashville branch, marketing manager Rebecca Johnson presented him with a pair of running shoes, jogging shorts, and a shirt. When Goldschmeding asked in surprise what those were for, he was taken to some place in Nashville, where to his great astonishment he was given the Olympic torch! Since Randstad was now a sponsor of the Olympic Games, his American colleagues had managed to arrange for him to carry the official torch for a distance of 1.2 miles along the route to the Olympic Stadium. Thirty minutes later, the 63-year-old director of Randstad was running through the streets of Nashville carrying the flaming torch. A camera man hired by Randstad Staffing filmed the whole event. At the end of his run, Goldschmeding handed the torch to the next relay runner heading for the stadium. Once it was over, the chairman of the board left the torch he had carried behind with his colleagues in America as a gesture of thanks for their extraordinary efforts in staffing the Centennial Olympic Games.

Frits Goldschmeding carries the Olympic torch toward the stadium.

randstad uitzendbureau

19 95 *These colorful posters appeared in the windows of the Dutch branches in 1995 and 1996 for the occasion of the Olympic Games in Atlanta, of which Randstad was a sponsor. The posters linked the first modern Olympic Games in Athens in 1896 with those held a century later in Atlanta.*

randstad uitzendbureau

the fire

The spectacular opening of the centennial games takes place in the Centennial Olympic Stadium in Atlanta, which was specifically built for that purpose.

On the evening of July 19th, the Olympic flame finally arrived at the 80,000-seat Centennial Olympic Stadium. To the monumental sounds of Beethoven's Ode to Joy, the torch was handed to the man who was to light the Olympic fire. There, high up in the stadium on a stage, stood boxing legend Muhammad Ali, who had been fighting a battle with Parkinson's disease for many years. Despite his trembling hands and encouraged by loud cheering, Ali lit the Olympic fire. The flame soared up a cord to the cauldron on top of the tower where the flame would continue to burn throughout the coming weeks. The choir sang its final *Götterfunken*, the Spark of the Gods,

and the huge fire was ignited; the Olympic Games had begun.

Two years of preparations were about to culminate in the two-and-a-half week long Summer Olympic Games. The number of Randstad USA temporary workers needed to stage the Olympic Games had soared from about 800 to 16,000 by the time the Olympic Games started. As *Official Staffing Service of the Centennial Olympic Games*, Randstad had become a 'spider' in the intricate web of the event. Approximately 1,400 people provided general, administrative and technical support before, during and after the Olympic Games, whereas 6,000 additional temporary

workers, including 3,200 bus drivers, provided transportation for spectators traveling to and from the competitions. Thousands more worked on the catering, cleaning, computer automation and management of this huge event.

All 16,000 temporary workers were clearly recognizable by their distinctive blue sport shirts bearing the Randstad name and logo. The relatively small Randstad Staffing Services organization, around seventy people,

received valuable backup from members of Randstad Nederland. This backup was essential, because the organization was faced with a massive workload during the event. The 3,200 bus drivers, for example, came not only from Atlanta but from everywhere throughout the United States. This meant that besides the fact that they sometimes took the wrong route because they were unfamiliar with the area, they all had to eat and sleep somewhere. Not only that, but they had to be accommodated in a city whose hotels were more or less fully booked due to the Olympic Games. Everyone did their best to find the last available rooms in Atlanta. They worked for 20 hours a day, seven days a week for several weeks in order to arrange things as efficiently as possible.

Despite the unavoidable organizational hassles, the event was a great success for Randstad. Research showed that brand recognition of Randstad USA had grown in Atlanta and the surrounding area from 15 to almost 99.5 percent. Within a short time, its database of potential temporary workers had expanded by 29,000.

Significant players in the region became familiar with the employment agency and its core business. Randstad's international image received a great boost as well: an estimated 4.5 billion people had watched the Olympic Games on television, which put Randstad very firmly on the international map.

Downtown Atlanta during the Olympic Games.

with an eye on the future

During the Olympic Games, Randstad Nederland had focused primarily on a decisive, new phase in terms of the legal status of temporary workers. In 1994, Wim Kok became Prime Minister of a new and ambitious Dutch Cabinet, known as the 'purple' cabinet because it was based on a coalition between the 'red' Dutch social-democratic party and two 'blue' liberal parties. The motto of the new cabinet was: *Work, work, work* and the ambitious coalition agreement was aptly titled *Choices for the Future*. The high unemployment rate was the Cabinet's greatest worry, totaling over half a million and including a record number of young unemployed.

The liberal parties considered the high unemployment to be partly the result of a lack of flexibility within the labor market and thus gave the subject high priority on their political agenda. The social democrats were somewhat more reticent. The labor market was based to a great extent on fixed

Dutch Prime Minister Wim Kok with Hans Wijers, his Minister of Economy, in the Dutch parliament.

contracts, which made it difficult, for young people in particular, to find employment. Younger workers had no experience and were therefore not being offered jobs, and the longer they remained unemployed, the harder it was for them to enter the labor market. Flexible employment contracts such as temporary staffing agreements solved the problem, but the social democrats felt that these employees should be offered a higher degree of secure and stable employment, and the opportunity to accumulate pension benefits.

And this was where the parties' apparently insurmountable differences lay: the liberals were focused on flexibility; the socialists on security. It was an incredibly tense time for Randstad; countless draft plans were being drawn up that might pose a threat to the future of temporary work in the Netherlands. However, since the government was unable to reach a solution, they decided to stick to the tried and trusted Dutch 'polder model' recipe of letting those most closely involved with the problem, in this case the unions and the employers, get together and solve the thorny issue themselves. Between December 1, 1995, and March 1, 1996, unions and employers, united through the labor foundation STAR, were given the time and the opportunity to suggest a solution.

the kitchen table

The 'kitchen table agreement' makes it to the front page of the Dutch daily newspapers.

As Randstad board member Fred van Haasteren (who was also the chair of the ABU's negotiating committee) was driving to the Dutch city of Haarlem, snow was falling. With him in the car was Niek-Jan van Kesteren, director of social affairs for the employers' association VNO-NCW. They were on their way to the home of labor union chairman Lodewijk de Waal. They had arranged to meet each other at a restaurant, but De Waal had been unable to arrange for a babysitter for his children and it was for this reason that the meeting took place at his home.

De Waal invited the visitors into his living room where the three men, all somewhat tense, sat down at what they assumed to be a kitchen table. It was an old boardroom meeting table that De Waal had taken home from the labor federation's offices because no one else had wanted it. Much was at stake, and each party was representing their own interests. Van Haasteren represented the interests of staffing agencies and of Randstad in particular. He wanted to prevent the temporary staffing agreement from becoming a normal labor agreement as proposed by Dutch Employment and Social Affairs Minister Ad Melkert. According to Melkert's plan, temporary workers would be entitled to a certain degree of secure and stable employment, job protection, and continued payment of wages when they were not on an assignment due to lack of work. However, his plan would also increase the cost of temporary workers, and Randstad and the staffing industry in general would have to pick up the tab.

Van Kesteren was there to make a firm stand in the interests of the employers, which put him in a difficult position that evening. His advisers had told him not to expect to reach an agreement with the union representatives. They had also pointed out that temporary work had been an extremely

The three main actors of
the Kitchen Table Agreement are
surrounded by their supporters and
constituents. Lodewijk de Waal
(first row, on the left) of the FNV
union is surrounded by fellow
unionists, Niek-Jan van Kesteren
(first row, fourth from the right) by
fellow members of the employers
association, and Fred van Haasteren
(first row, far right) of Randstad
by representatives of the staffing
industry.

controversial area for the last thirty years, and that nothing was going to change that. Van Kesteren, however, disregarded their advice. He saw this meeting as an opportunity to prove that employers' and employees' representatives were able to come to a mutual agreement. Van Kesteren was convinced that flexible labor was the perfect solution for many of the organizations represented.

As chairman of the largest union in the Netherlands, De Waal probably had the most difficult task that evening. He had to negotiate with the employment agencies, and the staffing industry was one with which his union had a history of disagreements. De Waal knew that his strongly divided followers were watching every move he made. Some of the people in his organization were not prepared to recognize temporary labor at all, while others were less

adamant. They appeared to be facing a problem that had no solution.

The three men understood each other's positions all too well. Their principles appeared to be incompatible, although they got on very well together on a personal level. It was partly for this reason that the evening in fact turned out to be very constructive. They worked out various scenarios on a notepad, discussed matters extensively, and finally managed to make a plan that did not present any of them with insurmountable obstacles. The temporary staffing agreement would be regarded as a contract of employment, but a special one. Van Haasteren was prepared to go along with the plan, but the freedom to terminate the contract upon completion of the assignment was not something he could compromise on. He went along with the unions'

proposal of allowing employees to accumulate more security and rights over time. After one year, temporary workers could work for eight additional three-month periods, after which they would be entitled to a permanent contract.

In return for this concession, the union was prepared to recognize the agreement as a special employment contract, and formally recognize the trilateral relationship between the employment agency, client, and temporary worker. The three men were delighted with the outcome of the evening and, after a celebratory beer, Van Haasteren and Van Kesteren set off for home; they had good news for their supporters.

bij Randstad als
verpleegkundige

en als
monteur
secretaresse
heftruckchauffeur
inpakker
aanpakker
kok
ober
winkelpersoneel
IT-specialist
productiemedewerker
commercieel medewerker
thuishulp
helpdesk medewerker
lasser

bij Randstad als
secretaresse

bij Randstad als
monteur

19 91 *Doormats shaped as a telephone, a syringe, and a wrench. These posters were informational as well as welcoming. Randstad could offer you work as a nurse, a secretary, a technician, and many other jobs.*

a polder model miracle

The *Kitchen Table Agreement*, as Van Kesteren had called it a few days later, solved the gridlock and allowed for further expansion on the agreement. This required more time than the negotiators had originally set aside however. Apart from the STAR (Labor Foundation) Flex Agreement, as is was officially known, other negotiations were also underway on a new collective labor agreement (CLA) for temporary workers in which terms were being determined regarding training, pensions and job security accrual when a temporary worker was employed over a longer period.

The three negotiators now had to convince their constituents of the value of the Flex Agreement, and that was not going to be easy. Van Haasteren was reproached by employment agency directors who argued that he had no mandate to recognize a temporary staffing agreement as an employment contract since this would place restrictions on the original concept of temporary work. On the other hand, temporary employment was now fully and definitively accepted by the trade unions. De Waal was therefore criticized as well for recognizing flexibility on behalf of the trade unions.

The practical interpretation of the agreement ended up taking so much time that the employers' and union's representatives had to ask for a month's respite. A swarm of lawyers for the unions, the employers' association and the ABU set about formalizing the legal structure of the agreement. On April 3, 1996, after countless draft versions, the Labor Foundation submitted a final version of its Flex Agreement to the Cabinet. From now on, the temporary staffing agreement would be regarded as a special employment contract. For the first three and a half years, employment agencies and their clients would enjoy the highly coveted flexibility, but after that, the temporary workers were entitled to a permanent contract, which provided them with greater security. In 1999, the Dutch Civil Code was amended to include the temporary staffing agreement. The Flex Agreement was now the 'Flexwet', the Dutch Flexibility and Security Act. The polder model had worked another miracle.

With the Flex Agreement, the Netherlands had become the first non-English-speaking country to liberalize its employment market. Types of flexible labor such as temporary employment were now a standard part of Dutch labor law, and the precarious balance between flexibility and security had been evened out. The way this had been achieved served as an inspiration for other countries in Europe and elsewhere.

In 1996 and 1997, the ILO worked on a new convention for labor mediation, flexible labor and temporary employment. Years of discussions and lobbying by the CIETT had influenced public opinion regarding flexibility. As an influential member of the ILO, the Netherlands presented its vision at a conference in 1996. The Dutch Flex Agreement showed how flexible employment could be integrated into a country's social and legal systems and be met with approval. In its new Convention 181, the ILO emphasized

*Gerhard Schröder,
candidate for the German
chancellorship, is educated
about the Dutch labor market
model by Frits Goldschmeding
and his successor, Hans Zwarts.*

the positive role played by employment agencies in the labor market and how flexible employment was an important condition for a well-functioning labor market.

There was an important difference between ILO Convention 96 of 1949 and the Convention of 1997: a significantly negative approach to flexible employment had turned into a positive one. From now on, tripartite cooperation between employment agencies, clients and temporary workers would be an internationally accepted form of employment. As of 1999, the Netherlands, Spain, and other countries ratified the Convention, and ten years later, ILO

Convention 181 had been ratified by twenty-one countries around the globe. Temporary employment had been accepted on a worldwide scale. Employment agencies were delighted, and the Flex Agreement served to inspire other countries too. Developments in the Netherlands were followed with much interest in Germany, where regulations were most stringent, and the impasse between employers and unions was most critical. German Social Democratic chancellor candidate Gerhard Schröder personally visited Randstad branches in Utrecht and Rotterdam. He wanted to understand the principles of the 'polder model' and the Dutch approach to flexibility

within the labor market. Schröder also asked Randstad to keep him informed of developments if and when he became Chancellor. He was obviously impressed, because in 2001, he appointed a committee to deal with the modernization of the labor market in Germany. Between 2002 and 2004, changes were made to the German labor market that were partly inspired by the Dutch example.

In 2008, important elements of the Dutch flex model were incorporated in Italy into a collective labor agreement. In Japan, the economic crisis led to intense debate about the staffing industry, in which the Dutch solution was examined as well.

adventure book for boys

Randstad Holding N.V.

On Friday, May 16, 1998, an enormous pavilion stood glistening in the spring sunshine next to Randstad's head office in Amsterdam. At 197 feet wide, 351 feet long, 105 feet high and with no less than 123 pillars to support it, the pavilion was the largest in the world. Three circus tents would easily fit inside, and it was strong enough to make gale winds seem like a summer breeze. The tent was aptly named *New Galaxy*.

Having reached the statutory retirement age of 65, the day had come for Randstad's founder and director, Frits Goldschmeding, to leave the company after 38 years of service. A total of 1500 guests gathered in the New Galaxy to celebrate this wonderful success story. The company figures said it all: when the agency had closed its first financial year in 1960, profits had amounted to a mere EUR 4.12. A year before he retired, profits had

In 1996, Frits Goldschmeding received the King William I prize from Prince Claus, Prince Consort of Queen Beatrix of the Netherlands.

Carin and Frits Goldschmeding and Hans Zwarts watch the firework at the founder's farewell party.

reached EUR 117 million with sales of no less than EUR 3.2 billion. Randstad had been the indisputable market leader in the Netherlands for the last 30 years. Moreover, by the time Goldschmeding retired, Randstad had become an enterprise with a strong international presence. In the 1960s and 1970s, new branches had been opened in Belgium, Great Britain, Germany and France. Branches in the United States, Spain, Italy, Portugal, Switzerland, Luxembourg and Denmark had also been opened in the 1990s.

The company had changed beyond recognition, and Goldschmeding had received various awards for his efforts. In 1995 he was made a Knight of the Order of the Dutch Lion, and on June 5, 1996, 'his' Randstad received the prestigious King William I Prize, a bi-annual award for outstanding performance; in Randstad's case it was for the high quality of its services. In 1999, he was made Commander of the Order of Leopold II for his outstanding contribution to socio-economic development in Belgium. On the eve

of Goldschmeding's departure a ceremony was held, and one of the speakers was Hans Wijers, Minister of Economic Affairs for the Dutch government. He compared Randstad's company history to a boys adventure book, "one of those books in which the protagonist tries to take on the world with courage, bravery and self-confidence." Wijers was aware that Goldschmeding had done more than just try, "He has left a powerful stamp on the staffing industry; I think you can safely say that when your company grows to become the third-largest of its kind in the world."

Goldschmeding's successor, the 57-year-old Hans Zwarts, called his predecessor "an incredible person, a professional, and a man with a keen eye for the big picture and for strategy." He also called him a man "with an unbelievable passion for the business of staffing and also for the people at the heart of the industry: the staffing consultants." As the evening reached its peak, Goldschmeding and his wife left to a storm of loud applause from everyone present in the pavilion,

and with that, an era had come to an end. The company founder did not accept a seat on the Supervisory Board that first year; the last thing he wanted to do was to get in the way of his new successor.

...en nu
weer

aanpakken!

...en nu
weer

aan de slag!

19
97 *The time for sunny
beaches is over: 'Back to work!'
With deflated plastic alligators
and giraffes, Randstad called
on young people to spend the
rest of the summer holiday
productively, and to earn some
money.*

the crown prince

Hans Zwarts, Frits Goldschmeding's successor.

Hans Zwarts had had a long and varied career, which included the positions of director of Personnel and Organization at Vredestein and at NMB Postbank. Following the merger of the latter with the Nationale Nederlanden insurance company, he became director of ING Bank Nederland, ING Lease and insurance organization RVS. It was during this period of his career, in the spring of 1997, that he was approached by a headhunter who wondered whether he might be interested in running the Randstad Group. The Supervisory Board had been given to understand that Zwarts, having had many years of hands on experience, was now ready to take the helm as CEO.

Zwarts understood people, and what was more, he had a wide network of contacts at various ministries, banks and unions. Just like his predecessor, he was a real 'Amsterdammer' with a keen sense of humor – one minute he was deadly serious, the next he was pulling your leg in his characteristically subtle way. On May 16, 1998, after an extensive period of orientation and full of enthusiasm, Zwarts took his place in the driving seat. His fellow teammates comprised the old stalwarts from Goldschmeding's days, Frits Drost, Cleem Farla, David van Gelder and Fred van Haasteren, as well as the relative newcomers Erik Vonk and financial director Bert de Groot, who had succeeded Theo Pruntel in 1997.

Zwarts wanted to further internationalize the company, tackle its organizational maintenance, and pursue the annual growth rate of twenty percent. The overarching goal was to register sales of 25 billion euros in 2005. Not only was it an ambitious target, Zwarts also found himself in the difficult position of a 'crown prince', expected to step into the shoes of the highly respected 'king' of Randstad. Newspapers and magazines wrote with some astonishment about the courage that this 57-year old must have had to take on the task. The chairman, however, considered his task to be primarily one of "keeping things going". In order to keep up the strength and enthusiasm he needed for the task, Zwarts refused to use the elevators at the head office. Instead, he took the stairs to his office on the tenth floor – day in, day out. From where he stood, the perspective was clear: the staffing industry was changing, and rapidly at that.

the flex industry in flux

In 1992, Europe took a big step forward towards a single European market. The European staffing industry was entering a new phase, and the CIETT appointed a special committee for EU-related matters, the Eurociett, which would later become an independent organization. Wim Ruggenberg (ABU), Fred van Haasteren (Randstad) and Annemarie Muntz (Vedior and later Randstad) from the Netherlands exercised a great deal of influence on its activities. In 1992, CIETT and a number of multinational employment agencies including Randstad submitted a complaint about prohibitive legislation in countries like Spain and Italy, and the highly restrictive legislation that applied in Germany. The European Commission decided to take action. Labor markets were just starting to become more liberalized and competition between large employment agencies had increased

accordingly. New markets were opening up for temporary work and everyone involved wanted to gain a firm foothold. In Spain, for example, temporary labor had been legal since 1994 (beforehand it had been merely tolerated), and rivalry was beginning to grow between international players such as Manpower, Adia and Randstad, all of whom wanted to lead the field. Randstad responded to the rivalry immediately. Under the supervision of David van Gelder, Edwin Schreur began pioneering work for Randstad in the Spanish market in 1993, ahead of the expected regulation. That same year, the first Spanish branch was opened in Madrid under the name *Randstad Trabajo Temporal*. At first, Randstad Spain came up against a great deal of resistance; although temporary labor had been legalized, it had not yet been accepted by everyone.

At the insistence of the European Commission, legislation prohibiting temporary labor in Italy was also dropped, allowing Randstad to enter the Italian market in 1999. One obstacle remained, however. Employment agencies were allowed to establish themselves on the proviso that they open at least four branches. Randstad complied with regulations by simultaneously opening branches in Milan, Vicenza, Bologna and Turin, with Rome following shortly afterwards. Marco Ceresa became managing director of this pioneering effort that was now 'Randstad Italy'.

The new opportunities in the labor market, in Europe as well as elsewhere, led to a wave of takeovers in the industry. The year 1996 saw the largest merger ever to take place between two staffing agencies. The Swiss company Adia, which had been established in 1957, was taken over in

Together we're the best

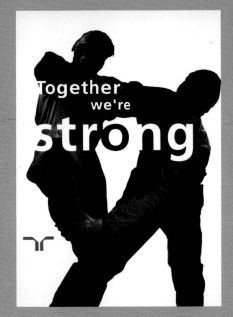

Together we're strong

1997 *The 'Together we're the best' posters created a furor in Switzerland. A woman in the francophone city of Lausanne was so upset about this English-language poster that she sent an angry letter to her local newspaper.*

Competitor Vedior steped up its globalization process in the nineteen-nineties. In 1996, it took over BIS, the oldest French staffing agency.

1992 by the German coffee and cocoa manufacturer Klaus Jacobs, who saw an opportunity in the market for HR services. Within four years, he was ready to take his next big step and in 1996, Adia merged with the French company Ecco to become Adecco. The ambitions of this new staffing giant were very clear indeed: to be the largest in the world. In 2000, Adecco took over the American Olsten Staffing, and in doing so, it overtook Manpower as the number one agency in the United States.

Other Dutch employment agencies also began to spread their wings, including Vedior. It took over the French company BIS in 1996, and in one fell swoop became a major player on the French market. As of that moment, fifty per cent of its total sales were registered in France. In order to spread its risk better, Vedior also decided to take over the top British brand Select in 1999. Select was widely known as a general staffing company, but it also specialized in recruitment, selection and referral of highly qualified staff. This made it into one of the main players in a strongly

fragmented British market. Vedior subsequently took over even more employment agencies, albeit on a somewhat smaller scale. The takeovers occurred all over the world and were used in order to gain access to national markets. Vedior focused in particular on companies involved in staffing and the recruitment and placement of professionals and specialists in areas such as information technology. Where most of the takeovers were concerned, Vedior was satisfied with a stake in the company of 60 to 80 per cent; the remaining shares stayed in the hands of local management. This growth strategy eventually resulted in the company having a presence in 52 different countries. Its philosophy was *think global, act local*, and at one point the company owned hundreds of brands. Vedior had become a truly global player and now ranked as the third-largest employment agency in the world after Adecco and Manpower.

The image of agency-supplied employees in Europe changed to an even greater degree during the 1990s. For many years, temporary workers

had been young, mostly under the age of 30, but the number of older workers gradually increased to include people over 50 and even some of retirement age. What was most remarkable, however, was that the workforce now included people who had traditionally been difficult to employ in Europe: minority groups, people with disabilities, and long-time unemployed. For them, temporary labor had grown during the 1990s into what was for many of them a *stepping stone*.

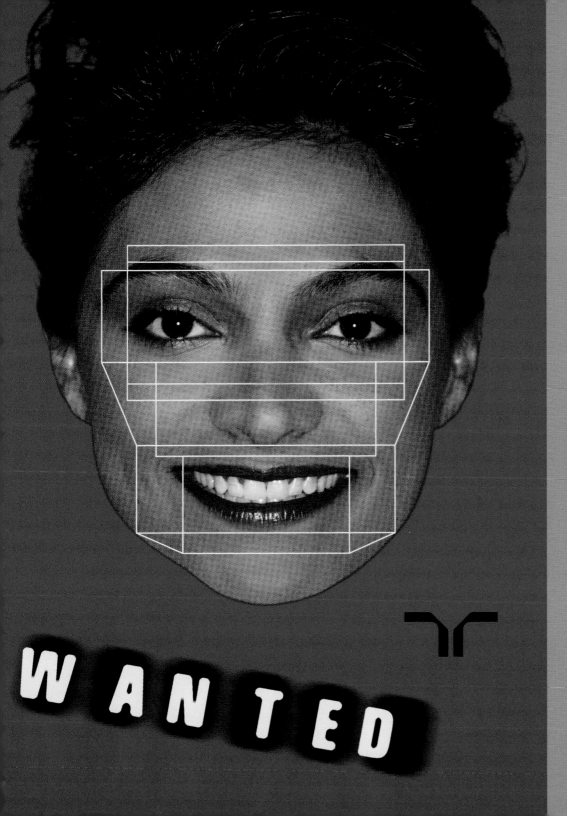

WANTED

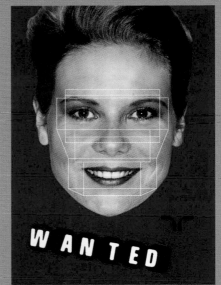

WANTED

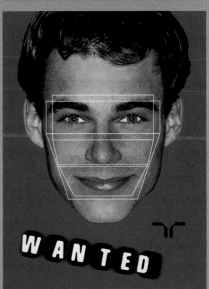

WANTED

19 96 *These posters have a clear and simple message: Randstad strives for a perfect match between client and staffer. Are you the staffer who meets all requirements? If so, we have a job for you.*

a breath of fresh air

Cleem Farla, a typical manager who stands among the people, rather than above them.

The increasing concentration of companies in the staffing industry, with fast-growing rival agency Vedior being one of them, spurred Hans Zwarts to take drastic action both internally and externally. The operating companies increasingly grew further away from the holding company. Regional directors were no longer based at the head office but in their own particular region, and cleaning and security activities were gradually spun off. Previously, the focus had been on the operational process, in other words the staffing consultants and the work process, but the entire organization had now become more outcome-driven: the end result became more important than the process. The RHB first became the EC (Executive Committee), and later in 2001 it turned into an Executive Board. Moreover, a new division structure was introduced in 1999, and the organization was also reorganized at the top level. A new level of management was introduced between the holding company and the various European countries: Randstad Europe, under the supervision of Cleem Farla. Radical changes also took place at the operational level through the updating of the ICT structure and the integration of various systems with each other.

Zwarts had been assigned the task of creating a strong management team for the Netherlands as well as internationally, and he achieved this partly through providing education and training. The market leader in the Netherlands, Belgium and Germany recognized that further strengthening of Randstad's international position was now required. Supported by the economy and initially by the stable stock market figures, Zwarts had launched himself into the field of potential international acquisitions almost immediately after his appointment. To do nothing would mean that the company would start lagging behind its big rivals. Randstad gained immediate success in the United States. On August 28, 1998, the company announced that it had purchased the medium-sized staffing firm Strategix for 850 million dollars (EUR 765 million). Strategix was the product of a succession of employment agency takeovers that had taken place within a five-year period. The integration was still in its early stages, which gave Randstad the opportunity to make its mark on the various parts of the company with ease.

Investors, however, had definite doubts about the takeover. Randstad had always presented itself as a company interested solely in autonomous growth, and suddenly it had purchased a company with three hundred branches and sales of three times that of Randstad Staffing Services. For a short period in October 1998, the share price dropped to below forty euros. Zwarts justified himself by pointing out the company's international strategy. Randstad wanted to be just as strong in America as it was in Europe, and as chairman of the board, Zwarts considered the cultivation of water lilies and autonomous growth insufficient to achieve that goal.

The Executive Committee did not allow itself any breathing space, and in the wake of the American takeover, Randstad also bought the Swiss staffing agency Life & Work, followed in 1999 by takeovers of the German company Time Power and the Spanish company Tempo Grup.

aces high

Under Zwarts' supervision, the Executive Committee presented the company with one challenge after another. Organizational structure, foreign expansion, brand politics, IT infrastructure…. it seemed as if the whole organization was being turned upside down. Frits Goldschmeding accepted the position of vice chairman of the Supervisory Board in May 1999, which was a comforting idea for the organization, but less so for the chairman of the board.

From 1999, business for Randstad was less positive than it had been previously. The integration of international takeovers such as Strategix turned out to be more problematic than expected, requiring extra financial investment and costing extra management time. The Internet added other new challenges. In 2000, Randstad launched a plan to bring together temporary workforce supply and company demand through a website. Staffing without staffing consultants was a revolutionary new concept. The virtual matching machine *Hedson* was established in 1999 under the supervision of Ben Noteboom, the successful manager of the new Capac concept. A second Internet initiative, the career portal *newmonday.com*, was supervised

by Jacques van den Broek, who had fulfilled various management positions in the company since 1988. Newmonday.com was a joint venture with the graduate-level job vacancy newspaper Intermediair, which was owned by VNU publishers. Multimillion euro investments were made by both parties, but despite the huge efforts, neither innovation bore fruit. Combined with the bursting dot.com bubble, this resulted in heavy losses for *Hedson* and *newmonday.com*.

In May 2000, Randstad introduced the Yacht brand in the Netherlands, Belgium, England and Germany. Yacht had been the result of a merger between Randstad Polytechniek, Randstad Automatiseringsdiensten and Randstad Interim Kader; the brand profile, however, was entirely new. Yacht was launched in the highest segment of the European recruitment and selection market and offered specialists in IT, management, engineering, and financial and legal services. The brand therefore positioned the company not just as an agency that found jobs for professionals, but as a career building coach. The new concept required significant investment. Unfortunately, the market for IT workers slumped in 2000, leaving Yacht with hundreds

of unemployed professionals on their payroll.

The accumulation of new activities, together with high staffing costs throughout the year 2000, started to become a thorn in Randstad's side, resulting in a 28 per cent drop in the share price in early November. Expected profits for 2000 could no longer be realized, and Randstad issued a profit warning. Stock market analysts were shocked: after seven years of double-figure growth, this was not like the Randstad 'overachiever' they had come to know. Moreover, following a comparison with other staffing firms, they were able to conclude that the problem had in fact been caused by the company itself and not, or at least not entirely, by the market. In their analyses, they even talked of a loss of trust in corporate management. The powerful strategies that Randstad had maintained through the years had become indistinct, and analysts thought the company's commercial focus was no longer credible. It was expected that 2001 was going to be an equally difficult year.

Needless to say, the internal organization also suffered as a result of these developments. With so many

We hebben tijdelijk werk voor je

Schrijf je in bij Randstad en maak kans op een workshop zingen met **Dignity**

⌐r randstad uitzendbureau

Ik heb tijdelijk werk voor je

⌐r randstad uitzendbureau

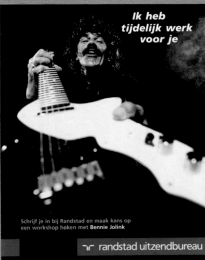

Ik heb tijdelijk werk voor je

Schrijf je in bij Randstad en maak kans op een workshop høken met **Bennie Jolink**

⌐r randstad uitzendbureau

19 99 *For the 'We have a temporary job for you' posters, Randstad called on Dutch celebrities. Upon signing on as a temp worker, you could be eligible for a singing workshop with Dignity, a tennis clinic with former doubles world champion Jacco Eltingh, or a workshop with the Dutch pop group 'Normaal'.*

plans and reorganizations, Zwarts had given the company quite a shakeup. Zwarts' aggressive strategy had led to further critical questions, however, and the fear that the company's flexibility might be stretched to its limit. The poor figures that were now emerging also served to create a pessimistic atmosphere. Many employees were wondering what was going on with the company they had once been so proud of. Zwarts beseeched everyone to have faith in his vision, but that did not stop him from becoming increasingly isolated.

The year 2001 progressed just as the stock market analysts had predicted. Zwarts and his Executive Board seemed unable to get their organization running smoothly again. In retrospect, the timing of the Strategix takeover had perhaps been wrong; the management had not been able to integrate a company of that scale while simultaneously implementing changes to the company on every front. "Zwarts wanted too much," was the conclusion. Zwarts had been forced to issue a second profit warning, and in late March it seemed that another one was due. Zwarts, however, refused to issue a third warning. In the autumn of 2001, he decided to do the honorable thing,

and on October 2nd the Supervisory Board announced he would be stepping down as of January 1, 2002.

Hans Zwarts had initiated great change within the company. During his term of office, company sales had increased from 4.3 billion euros in 1998 to 5.8 billion euros in 2001, sixty percent of which had been registered abroad, and Randstad, Yacht and Capac were now independent divisions. In the staff journal 'Terzijde', Zwarts departed with the words, "I can proudly confirm that during the time I have spent as CEO, Randstad has grown from a Dutch market player with international activities, to an international organization with a strong position on the home market."

Randstad stories
, Patrick Maloney 32 trust,
ou 33 first aid for movers,
childhood dream, Violetta
ive life to the maximum,
th Randstad, Juan Manuel
so 37 work, sail, laugh, cry
Yazicioglu 38 hidden gems,
work of the devil, Fermín
the courage of Randstad,
Catelene Passchier

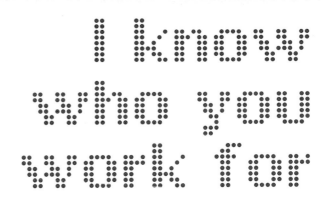

I know who you work for

the taxi

Patrick Maloney, then director of Regional Operations at Randstad in the United Kingdom, was traveling by taxi from Schiphol Airport to De Hoge Veluwe National Park, a peaceful woodland area where he was participating in an international managers meeting. He was sitting next to the driver, and chatted with him about his life as a taxi driver, his family and his daily experiences.

After about 45 minutes, the driver suddenly said: "I know who you work for." Maloney looked at him in surprise. "Really? Who do you think I work for?" he asked. "For Randstad," the taxi driver answered. "How do you know that?" asked Maloney. "Easy," replied the taxi driver, amused. "By your attitude. I often drive top managers for large, international companies from Schiphol to various places in the Netherlands, but only Randstad managers come up and sit in the front. You're all so friendly; you chat and always take an interest." Half an hour later, they arrived at the conference center. Maloney went off to his meeting feeling proud of the strength of character that characterizes the people at Randstad.

Patrick Maloney (left) – Managing director of Randstad Education, United Kingdom

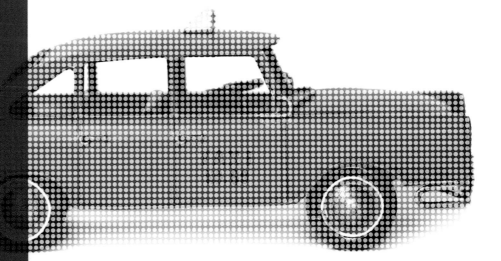

Randstad saves lives

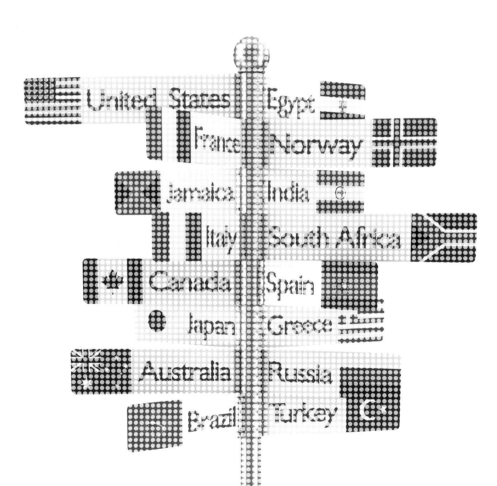

trust

"Many employers in Greece consider people older than fifty too old and too expensive. They expect them to be inflexible and unable to adapt to changes. Randstad offers experienced people a chance to find work. I had a candidate who moved back to Greece when she was 52 years old. She found it impossible to find employment. It took her seven months to get interviewed, and even when she did, she only got no for an answer. She was desperate when she signed up. We immediately realized her added value: international experience, and perfect command of several languages. We were able to place her immediately in an embassy in Athens, where she is now regularly employed."

"This story demonstrates our importance. Randstad offers people like her a chance to find goingful employment, while most other employers reject her just on the basis of her age. She is immensely grateful for our trust in her: she literally said that Randstad has saved her life. And our reward? Our reward is expressed in her trust in us. She rejected an offer for a job elsewhere."

Kiki Avgoustatou (middle) – Operations manager
Randstad, Greece

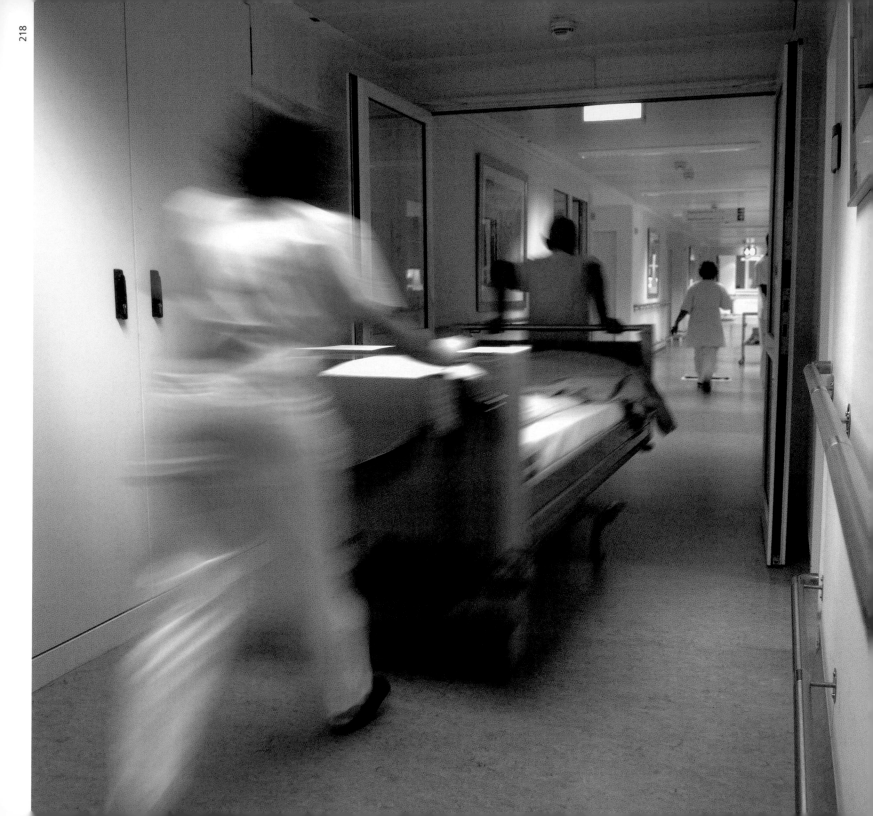

33

mission accomplished!

first aid for movers

It's never as busy as when one has to move. This certainly was true for a hospital in the town of Swindon in the United Kingdom. The treatment of the patients had to continue throughout the process of moving into the new facility. As the first steps towards the move were made, it became obvious that there was an acute need for more personnel, in particular in the domestic service.

"Randstad is very good at providing qualified workers with short notice, so we got involved, and provided 100 workers within two weeks as part of our *Operation Move*", says branch manager Mel Churchward. "Many people remained employed after the opening of the new hospital in the function for which they had been hired." "Mission accomplished" would be an understatement!

Mel Churchward – Branch manager Randstad, United Kingdom

what do you want to be when you grow up?

34

a childhood dream

"The best matches I made were for someone who came to us through social services. When he first appeared at my desk, he looked like a real down-and-out. He had not worked for seven years and had problems with everything and everyone; the man had obviously had many disappointments to deal with in his life."

"The first thing I ask every candidate is 'what have you always wanted to be?' I'm convinced that the things people are good at, and persevere at, are the things they love doing. When I asked this man that question, he looked up and said with a smile that he had always wanted to be a truck driver. I said to him, 'Let's make a deal: if you work for the city's sanitation department for at least six months, I will arrange an interview with Randstad's transportation services. That way, you will be able to get your heavy vehicle driving license at our expense'."

"Since then, he has looked fresher and fitter every time he comes to hand in his weekly time-sheet. He seems to have flourished at the thought of being able to make his childhood dream come true. Now, a few years later, his dream has come true: he is a truck driver."

Violetta Permis Levyssohn – Staffing consultant
Randstad, the Netherlands

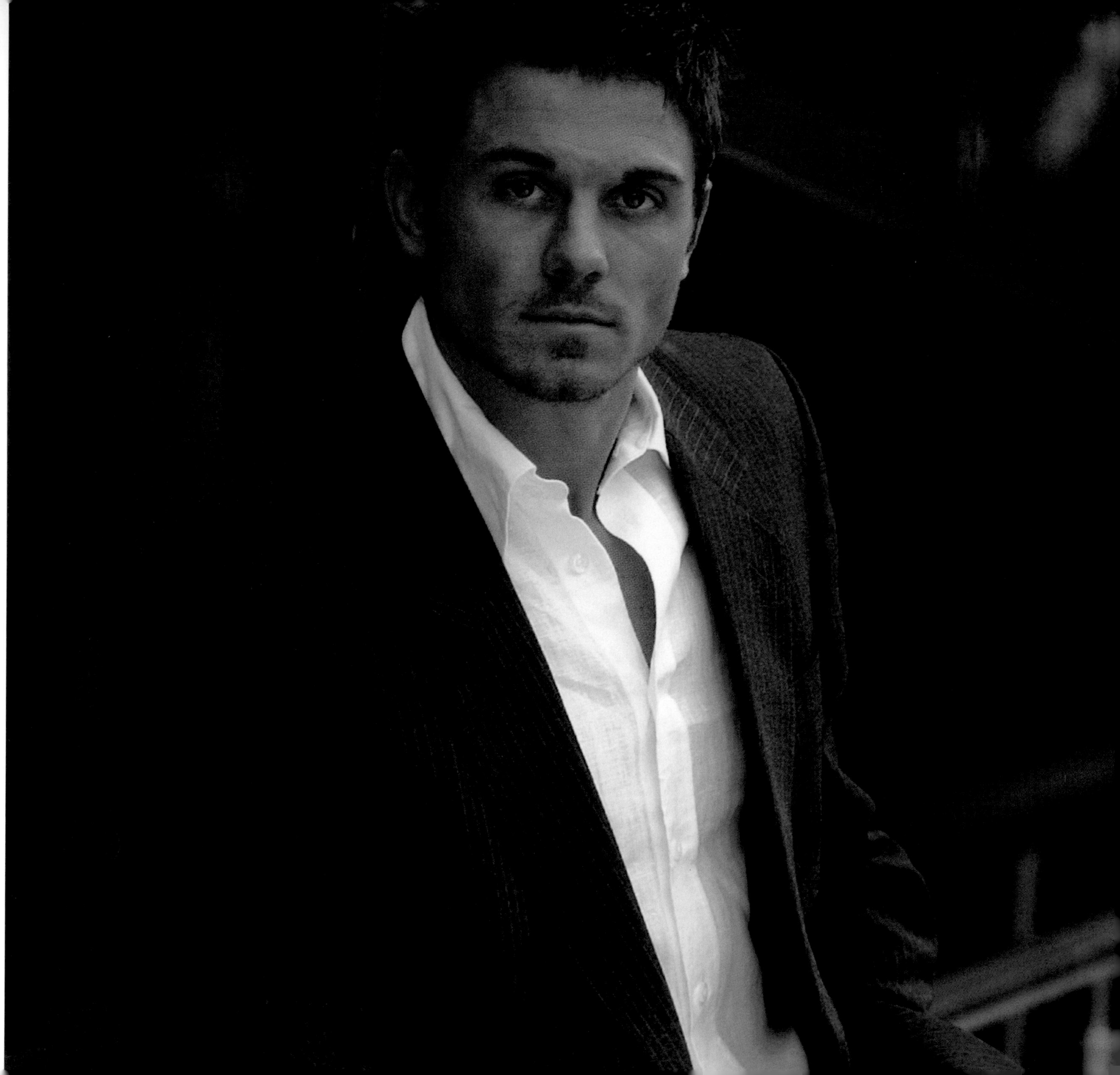

35

live life to the maximum

Eli Ellwood is a humanities teacher, a photo model, and a student at the East 15 London drama school, and likes traveling around the world. It is not easy to combine all these activities and interests with a regular job. This is why Eli chose for flexibility: he works via Randstad Education as a high-school teacher.

"This was a very deliberate choice. Apart from the fact that this gives me flexibility, I no longer need to dread the thought of working for forty years for the same employer before retiring. That would not be right for me. Sometimes I work in a school for a week, and sometimes for a year, depending on my studies, modeling assignments in South Africa, or photo shoots for television commercials. Randstad Education allows me to get the most out of life. I'm paid nicely on time, they take care of tax payments, and I am building up my pension fund. A perfect combination!"

Eli Ellwood – Humanities teacher Randstad Education (until recently: Select Education), United Kingdom

a very conscious choice

Randstad plays a round

scoring with Randstad

"One day, my colleague entered my office very enthusiastically. I wondered what might be going on. He pointed at his cell phone screen. On the display was a picture of a soccer field surrounded by Randstad's advertising billboards. 'I saw this game from Spain this weekend. Isn't it great that our company name is all over the place?', he said. This was the first time that my colleague from Randstad Mexico – formerly Vedior Mexico – realized he was part of a global corporation with a strong brand presence."

García de León had already realized that when he was on a trip in Europe with his family. He had made a detour in order to see Randstad's head office in Diemen. Soon thereafter he came for a management meeting of CFOs, the first such meeting after the merger with Vedior. A cup of coffee with CEO Ben Noteboom was immediately arranged. "I was impressed by his openness and his knowledge about our operations in Mexico. But later I'd learn that that was typical for Randstad."

"Many Mexicans love soccer. We watch our national championships, but we also watch the English and Spanish league. We'll enjoy watching them even more, now that we know that Randstad too is a player in the field."

Juan Manuel García de León del Paso – CFO Randstad Mexico

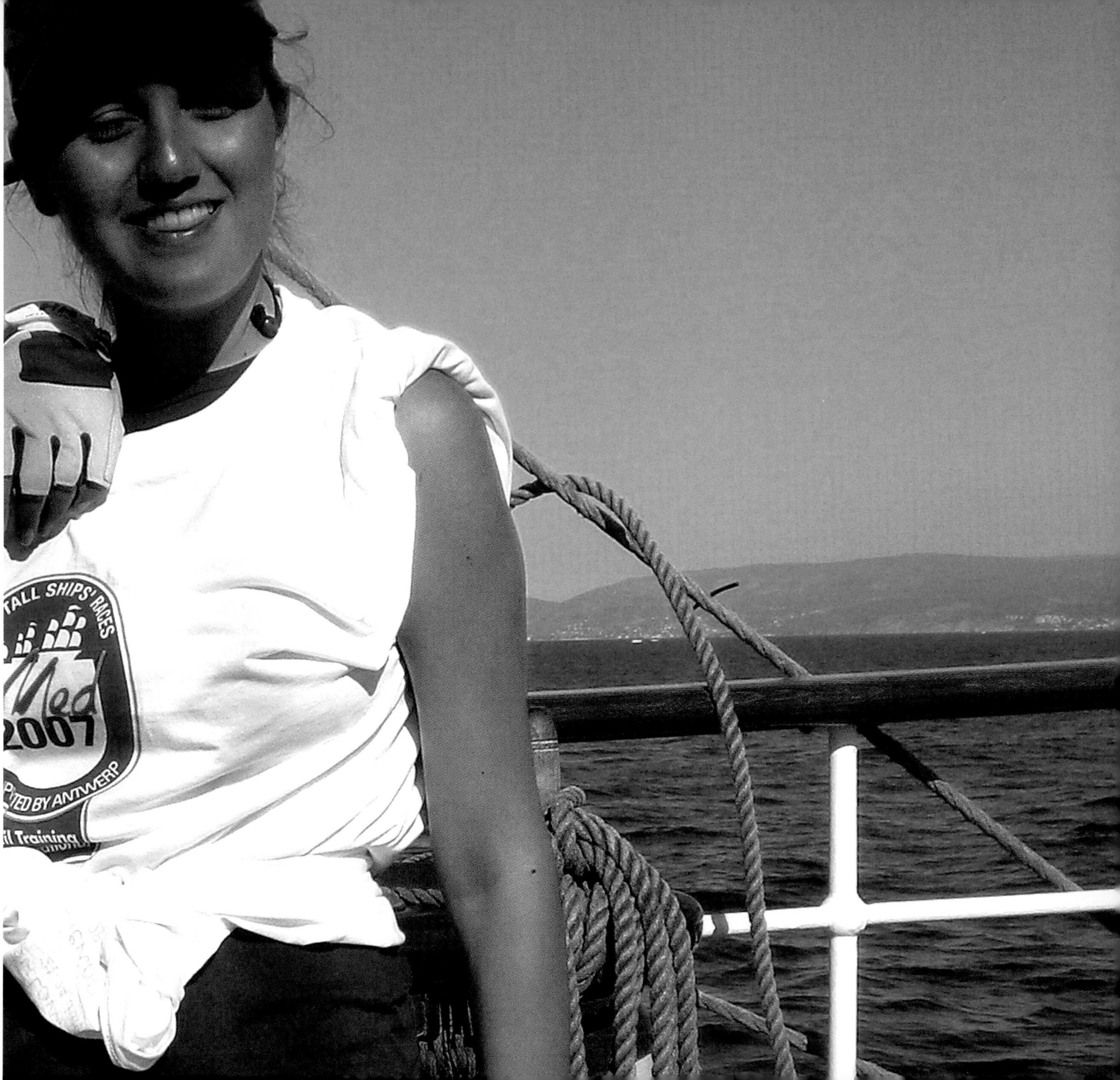
TALL SHIPS' RACES
Med
2007

37

I decided never to be afraid again

work, sail, laugh, cry, and admire

Out at sea, with her knees trembling, Turkish-born Zeynep Yazicioglu climbed ten meters up the ship's mast. For someone suffering from vertigo, reaching the top was a huge achievement. "At that moment I decided that I would never need to be afraid of anything ever again", she told us later. For her, it was one of the highlights of the *Tall Ships Race 2007 Mediterranea* from Toulon to Genoa, in which the Randstad Clipper took part. As top salesperson in her branch in Istanbul, Zeynep Yazicioglu was given the honor of being asked to join the ship's crew, together with 44 colleagues from 16 different countries.

"It was a tough but unforgettable experience, particularly the night shifts that we did in four-hour blocks. But it is the mutual responsibility for such a large ship that creates a real bond between crew members. I learned a great deal about the art of sailing from the professional crew on board during those seven days at sea. Every day we were given various tasks to perform, such as trimming the sails, charting the course, baking bread, and cooking meals."

"Most important to me was the contact I had with so many different Randstad colleagues. I still keep in touch with my three 'cabin mates' from France, the Netherlands, and Spain. On the last day of our sailing trip, the imminent parting caused many a tear to be shed. My father was waiting to pick me up when I arrived at Istanbul airport. He greeted me anxiously, saying 'What on earth is the matter?' I wiped away some more tears, but this time they were tears of joy."

Zeynep Yazicioglu – Staffing consultant Randstad, Turkey

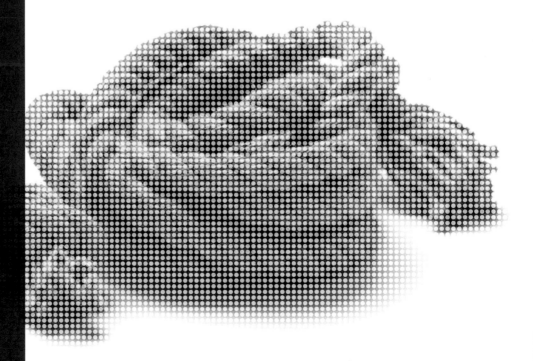

shaping the world of work in its purest form

38

hidden gems

Ayers Rock, a huge monolith of red sandstone, stands towering above the desert deep in the heart of Australia. It is a breathtaking environment and eminently suitable for unique meetings such as the four-day training course that was held for potential management talent at Randstad Australia. Peter Tanner was present at several of these courses: "The huge scale of Randstad has many advantages. The company can take the time it needs to seek and train 'hidden gems'. What's more, it can do this in amazing places where people can be far away from their normal working environment; places like the magical Ayers Rock."

"One of these 'hidden gems' was present at a training course I attended. He was incredibly shy; he barely dared to look people in the eyes, and yet we sensed that he had talent. In various sessions we challenged him to overcome his shyness in the safe and trusted surroundings that we had created. This method worked, and the man turned out to be the most talented member of the entire group. On that last evening, the man sitting there at dinner under a starry sky was a changed person. He is now one of our top managers; for me, that is *Shaping the world of work* in its purest form."

Peter Tanner (eighth from the left) – Managing director HR consulting Randstad, Australia

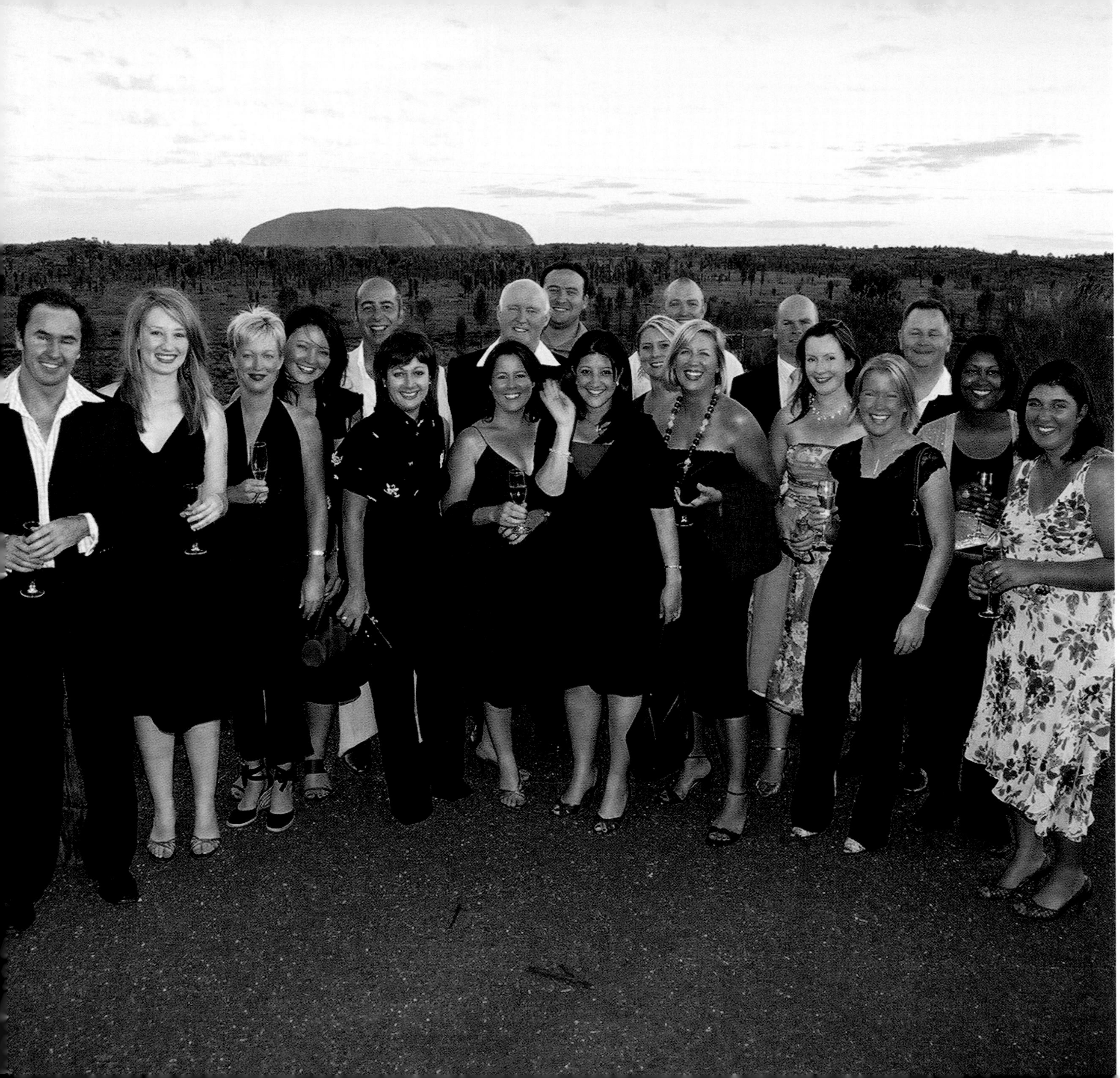

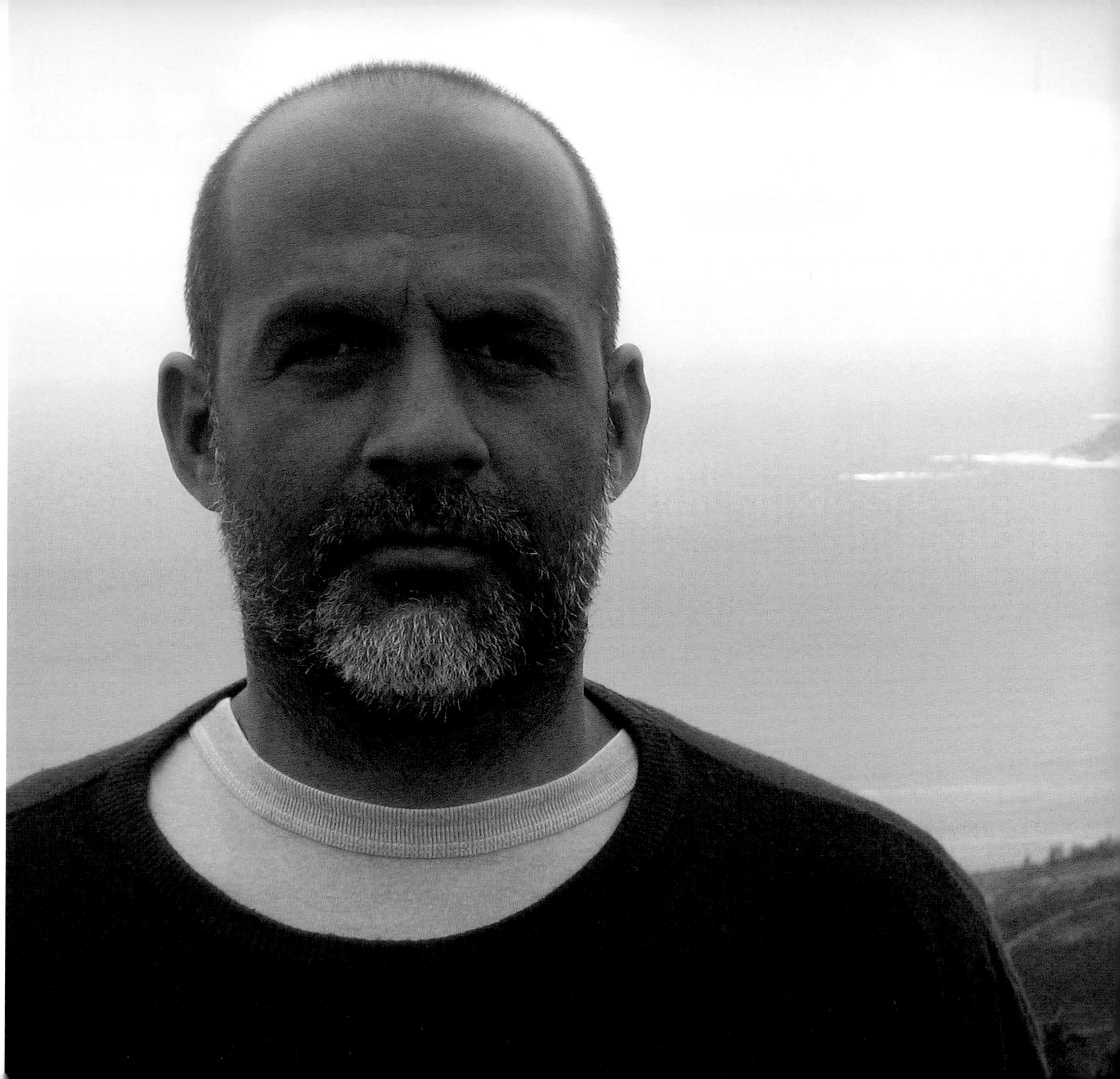

they treated us like demons

the work of the devil

In 1993, the Spanish labor market was totally inflexible. Governments and trade unions thought exclusively in terms of permanent employment contracts. Urged by the European Commission, however, a new law was passed that would make labor more flexible. Randstad seized the opportunity, and so it happened that two members of staff, who had previously worked together at the Dutch Chamber of Commerce in Spain, sat down in a spacious office in downtown Madrid and began a campaign to win corporate Spain over to the idea of temporary work.

One of them was Fermín Abella. He looks back at that initial turbulent period: "At first we were made out to be devils, but gradually, we managed to persuade employers of our value by recounting the successes that had been achieved in other countries. The first company to make use of our services was a large road construction company in need of flaggers. We knew then that we had broken the ice. Recruiting candidates was much easier; unemployment was high at the time, and people soon gained trust in our ability to provide work. Word-of-mouth did the rest."

Fermín Abella – Ex-employee Randstad, Spain

Fermín Abella is a true pioneer. He was the second person in Spain to be put on Randstad's payroll after his boss, Edwin Schreur. Abella is no longer with the company today: Randstad has become an established name in Spain over the last 15 years, and Abella felt he was ready for a new challenge.

crazy guys, those dutchmen

the courage of Randstad

"'How strange the Dutch are.' That is what most foreigners think about Holland's liberal attitude towards prostitution. What I think is most remarkable, however, is how even a reputable mainstream staffing agency like Randstad is happy to reply that 'We rehabilitate former prostitutes who are looking for work in the regular labor market,'" says Catelene Passchier, secretary of the European Trade Union Confederation. "Randstad lends, so to speak, its reputable and reliable image to people that desperately need it to be able to be rehabilitated into the regular labor market; people like former prostitutes. It takes courage to do that, but it works. Clients are prepared to take a risk for the simple reason that the flexworker has been sent to them by Randstad. I have great respect for that courage, because Randstad provides people like these with a chance of getting a regular job."

Catelene Passchier – Confederal secretary European Trade Union Confederation, Belgium

inspiration
and vision

Randstad started the new millennium with strong ambitions. Companies were taken over and new activities were started. Randstad had to learn a lesson: ambition alone is not enough; an international scope requires a strong foundation. Strong *building blocks* were laid to support the rapid growth. By 2008, the company was ready to start a new chapter in its history: the merger with Vedior resulted in the second-largest HR company in the world. With this reinforcement, Randstad continued *Shaping the world of work*: making the dream a reality is a never-ending process.

CFO Robert-Jan van de Kraats
(left) and CEO Ben Noteboom
at a press conference about
the 2008 annual report.

trust

In October 2001, Cleem Farla was asked to succeed Hans Zwarts as CEO of Randstad Holding. For Farla, it was the crowning glory of a long and successful career. He began his career with the company in 1973 and went on to follow the perfect career path of branch manager, area manager, district manager, head of marketing and then regional director. In 1990, he joined the management board of Randstad Holding, a position in which he assumed responsibility for some of the company's international operations, and in 2000 he became head of Randstad's European division. With this background, 56-year-old Farla was the obvious contender for the position of CEO. He knew the organization like nobody else, he was a consummate team player, and he took up the gauntlet. On 1 January 2002, he became Chairman of the Board of a company that, at the time, employed no fewer than 14,000 people. The Executive Board consisted of Leo Lindelauf, Ben Noteboom, the American Jim Reese, who had been responsible for Randstad North America since 1998, and Robert-Jan van de Kraats, who had served as CFO since 2001.

The financial press welcomed the appointment and described the new CEO as a bridge builder and someone who would handle the company with care. Elan magazine quoted Farla saying that he was not a 'macho manager' who liked to speak in one-liners. The Executive Board saw the reintroduction of the old Randstad values as its main challenge, but also sought to develop an adapted strategy for the company's further internationalization and growth. Farla and his fellow board members thought that Randstad had to return to organic growth and straightforward corporate management. The Hedson and newmonday.com activities were discontinued in order to cut costs. Internationally, the number of brands was

Cleem Farla in 2002.

reduced to just Randstad and Yacht. The Tempo-Team, Otter-Westelaken, and Capac Inhouse Services brands continued to operate on the Dutch market. These measures resulted in a reduction of EUR 70 million in costs for 2002. That was a good start, but the new CEO was acutely aware that there was still a very long way to go.

back to basics

Over the years it had become something of a tradition for the board members of Randstad Holding to discuss company planning and strategy during a strategic retreat. Brainstorming sessions lasted for several days, meetings in which finances, strategies for the various operating companies, and future plans for the entire organization were discussed; any ideas that seemed feasible were developed further.

During the January 2002 meetings, the Executive Board spent much of its time considering the future of the organization. They started by looking back and asking themselves what had gone wrong in previous years. Board member Leo Lindelauf said: "Companies that have experienced periods of unbelievable setbacks often come out stronger in the end. We were dealt a massive blow at the end of the 20th century. Frits Goldschmeding left, then came the Internet hype; there was panic in the air due to emergence of an entirely new world, a world we had to join quickly or be left behind. We were doing all kinds of things at that time, and the biggest mistake we made back then was taking on everything at the same time. The staffing consultants – the very basis of our company – felt acutely how the heart and the mind of the organization were being torn apart. The lesson we have learned from that difficult period is that if you plan to change the internal structure of the organization, for heaven's sake, leave the processes alone. Likewise, if you change the processes, leave the structure for what it is. In other words: don't try to do everything all at once".

Ben Noteboom also thought that the company had made too many changes. "We were dealing with takeovers and integration while also investing in organic growth. Doing just one of those things and doing it well would have been a mammoth undertaking. Successfully doing both at the same time would be entirely exceptional." Another conclusion they drew was that the company had been highly dependent on the Dutch staffing market. Randstad's top management was predominantly Dutch. According to CFO Robert-Jan van de Kraats, "To make our mark internationally we will need an international crew, like the one we now have following the takeover of Vedior. Back in the days of Goldschmeding and Zwarts, the chairman of the board held formal powers, rather than the board itself. Later, the Supervisory Board handed over formal powers to the Executive Board. If anything went wrong, the entire team could be held accountable, legally or otherwise. Responsibilities are now shared equally, and we can develop and implement company strategy as a team. Indeed, we now run the company together, as a team."

The most important question the Executive Board asked itself during that strategic retreat was why the company had achieved double growth figures nearly every year for two whole decades, but failed to do so in recent years. The solution was to get back to basics. What the organization needed now was clear guidelines. In practice, this meant a complete reappraisal of the key role played by the staffing consultants. The core process, the matching of clients with temporary workers, was to become the company's main focus again. After all, bringing together supply and demand in the labor market was Randstad's core business; it was also the business in which Randstad had been excelling for several decades.

*A conference room at a Randstad
branch where staffing consultants
can host their visitors.*

Building blocks

strong concepts

best people

excellent execution

superior brands

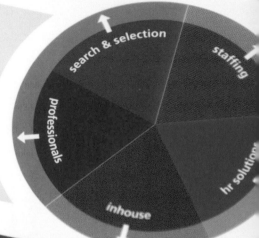

search & selection

staffing

professionals

hr solutions

inhouse

targets
- EBITA margin of 5% to 6% through the cycle, not below 4% in normal down
- mid-term EBITA margins of 4 to 5% for inhouse services, 5 to 7% for staffing
- continuous market share gains
- sound financial position; leverage ratio of between

2009 is th...

annual report 2009

randstad

ready for your future

hr randstad

key points 2009

- The integration of Randstad and Vedior was successfully completed
- The synergy targets came in ahead of schedule and ahead of target
- In the sharpest downturn in the history of our industry, revenue declined by 27% to € 12.4 billion
- Our extensively prepared 'managing through the cycle' approach worked
- Operating expenses were reduced by 22% to € 2.1 billion, backed by natural attrition, synergies and restructuring, extensive global footprint maintained
- Cash flow was strong and net debt was reduced by over € 600 million to € 1.0 billion
- It is proposed to further strengthen the balance sheet and not to pay dividend
- Classical recovery patterns became visible in Q4

ready for your future

The 'new' Randstad, ready for your future
For the theme of this year's annual report, we look back on how today's world of work has been shaped, and how we have shaped the 'new' Randstad to benefit from current and future drivers of growth. We outline our vision on the employment markets of tomorrow, and describe our readiness to achieve our mission of taking the lead in shaping the world of work of the future.

**20
09** *Since their introduction in 2002, the building blocks have been a standing subject in Randstad's annual reports. 'Strong concepts', 'best people', 'excellent execution' and 'superior brands' get a close look every year: how is Randstad performing on these specific points?*

Most recently this was done in the annual report of Randstad Holding nv for 2009. The graphic (second from left) shows the key points of that year: Randstad is ready for your future.

building blocks

It was February 2002 and one by one, some one hundred senior managers from all countries with Randstad representations began to take their seats in the conference room at Randstad's head office in Diemen. They had been invited by the Executive Board; the primary agenda item was the company's policy for the years ahead, and the board wanted the senior managers to be the first to hear about the new direction the company was about to take. Randstad now ranked fourth in the world after Adecco, Manpower and Vedior; it had built up a reasonable international foundation with branches in 13 countries across Europe and North America. This position now had to be expanded further in order for the company to become a genuine global player. What the Executive Board had to say was short and to the point: "We are ambitious, and we have great plans for the company." The company strategy fits on a single sheet of paper. Four principles were stated as strategic building blocks: strong concepts, best people, excellent execution and superior brands.

The first strategic building block, strong concepts, consisted of Randstad's three different service concepts. The first is staffing, the traditional services provided by Randstad and Tempo-Team, services ranging from administrative to industrial staff. The second concept was in-house services. The brands Randstad Inhouse Services and Capac Inhouse Services supplied large numbers of temporary workers for a limited number of positions within large companies or projects. The third concept was professionals. Using the Yacht brand, Randstad focused on highly educated professionals in the Finance, Management, Technology and ICT sectors. In 2004, the concepts search & selection (for the placement of highly trained personnel in permanent positions) and HR Solutions (a wide package of tailor-made solutions for administration, payroll, and process management) were also added.

The second building block was best people. Everything depended on the quality of the people working for Randstad, including the staffing consultants. These were the real heroes! They looked after the interests of both clients and temporary workers, and were able to combine the supply and demand for flexible workers thanks to their excellent knowledge of local markets. Their daily work consisted of matching the most suitable temporary workers to individual clients and bringing substance into the abstract principles comprising the strategy. At higher levels in the organization, the best people credo was made tangible by setting a target stating that 80 per cent of management positions were to be filled from within the organization.

The third building block, excellent execution, went hand-in-hand with 'striving for perfection'. Wherever possible, the company aimed to standardize work processes to achieve the highest possible quality. This also made it possible for the company to enjoy operational benefits such as lower costs, more effective internal and external communication, and faster decision-making processes.

The fourth building block, superior brands, is linked to the first building block, and completes the circle. The chosen concepts had to be strong, consistent, and suitable for international implementation. The Randstad brand was now becoming a major international brand and was universally expressed in the same way. Clients worldwide recognized its high quality and employees were highly aware that they were working for no less than a global player.

The four strategic principles signaled a new start for Randstad. Cleem Farla knew as no other how to restore that Randstad feeling, and he did it in just a few short months. He and his team managed to reverse the company's downward spiral quickly, through a combination of good leadership and enthusiastic employees who were willing to follow the new course with confidence and conviction. August 2002, however, brought the unexpected bad news that Cleem Farla was seriously ill and had decided to step down temporarily. Ben Noteboom stood in for him as of September 2002, but in early 2003 it became clear that Farla would not be coming back. He nevertheless remained

involved with the company as advisor to the Executive Board until his death in 2007. Ben Noteboom was appointed as new CEO on 1 March 2003. The Executive Board then consisted of Robert-Jan van de Kraats, Leo Lindelauf and Jim Reese until 1 June 2005. Jacques van den Broek joined the board in 2004.

YACHT | TECCON
a Randstad company

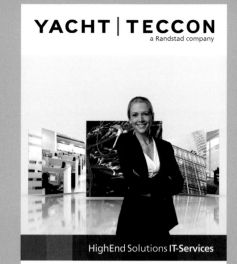

HighEnd Solutions **IT-Services**

HighEnd Solutions **Aerospace**

20 09 *Yacht Teccon is the specialist in interim professionals for the technology sector in Germany and in France. The 2009 ad campaign shows professionals, with their field of specialization in the background. We see airplane engines and advanced network technology. Yacht makes the difference in every complicated project.*

Randstad Holding nv's board in 2009: Greg Netland, Ben Noteboom,

Robert-Jan van de Kraats, Brian Wilkinson, Leo Lindelauf, and Jacques van den Broek.

how to become a CEO

It was early February 2003 and the conference room at Randstad's head office in Diemen was packed with students from the AIESEC international student organization. They were there for their annual international conference and Randstad had offered them the use of the premises; Ben Noteboom acted as host and opening speaker. The students waited patiently, some slouching lethargically in their chairs – nights could be short for students studying in Amsterdam, a city that never sleeps. The chairman of the board then took the floor. His opening words, "I'm going to start by telling you something about Randstad" instigated only minor interest, but when, after a short silence, Noteboom continued "… and then I'm going to give you a short course on how to become a CEO", a visible stir went through the audience. Students sat up straighter and began taking notes. Noteboom gave the students a brief history of the company before starting the 'course'; he was clearly enjoying himself. He carefully glanced around the audience, and then he began his lecture. "First," he said, "I am a firm believer in common sense. If you can't explain something in a simple manner, forget it. Second, I believe in independence. Nothing will work if you can't think independently." With the students hanging on his words, the chairman continued, "Course completed!" As he left the floor, the students looked at each other in astonishment; that was indeed a very short course! But Randstad's chairman of the board had made his point. His strength lay in his ability to bring everything down to basics and communicate concisely and with clarity.

a process for success

A career in the staffing industry was certainly not the career that Noteboom had expected to pursue. The new CEO was a martial arts enthusiast, and had always aspired to a career as a sports instructor. However, his fellow students' lack of motivation made him decide to rethink his ambitions. He chose to study law in Rotterdam, as this was likely to open up many doors to him in the future. After graduating in 1982, he went to work for Dow Chemical, an international chemical company. He worked for Dow in various operational management positions around the world.

He was introduced to Randstad in 1993. The company's management was impressed by this man who had worked so quickly to make an international career for himself, and likewise Noteboom was impressed by what he had seen of Randstad. In fact, he was so impressed that he decided to take an unprecedented step in his career by signing a contract without knowing precisely what he was going to do. In May 1993, he started working as a temporary staffing consultant at a branch in Bunnik, just as many managers before him had done. He was tossed in at the deep end, since one of his colleagues was on holiday and the member of staff assigned to show him the ropes had called in sick for a few days. Noteboom had to keep the branch up and running. His training came to an abrupt end after just a few months, however, when Randstad needed him for a special operation. Werknet, which was part of the newly acquired Flex, had to be integrated with Tempo-Team, and in France, Flex Intérim was being merged with Randstad Intérim. These successful integrations provided Noteboom with an experience that would prove to be very useful later in his career.

In 1997, the opportunity arose for him to make his mark on Capac Inhouse Services. This brand served the major industrial clients that required large numbers of temporary workers for a limited number of positions. Capac therefore opened a branch at the client company and ultimately took over partial management of its human resources. At Capac, Noteboom learned all there was to know about standardization. "To achieve fast growth in the service industry, you must be able to replicate effective processes. This involves the ability to explain how things work in a clear, simple and comprehensible manner so that people catch on very quickly. I have often seen people working very hard when the telephone rang, but actually it was too late by then. You have to know what to do before the telephone rings; it should be predictable. So, what we did was to make the clients' needs predictable. The concept was a great success and we now work in a far more analytical fashion than what used to be the norm in the services and staffing industry. We grew very quickly; even in that first year we made a profit of a million Dutch guilders, on a turnover of 40 million. In the second year, the turnover was 212 million Dutch guilders. That was quite impressive, you could say."

Randstad en Capac:
samen sterk

20 08 *Capac focused in particular
on industrial clients with a need
for large quantities of flexible
employees. Capac often had a
branch at a client's location.
Parts of a client's HR needs –
and sometimes all of them –
were often managed from
such on-sites.*

*In 1996, Studio Dumbar in
Rotterdam was asked to develop
a corporate style for Capac.
Concrete language indicated
the efficiency offered by Capac
in a production environment.
A three-dimensional logo showed
that Capac was the indispensable
link between flexworkers and
clients.*

*From 2008 onward, Capac
continued as Randstad Inhouse
Services. The logo is no longer
in use, but the typical yellow
'Capac' color was maintained.*

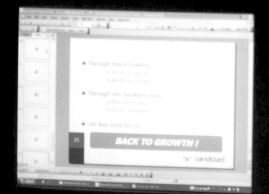

A meeting of Randstad's General Managers in April 2010.

best practice works

CFO Robert-Jan van de Kraats told us that "there was always much discussion within the company about how we provide our services. One operating company said it should be done one way, another wanted it another way. As a board member, you always want to add value to your company and it was with this in mind that the idea emerged to standardize our services to the highest degree possible. We did this by using best practices as a basis; collective learning processes emerged and these were summarized in process descriptions. Our new employees were almost all educated at graduate level, but they had relatively little experience. If you told someone to 'go ahead', they had no idea where to start, and how could they? Standardized processes would provide the helping hand they needed. This is how you assess the market; the results are entered into the database; if you win a new client, you take a give-away with you. We turned those activities into routine tasks and that gave our staff confidence so they could use their creativity for other business issues. We supplied the rhythm and the key, and the staff could subsequently make their own music. And that is the secret of our success!"

Randstad was highly successful in standardizing its services and translating them from one market to the other. Rolling out best practices on an international scale is a skill in its own right, after all. Board member Jacques van den Broek had the following to say about it: "It is very important that we are also successful outside of the Netherlands; we have to make a profit in each of the countries in which we operate. We are growing faster than the market in most of those countries. One of the main things we have learned is that we can recognize a concept. We used this knowledge successfully at an airport in France; once established and applied, we then had an airport concept that we could use for other market applications, and it works everywhere.

The idea is that we build upon a theme using the same foundation, to which we add specialized marketing knowledge. We are constantly creating new solutions in this way; recognizing, recording and implementing a concept worldwide is a competence rarely seen in our line of business and, fortunately, we have become very good at it."

5, 4, 3...

The renewed focus on Randstad's core business and the crystal clear strategy they embraced resulted in a net profit of EUR 77.1 million in 2003, which was 36 per cent higher than in 2002. Furthermore, by 2005, the EUR 500 million deficit from 2001 had been turned into a cash surplus of 200 million.

The international character of the company was underlined in grand style during the company's 45th anniversary in 2005. A huge party took place for Randstad employees across the globe, held simultaneously in 10 different countries. The pinnacle of the event was when Ben Noteboom's speech on the behalf of the Executive Board was broadcast live from the Netherlands by satellite to the parties in the other countries. After the speech came the countdown, "… 5, 4, 3, 2, 1, 0!" At the count of zero, 10 bands began to play, each in its own country and each on its own stage. They played 'Good to know you', a hit written by Billinger & Marsman and produced by the Dutch hit record producers Jochem Fluitsma and Erik van Tijn. The lyrics to the song were the same everywhere but the style was individual to each country. And in the United States there was an additional reason to celebrate: the anniversary year had been particularly successful for the American branches of Randstad thanks to the recovering economy.

Supported by the good results, Randstad decided to spread its wings and go even further. Members of the Executive Board traveled around the world seeking contacts in new markets. In early 2004, Ben Noteboom and Robert-Jan van de Kraats made a trip to China and India together. The visit was an eye-opener: both countries had a highly dynamic market and they immediately decided to pave the way for operations there. Randstad entered India in 2005 with the takeover of EmmayHR and Team4U, making it the third largest company of its kind in this country. That same year, Randstad also entered the Chinese market, the fastest-growing economy in the world.

Randstad kept up the pace by entering into three new countries each year on average, expanding from 12 to 20 countries in just a few years. The company sent its experienced managers, the old stalwarts, to do the pioneering work. French veteran manager Guy Mallet was asked to open Randstad Portugal in 2000 and Henk Janssen, who had spent many years working for companies including Tempo-Team, later took over the helm. Another veteran manager, David van Gelder, opened branches in Hungary in 2004 and in Turkey in 2006. In 2004, Pierre Adida, former director of Randstad France, opened the first branches in Poland. That same year, Randstad became the market leader in Poland following the takeover of Intersource and Job Net.

Randstad continued its journey along the takeover path. In 2005, it took over the British company Martin Ward Anderson for EUR 48 million. The takeover of Bindan and Teccon for EUR 148 million followed in 2006 in Germany, where Randstad had been the market leader since 1997, and allowed it to gain maximum benefit from the newly gained flexibility of the German labor market. In 2006, Marcel Wiggers of Randstad entered the Japanese market.

Between 2003 and 2007, the Randstad organization performed better than its immediate competitors. In 2006, it surpassed its rival Vedior and became the third-largest staffing and recruitment company in the world. Accelerated consolidation in the sector during this period resulted in a divide between one group comprising thousands of small staffing firms and another, leading, group, consisting of just four large companies. The largest of these was the Swiss company Adecco, which had been created by the merger of Adia and Ecco in 1996; the second largest was the American firm Manpower. The race for the top had begun.

Randstad proves it can party at its
45th anniversary in 2005. Parties were
held in ten countries simultaneously.

At a last-minute press conference, Randstad and Vedior explain their plans. From left to right: Tex Gunning, Ben Noteboom, Robert-Jan van de Kraats, and Frans Cornelis.

Vedior the sunflower

"Are you serious?" Tex Gunning asked Ben Noteboom. Gunning, the CEO of staffing giant Vedior, had invited Noteboom to his home in The Hague. USG People, a major rival of both Randstad and Vedior, had previously expressed interest in a merger with Vedior, but nothing had come of it. In late October 2007, Gunning had heard rumors in the market that Randstad was considering a takeover of Vedior. Vedior's CEO had therefore decided to invite the company's head man to his home and ask him about Randstad's plans face to face. Vedior had just experienced a period of great growth, with fifty acquisitions between 2001 and 2007. The company had operations in over 50 countries and their turnover had increased from approximately 6 to 8.4 billion euros between 2003 and 2007. International, successful and thoroughly sound, Vedior would make an excellent partner for Randstad.

In his typical succinct fashion, Noteboom explained his plans. Under the codename Sunflower, Randstad had ordered analyses to evaluate whether a merger with Vedior might be successful. The conclusion was that the two companies complemented each other perfectly. By taking over the number four in the world, Randstad would become the second largest company of its kind. Moreover, strategic markets such as Japan and Brazil, where the presence of Randstad was still very limited, were waiting to be tapped. Another interesting consideration was that Randstad, unlike Vedior, had never had a strong presence in the upper market segments in the UK and in the US. The new combination would also suit the wishes of international clients who preferred to work with a single entity.

In many respects, Vedior was Randstad's opposite. Vedior was very much a decentralized organization whereas Randstad's organizational structure was more centralized.

Vedior had over 125 different brands, whereas Randstad concentrated on a single strong brand with just a few smaller brands alongside it, and it excelled in the professionals segment. Vedior had a powerful position in the recruitment and selections market and had a supply of highly trained specialists, including lawyers and doctors in the US and the UK. Randstad, on the other hand, excelled in the business of general staffing. Vedior recorded 90 per cent of its turnover outside of the Netherlands, compared with Randstad's 65 per cent.

The dialog between the two CEOs was a conversation between equals; the scope of the two companies did not differ greatly. A joining of forces could result in a highly effective combination and the second place among staffing companies worldwide. It was a tempting prospect. Noteboom therefore answered Gunning's question with a bold and sincere "yes". Vedior's top man was impressed with the Randstad model and, although much still had to be decided for, little seemed to stand in the way of an enthusiastic cooperation between the two.

From that afternoon onwards, Noteboom and Gunning concentrated their efforts on the possible consequences of the merger for both organizations, the market and competition regulations. "I think", Gunning later said, "that that first conversation set the tone for our entire relationship. Ben and I kept our heads cool all along and kept in touch by telephone and text messages right up to the final date of completion. I never lost faith that we would make the merger happen."

In late November, however, there was a hitch when the news leaked that Vedior was negotiating a takeover. Vedior shares skyrocketed as the stock exchange opened for business on Friday, 30 November 2007. Both companies were dismayed by the news of the leak and felt obliged to come forward with an explanation. Fortunately, it had no influence on the relationship that the partners had built up. A team of almost 100 people worked day and night for a whole weekend, preparing everything that they needed to close the deal. On the evening of Sunday, December 2nd, Noteboom and Gunning both signed an agreement of intent for the takeover of Vedior by Randstad for the price of EUR 3.51 billion. The merger was made public on Monday, December 3rd, at a hastily arranged and well-attended press conference held at the Amsterdam Hilton Hotel.

Three obstacles still had to be overcome, however, before the merger could be finalized. Firstly, Randstad had to verify the bid made to Vedior in December 2007 within a given period of time. For every Vedior share, 9.50 euros in cash and 0.32759 Randstad shares would be tendered. 2 April 2008 was the first day of trading and also the day on which it would become clear how many shareholders would be tendering their Vedior shares; 67 per cent of the shareholders would have to do so to satisfy the Randstad offer. That threshold was reached comfortably, and by May 7, 93.46 per cent of the Vedior shares had been tendered.

The second obstacle that had to be overcome were the Vedior and Randstad shareholders' meetings at which an entire list of resolutions had to be dealt with in order to make the merger legally possible. Nevertheless, everything went without a hitch and the resolutions were adopted with comfortable majorities.

The third obstacle, however, was beyond the control of either Vedior or Randstad. The takeover would result in a company of such magnitude that the European Commission in Brussels was required to determine whether or not it would upset the balance of competition in the staffing market. After an extensive investigation, the Commission confirmed that there was no question of the new company gaining a monopoly in any relevant market except in Portugal, where the new combination's market share would be too big. The Commission was only prepared to approve the merger if Randstad would sell its Portuguese branches, a measure that Randstad eventually agreed to, albeit with a heavy heart. By 1 July 2008, the merger between Randstad and Vedior was official.

Vedior s'appelle maintenant Tempo-Team

seul notre nom change

www.tempo-team.be

Rowlands s'appelle maintenant Tempo-Team

20 10 *After the merger with Randstad, the Vedior branches in Belgium and Luxembourg were renamed Tempo-Team. In doing so, Randstad maintained its strategy of introducing a second strong brand in countries in which its market share is high (like the Benelux countries).*

The public was informed about the name change by way of a publicity campaign: seul notre nom change – only our name is changing.

 Accountants Intl.™
a Randstad company

 advancers executive
groupe ⌐ randstad

 l'appel medical
groupe ⌐ randstad

 bbt beresford blake thomas
a Randstad company

 capsecur conseil
groupe ⌐ randstad

 CLINICAL ONE
a Randstad company

 expectra
groupe ⌐ randstad

HR*i* Human Resources Intl.™
a Randstad company

 jbm
groupe ⌐ randstad

JoslinRowe
a Randstad company

 ma foi
a Randstad company

martinwardanderson
a Randstad company

minvesta
a Randstad company

 Reliance Care
a Randstad company

⌐ randstad education

SAPPHiRE
a Randstad company

 select
part of the randstad network

tempo-team

YACHT
a Randstad company

YACHT | TECCON
a Randstad company

20 10 *Some of the brands carried by Randstad after its merger with Vedior. The logos show the enormous diversity of the activities of this international corporation. From industrial and administrative flexworkers through technology specialists, and from call center operators through accountants: Randstad is the place for any type of employee. Most brands clearly display their link with Randstad by adding the phrase 'A Randstad company'. Moreover, every brand implements Randstad's house style, in order to maintain unity despite the diversity.*

get to know you

Tex Gunning was given the task of overseeing the smooth integration of the two companies. He explains how cultural differences and conflicting corporate values played an important role: "There are always going to be significant differences, but a multinational has to learn to recognize and appreciate them. Argentineans will never be Americans, Americans never Europeans, and the Germans will never be like the French, but that doesn't have to be a problem. You can always communicate with each other using the language of trust and respect. The way in which people connect and interact with each other has less to do with culture than with human nature."

In order to bring people together and build relationships, Tex Gunning used personal lifelines. Relationships are built through conversation, and in this case, those conversations took place through personal lifelines in which people told each other their own stories; stories about how they had become who they were, from early childhood right up to the present. Respect for each other's lifeline would help creating trust, and would be the ideal way to form ties with each other. The principle of lifelines was applied first within the Executive Board and then to the top 200 most important people in the organization. 'Get to know you' sessions were held around the world wherever Randstad and Vedior were working together, giving their employees the opportunity to meet new colleagues and swap stories of their individual lives. They got to know each other personally in a very short time and the 'Get to know you' sessions soon created a sense of unity among the participants.

The merger obviously required a significant change in perspective from everyone at Vedior and Randstad. After all, the former rivals, particularly in the field of general staffing, had suddenly become colleagues. It was also important that the staffing consultants from both organizations dealt carefully and sensitively with their client databases before the legal merger took place, although initial introductions had already taken place and some people were already working together.

The merger was received well by the thousands of employees at Vedior. A survey held among Vedior employees in eight countries in June 2008 showed that 80 per cent thought the merger was a logical step forwards. Responses varied from "Exactly what Vedior needed" to "It is the great diversity that makes this merger so valuable", "Together, we have become the largest recruiter in the world!", "We can now offer our clients even more specialized services" and "We might be rivals, but it is now a future of sibling rivalry we can look forward to". Their attitude was not only positive; it was the key to the great success of this merger.

a world player

The merger of these two staffing giants was a historic event; never before had the industry experienced such a large merger. Randstad had doubled its size and become a true global player, and thereby achieved the main goals set out by the Executive Board during the strategic retreat of 2002. In 2008, with sales of EUR 17.3 billion, Randstad became the second largest staffing company in the world after Adecco, with sales of EUR 20 billion. Manpower was the third largest with sales of EUR 15.1 billion. Randstad now had branches in over fifty countries worldwide and was the top staffing firm in the Netherlands, Germany, Belgium, Portugal, Poland, Luxembourg, Canada and India. A total of 5,400 branches with over 36,000 staff members provided jobs for almost 700,000 temporary employees.

The merger also resulted in the expansion of the Executive Board, as two new members from Vedior joined the board: Greg Netland, manager of Vedior North and South America, and Brian Wilkinson, who was responsible for the United Kingdom, British Commonwealth, Ireland and Hong Kong. The Board of Supervisors was also joined by new members from Vedior, which meant that the board was now composed of an international team comprising several Dutch members, one Greek, one British, one German, and one French member.

A broad spectrum of services was offered following the merger. 21 per cent of the company was now geared towards the contract staffing of highly skilled professionals for middle and higher management, a market that had grown rapidly in the previous ten years, and in which Yacht had been the driving force since 2000. The expertise in the field of professionals, which had always been Vedior's strong suit, was increased further through the absorption of companies such as Select Education, HillMcGlynn, Beresford Blake Thomas and Sapphire Technologies. Highly trained specialists were contracted out in the financial, medical and legal sectors in particular. These forms of flexible employment catered to the needs of many young and highly educated people looking for varied careers and a healthy balance between work and leisure.

In addition to the placing of professional staff, 11 per cent of the company focused on the market for inhouse services, 66 per cent worked in the market for traditional recruitment and selection, and two per cent targeted the market for other HR Solutions such as outplacement, career development and human resource management. This wide-ranging package of services was essential for an international company with an international client base; there was a growing need among larger companies for a single, worldwide package of services in the field of human resources, which would be provided by one supplier. With its capacity doubled, Randstad was now able to fulfill that need.

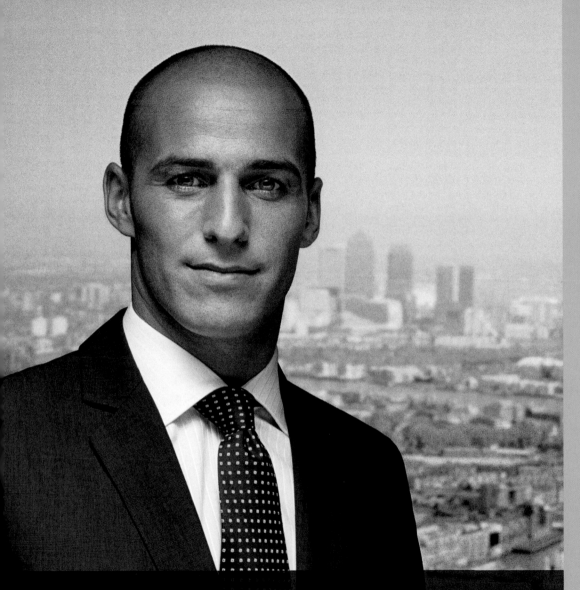

professional recruitment specialist

martin**ward**anderson

work for us

financial recruitment specialist

martin**ward**anderson
a Randstad company

20
08 *Martin Ward Anderson is a genuine professionals company in the United Kingdom. It focuses on the recruitment and selection of highly educated financial specialists. Its clients are banks and accountancy firms.*

The personnel recruitment campaign in the advertisements focuses on confident professionals. People who's natural working environment is the metropolitan downtown. In the background we see an overview of London, the financial heart of Europe.

good
to know
you

ᴙᴙ randstad
work solutions

ŞAKIRPAŞA İŞ HANI
89-91

Randstad opens its first branch in Turkey, Istanbul, in 2006.

a world market

Randstad's spectacular growth ran parallel with that of the staffing and recruitment industry as a whole, and in just 50 years, a global market had emerged. In 2008, there were 70,000 staffing firms with a total of 170,000 branches worldwide and combined sales of EUR 229 billion. Approximately forty million agency-supplied employees were placed annually.

Ranstad's futher growth depends on a number of developments. Primary among those is the degree of success in implementing its strategic building blocks, namely strong concepts, best people, excellent execution and strong brands. A second factor is the growth of the economy. In times of economic prosperity, Randstad's clients increase their production capacity by hiring qualified staff on a temporary basis. In the short term, economic cycles have a significant influence on business; the 2008/2009 credit crunch resulted in a sharp downward trend in Randstad's results. The staffing sector, however, has traditionally come into its own when business cycles begin to follow an upward trend. The sector is a breeding ground for employment growth. The third factor is the development of flexibility in labor markets worldwide. Flexibility is a valuable resource in the labor market and the lifeblood of modern, globalizing economies. Supply and demand are better matched thanks to the role played by staffing companies and recruiters. The final factor concerns the area in which relevant regulations are developed for staffing and placement activities. Randstad is in favor of lifting or relaxing certain regulations where necessary and of the introduction of new rules as required.

Randstad was a true authority in the public debate on temporary employment and the increase of labor market flexibility. Randstad was taken seriously by influential politicians such as former Dutch Prime Minister Wim Kok who, having consulted Randstad on a number of occasions, suggested in a 2003 report for the European Union that staffing firms could fulfill the role of human capital manager. The International Confederation of Private Employment Agencies, CIETT, has predicted that, given normal economic conditions, 1.6 million new temporary jobs will have been created in Europe alone between 2007 and 2012 as a result of increased flexibility. A further 570,000 extra jobs could be created if labor markets in Belgium, France, Germany and Spain also became more flexible. Most of these would involve activities that were not carried out by permanent staff in the past. The European Commission recognized the importance of flexibility for the labor market and the economy. Randstad received significant backing in 2008 when the EU introduced a directive according to which obsolete and outmoded impediments to temporary work will have to be abolished by all member states by 2012. This directive will ensure that flexible work will become an accepted form of employment in all European member states. Moreover, they will help reduce unemployment levels in those countries.

The future of European labor relations will be determined by the concept of flexicurity, which represents the balance between flexibility and security. Flexicurity aims at replacing the current emphasis on job security with a new emphasis on work security. Flexible contracts would allow companies to adapt to changes faster, and to optimize operational management. All employees would receive adequate social security, whether they are employed on a flexible, permanent, part-time or full-time basis; they would be assured of a steady salary and be able to combine work and leisure arrangements more easily. Continuous efforts are made to enhance people's employability through lifelong learning, and modern flexible contracts are designed to support the integration of newcomers into the labor market. Employer and employee representatives (industry organizations and trade unions, respectively) and government together fulfill a key role in introducing flexicurity into their own countries.

a world brand

Randstad's story is crystal clear. It is a story about concepts, accomplishment, people, and a brand. Marketing was given high priority in 2002, when the organization realized that the Randstad brand deserved the same amount of attention it had received at its beginning. The first step was the launching of the international concept Good to know you. This slogan invoked the company's core values: to know, serve and trust. If someone says "Good to know you", it shows they are taking pleasure in serving their clients through their love of people and the love of their work, which results in trust between clients, candidates and colleagues.

At the beginning of 2007, the Randstad brand was positioned at around four hundred in the list of the most valuable international brand names. Coca Cola had always headed the top one hundred places in the ranking of best world brands. "That's where we should be", was the firm opinion of Frans Cornelis, director of corporate communications. "There are two service providers on the list, Oracle and Accenture, with marketing budgets comparable to ours. If they can make the top one hundred, why can't we?" That question led to another one that summed up the essence of Randstad's ambition. "How can we highlight our role as the authority in our industry in the coming years?"

Randstad approached Interbrand, a renowned international brand consultant, who advised Randstad to position itself on an equal footing with the top world brands. The Randstad brand name had to be positioned center stage in every segment, including that of professionals. The addition of a product or capability line in all its communication crystallized what Randstad meant to its clients: Staffing, Professionals, Search & Selection, HR Solutions and Inhouse Services.

Since 2006, Randstad has sponsored the AT&T Williams Formula 1 team. This popular spectator sport guarantees Randstad worldwide attention for its brand.

good to know you

**20
07** *Visual identity is important
for Randstad: it determines the
image of the company. Ever
since it was founded, Randstad
has been giving this much
attention. Posters, billboards,
brochures, packaging,
calendars, the interior design
of the branches, and during
the last decade the websites:
every expression must align
with the prescribed house style.*

 randstad

Staffing Solutions | Professionals | Search & Selection | HR Solutions | Inhouse Services

A world brand needs a global mission, and a company needs to have a clear story to help it reach markets and target groups. In order to achieve this, Randstad drew on its significance in society and its authority on matters relating to the development of the global labor market. Significance and authority were brought together and summarized in Randstad's new mission statement, Shaping the World of Work. Randstad wanted to be recognized as the number one worldwide authority on labor markets. The company was in the perfect position to achieve this, due to its longstanding and extensive knowledge of international and local labor markets. Randstad was in continuous dialogue with all the relevant parties in the world of employment. Employees all over the world simultaneously looked after the interests of clients, candidates, staffing service providers, suppliers, governments and unions. At the macro level, Randstad was engaged in a social dialogue on optimum legislation, flexible labor markets, social acceptability and corporate social responsibility.

The mission gained a global perspective with the takeover of the internationally strong Vedior organization. In one fell swoop, Randstad expanded its working environment to include almost thirty new countries. The new brand policy, however, left no doubt as to which brand was to be the main brand: that was Randstad. The choice was a logical one. Vedior had always adopted a multibrand strategy, so its name did not develop into a recognizable brand. It was decided that the name should be changed quickly, and 106 rebranding exercises were initiated. The names of the former Vedior staffing agencies in Spain, England, Italy and Germany were changed to Randstad; in the Netherlands and Belgium, the Vedior brand continued to operate under the name Tempo-Team, and Dactylo was integrated with Randstad in the Netherlands. In France, Vediorbis was also renamed Randstad.

Vedior had always enjoyed a prominent position in the professionals market segment. Following the merger with Randstad, this segment became one of the most important pillars of the 'new' Randstad. In 2009, an integrated group of Vedior and Randstad marketers took just four months to develop a new concept for the Professionals house style. Almost all the staffing companies that handled professionals, including Select Education, HillMcGlynn and Beresford Blake Thomas, were given their own version of the new house style that incorporated their own photography and resources, but which was still recognizable as part of Randstad. By the end of 2009, the Vedior brand change was 95 per cent complete, and the efforts involved did not go unrewarded.

Of the three major staffing firms, it was the Randstad brand that grew fastest in familiarity and image. In 2008, Randstad was the most frequently cited company in all publicity about the industry. Randstad believes in the power of its brand. This became evident in the deepest recession months of 2009, when the Randstad brand managed to maintain a continuous presence on television in the Benelux countries (for instance with the Clipper Stad Amsterdam) and in France during the Formula 1 championship, and again, together with the NOC*NSF, during the 2010 Olympic Games in Vancouver. The real strength behind the Randstad brand, however, is in the strength of its employees. It is their constant dedication and commitment that give shape and meaning to the brand; they are Randstad's true ambassadors.

shaping the world of work

The new mission represented the task that Randstad set for itself back in1960. The hard work was paying off, and flexible employment was increasingly implemented strategically rather than simply during the usual seasonal peaks and periods of sick leave. A flexible workforce allowed companies to deal better with economic swings, conduct reorganizations more quickly, guarantee quick start-ups, or enter new markets. The professionals were a relatively new addition to the flexible workforce. During the previous fifteen years, professionals had increasingly used Randstad as an instrument with which to gain short-term experience with a variety of companies and at the same time extend their networks; the merger with Vedior saw a major increase in the size of this group.

Flexibility is an indispensable instrument for operationally efficient companies. By hiring flexworkers and professionals, companies can expand their structural capacity with skilled staff in essential areas. Board chairman Ben Noteboom said "We supply companies with expertise, capacity and efficiency, and the structural use of flexibility; this can mean the difference between making a profit or facing bankruptcy."

Randstad survived the economic crisis of 2008-2009 with opportunities intact and flexible workers continuing to fulfill an important role. Randstad was able to offer expertise that went further than just a flexible outer layer; it also took care of personnel management for companies by drawing on its comprehensive knowledge of the labor market and by supplying, coaching and training employees for various corporate activities. Companies were keen to make use of this expertise so that they could concentrate fully on their core activities. Randstad had developed from a staffing agency into a strategic HR partner.

The value of temporary work is not only economic; it also has significant social importance. Minority groups, young people without work experience, and the long-term unemployed can find placement that leads to work, a stepping stone out of unemployment. Temporary jobs provide these people with the opportunity to prove themselves in companies for which they would not other-wise work, to gain valuable experience, and in many cases, recognition. The degree of labor participation, or the percentage of the population that is gainfully employed, is thereby increased. This creates a situation that is desirable and meets one of the European Union's objectives. In order to meet the demands of the increasingly aging population and the decreasing birth rate, the degree of participation in employment must increase from 60 to 70 per cent by 2010 and eventually even to 75 per cent.

Randstad is aware of the fact that, with its core activity of staffing and recruitment, it plays an important role in society. After all, its core business contributes to an

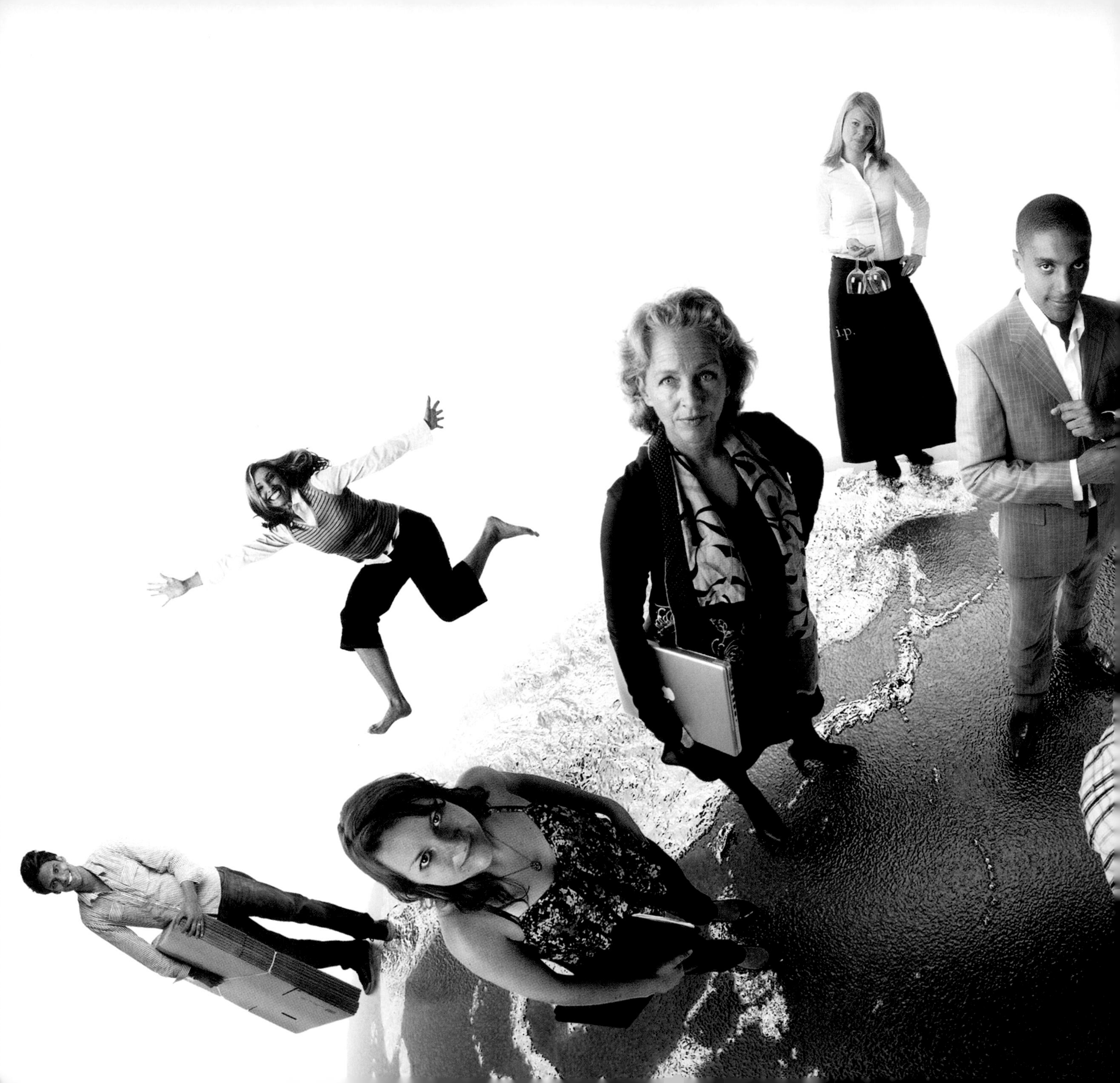
i.p.

improved functionality of the labor market, creates jobs, and provides a route into the labor market for people who are difficult to place. This creates responsibilities; Randstad has always felt very strongly about corporate social responsibility, which is linked to its central philosophy of simultaneous promotion of interests. A safe working environment, respect for human rights, and sustainable business practices are just some of the aspects which the organization continues to address on a worldwide scale. By 2010, 27,000 employees in over forty countries provide work to hundreds of thousands of people.

Work is a unifying force in the world, and with its mission of *Shaping the world of work*, Randstad stands firmly at the very heart of that world. The mission motivates staff and creates a feeling of communal destiny: "We will do something never done before in the staffing industry by taking the leading role in shaping tomorrow's worldwide labor market."

41 unforgettable
flowers, Christine Van
Jesús Beltejar Campos 4
Betschart 45 a passage
a couple of weeks of
Mohammed and Michel
Sun 49 best matc
Dagmara's secret, Dag

Bernadette Tilman 42 blue Helleputte 43 a love affair, career partner, Christelle to India, Santhosh Nair 46 , Kata Gombos-Kovács 47 e 48 night and day, Selina , Rafael Diaz-Cañabate 58 mara Chudzinska-Matysiak

the maximum out of sports and career

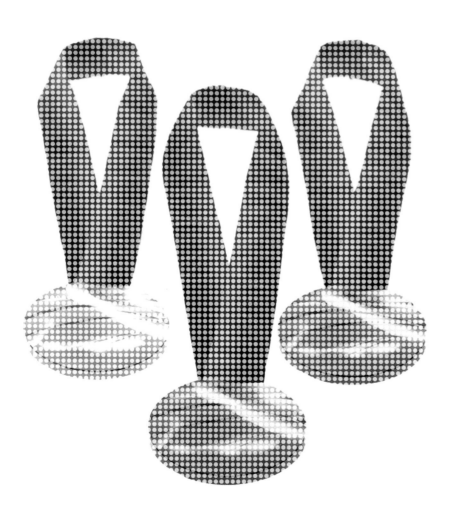

unforgettable

What do Atlanta, Nagano, Sydney, Salt Lake City, Athens, Turin, Beijing, and Vancouver have in common? All eight cities have hosted the largest sports event in the world, the Olympic Games. And Randstad was there, every time. The shining Dutch focal point during every Olympic Games is the Holland Heineken House, the prime meeting place for athletes and fans. The recruitment, selection, and training of the crew members working at the Holland Heineken House are provided by Randstad.

Bernadette Tilman, manager sponsoring & events: "We do not only look for people among our own staff. The motivation to work at Holland Heineken House is great. We receive about 1,300 applications every time. Not just in the form of résumés on a letter-sized piece of paper, but sometimes in exceptional shapes or forms. We have even received carefully-crafted papier-mâché constructs, meant to stand out in the pile of applications. Unfortunately, Randstad can only make 160 people happy."

"The people who end up working in the crew are carefully selected. The work is quite demanding. It is four weeks of hard work among sports celebrities, politicians, and occasionally a member of the royal family. Or as one employee put it recently: 'It is an unforgettable experience.'"

Bernadette Tilman – Manager sponsoring & events
Randstad, the Netherlands

flowers open doors

blue flowers

Interlabor, one of the former Randstad brands in Belgium, is growing rapidly. In 1976, Christine Van Helleputte started in Ghent with seven flex workers. In less than two years, her branch dispatched 312 workers. Interlabor kept expanding. Almost weekly, Van Helleputte would get a call from management assistant Didier de Laminne de Bex, who would tell her that they were opening a new branch. All colleagues in Flanders and Wallonia were called on to help out with the introductory days of the new branch.

Van Helleputte: "The point of these introductory days was to inform all businesses in a city or in an area about the opening of our new branch, and to visit them. We would always take along a plant when we would go visit a potential client, one which would produce pretty blue flowers. On the pot it would say 'Hello Kortrijk' or 'Hello Bruges', and underneath that would be our phone number. The flowers opened doors in ninety per cent of the cases, a conversation with the company ensued. Some companies would tell us later that they had kept the plant for more than two years!"

Christine Van Helleputte – Business development manager Randstad, Belgium

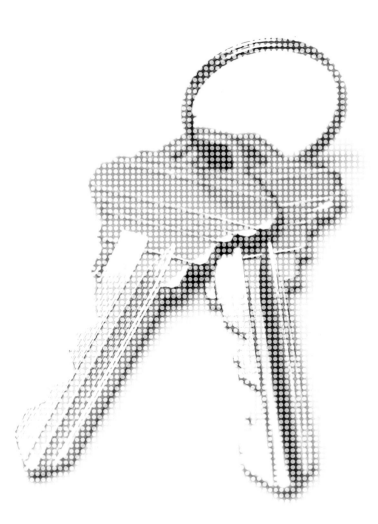

he made an enormous impression on me

a love affair

In 2000, after Randstad had taken over Umano, a Spanish staffing agency of which we were a client, someone from Randstad visited us in order find out who we are. I only met this person once, but he made a lasting impression on me. It was the first time that anyone was able to explain to me in detail the benefits that our company could gain from using flexworkers, and it took him less than an hour to do so. What a vision statement! I immediately thought to myself: that guy is so good that the company behind it must be excellent too.

The love affair between me and Randstad is enhanced by my two contacts. They provide excellent help with brainstorming about how to deal with capacity issues. If the production line is at risk of coming to a standstill, Randstad arranges extra staff post-haste. It feels as if we are constantly on a honeymoon!'

Jesús Beltejar Campos – HR manager Nutreco, Spain

Nutreco is a Dutch multinational with annual sales of almost EUR 5 billion. The company has approximately 25 production sites in Spain, and one of its major challenges is to keep all its production lines permanently operational. Seventy-five percent of the company's staff work in production. The flexworkers that Randstad supplies are therefore primarily industrial workers who provide cover for absence due to sickness or annual leave.

career partner

Christelle Betschart got her MBA in 2002. It was not easy to find a job, though: in interviews she was repeatedly told that she had too little work experience. But then, Betschart found out about a different career path: Expectra, a company that dispatches highly-qualified professionals to large companies.

"To tell you the truth: I did not expect too much from Expectra. I thought that staffing agencies only placed administrative and industrial staffers. But the opposite is true. After I signed up, I could start almost immediately as a technical purchaser at the Research & Development department at Renault Automobiles, where the newest technical features are developed."

"Since then I have always worked for Renault. Occasionally there are times that there is no work, and then, as a flex worker I temporarily have nothing to do. However, in the meantime, my network inside Renault is so strong that I will soon have a new contract, And if you wonder what role Expectra has in this, I consider them to be my career partner: I do the work, and they do the administration around it!"

Christelle Betschart – *Technical purchaser for Renault, France*

turbulent, chaotic, hectic, colorful, and enterprising

a passage to India

Turbulent, chaotic, hectic, colorful, and enterprising; there is no more succinct way to describe the Indian temporary employment market. Everyone who wants to start a temporary employment agency can just go ahead and do so, and rules do not form a barrier because the few existing rules on temping were drawn up forty years ago. New companies pop up all the time, many of which to disappear just as quickly.

Santhosh Nair: "India was running its economy at full tilt, which enabled someone like me who started out managing a five-member team a few years ago to manage a five hundred-member team now. Under Vedior, however, Ma Foi was not particularly strong in recruiting major international clients; it was, in fact, 'too Indian'. International clients require staffing service providers who are familiar with the world of multinationals, and Randstad India is taking a giant leap forward. We now have streamlined processes, international client teams and strong marketing." Randstad India now provides international clients with the clarity and structure needed for a successful *Passage to India*.

Santhosh Nair – Business head Randstad, India

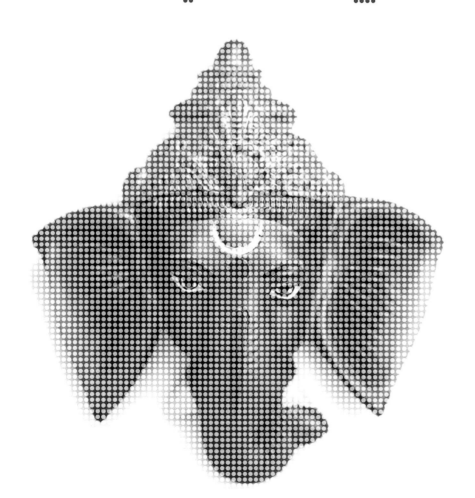

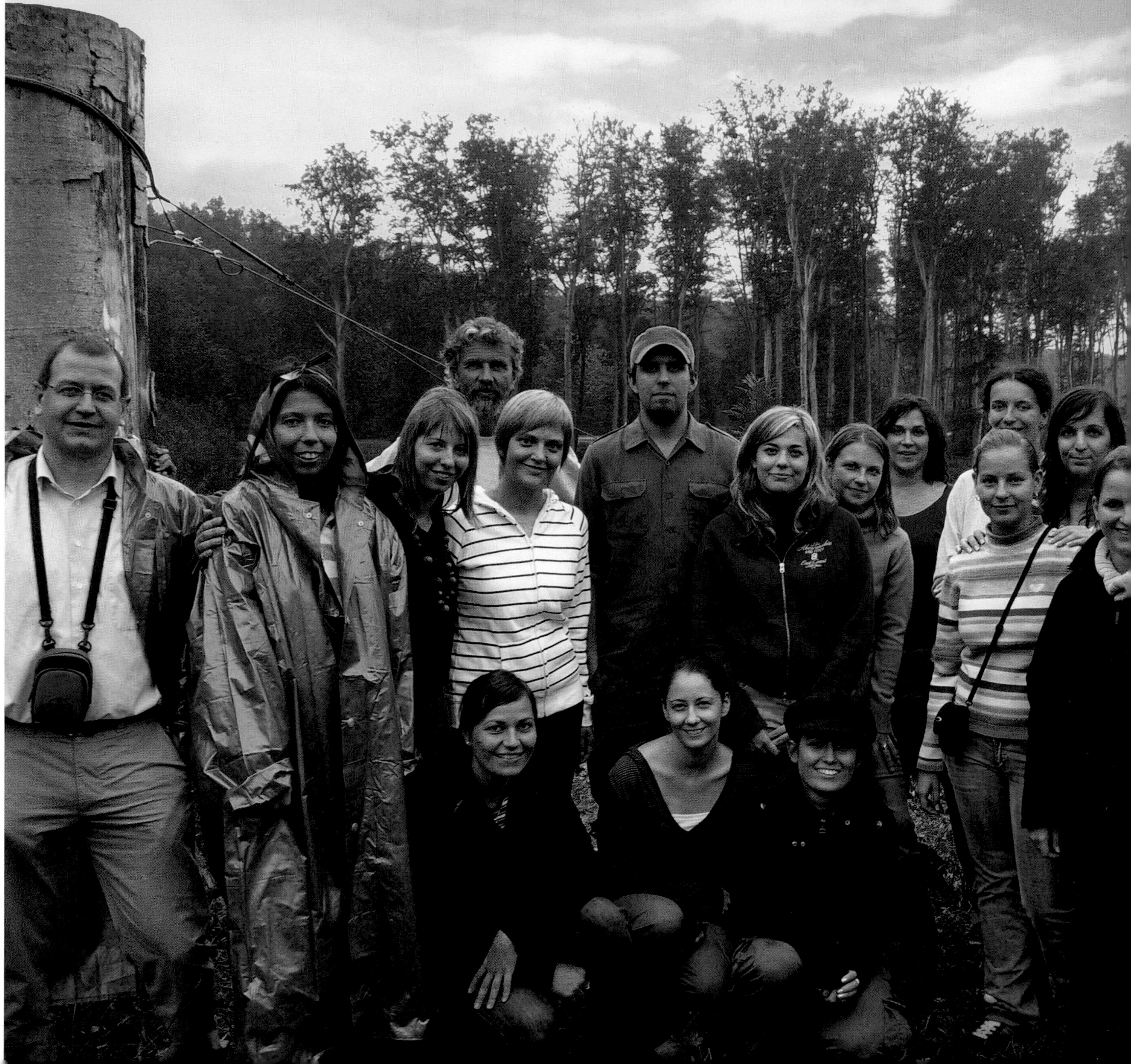

46

a couple of weeks off

Kata Gombos-Kovács appeared to have landed on her feet in 2007 when she started working for Randstad Hungary, a relatively small business in the capital city of Budapest comprising 32 staff members. She was immediately able to take part in a teambuilding session at an attractive location outside the city. After a day packed with activities, the program was rounded off in the evening with dancing at the hotel.

"I was feeling wonderful. Everyone was dancing and having fun. And then, at one point, I jumped onto a low bench without paying attention to my step; I slid, and crashed onto my ankle. At first, I didn't make a fuss, not wanting to spoil the fun, but my colleagues soon saw that something was wrong. I was in so much pain that I couldn't walk. Tears were streaming down my face. A male colleague of mine lifted me up and carried me back to the hotel room. I lay on the bed surrounded by the concerned faces of my entire team, who then proceeded to almost fight about who was going to take me to hospital. I had to stay at home for a couple of weeks and I received telephone calls and emails from the office almost every day. Breaking your ankle is never any fun, but the kindness shown by my colleagues at the time made it feel a lot better. They really made me feel like a member of the family. And I had only been working at Randstad for a month!"

Kata Gombos-Kovács (sixth from the left) – Staffing consultant Randstad, Hungary

I want Mohammed, I want Mohammed!

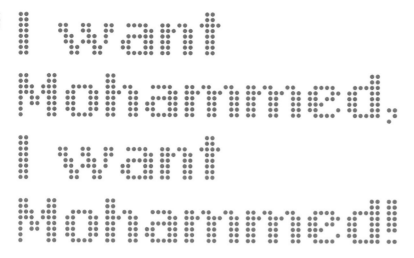

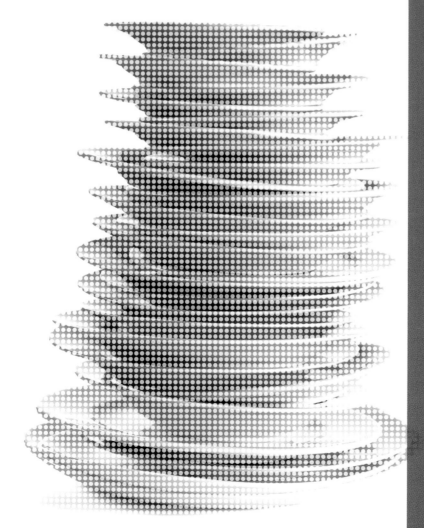

47

Mohammed and Michelle

The story of Mohammed and Michelle is one of contrasts: one senior (58 years old) and one junior (27 years old), one flexworker and one staffing consultant and one who immigrated from Tunisia years ago and the other born in the Netherlands. Despite their different backgrounds, Mohammed and Michelle get along like a house on fire; they make an unlikely yet successful pair.

Mohammed, who is a flexworker in the catering business, told us "I have a permanent job during 30 hours a week at a hotel in the Dutch beach resort of Noordwijk aan Zee. I'm a flexworker the rest of the time because I like to keep busy. I never refuse when Michelle calls me about a job; she and her colleagues are always pleasant, spontaneous and friendly; they always start by asking how I am doing. I am a hard worker and have a lot of experience; people always say 'I want Mohammed, I want Mohammed!'"

Michelle added that "clients always ask for Mohammed. He's a fantastic flexworker and definitely one of my favorites. He is always cheerful, a hard worker and simply a very nice guy."

Mohammed (left) – Flexworker Randstad, the Netherlands
Michelle – Staffing consultant Randstad, the Netherlands

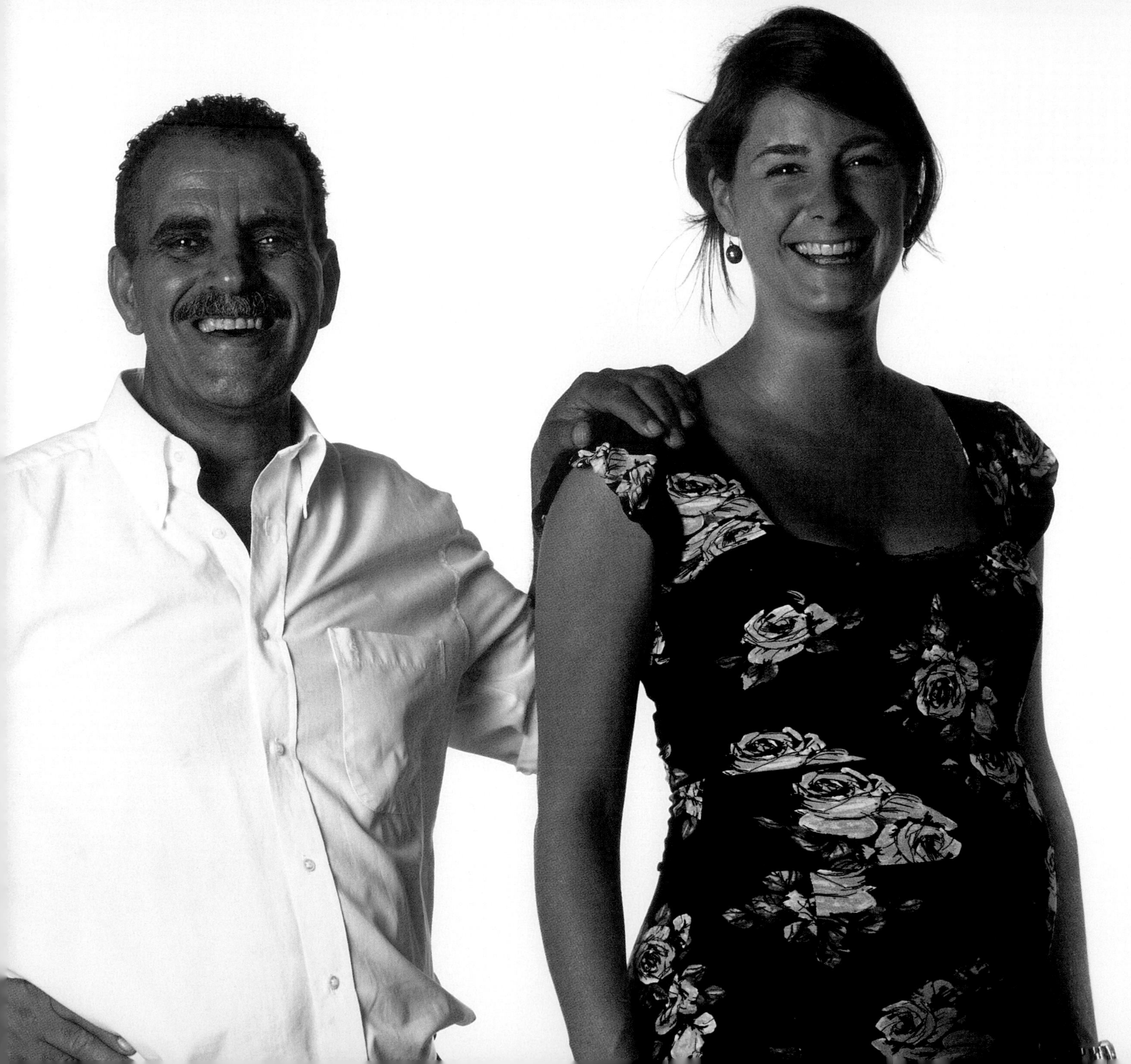

48

night and day

If anyone is in a position to make a comparison between the Netherlands and China, it is Selina Sun. When she was eighteen, she left China to pursue further study in the Netherlands. In 2007, after having gained her Masters degree in HR, she started working for Randstad as a management trainee. Her aim was to return to China some day and work as a pioneer for Randstad.

"For eight months, I followed a program of working at a branch and intensive training at the head office in Diemen. In between I worked at a branch in Amsterdam to gain more knowledge about this industry and Randstad. After that, I returned to Shanghai to start working as a consultant. Three months later, I was promoted to manager. Together with my consultants, we search and select candidates for clients."

"The Netherlands and China are as different as night and day. The employment market here has a working population of almost 810 million people! Randstad is a recognized authority in the Netherlands. This makes it so much easier to recruit clients. In China we are only at the beginning, and the market is full of competitors. Only through very hard work will Randstad be able to be as successful in China as it has proven itself to be in other markets!"

Selina Sun (second from the left) – Selection manager Randstad, China

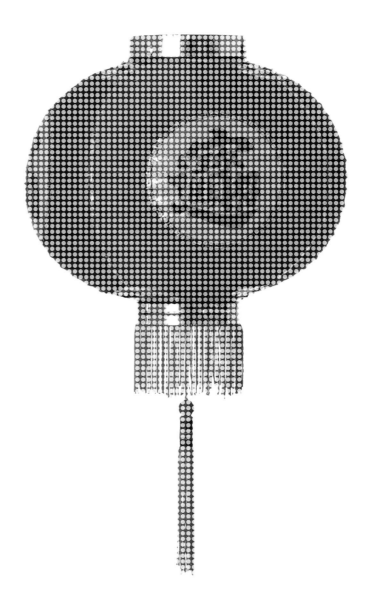

my most important conquest

best match

Lawyer Rafael Diaz-Cañabate takes his job seriously: "The success of Randstad in the Spanish labor market depends on the removal of restrictions and bans in our legislation. For example, Spain still has an exclusivity law: a staffing agency may only do staffing work. Other activities, such as recruitment and selection for permanent positions, are prohibited. We would obviously like to see a change here."

"We would like to offer our complete palette of services through the same company: staffing, professionals, recruitment and selection, HR Solutions, and inhouse services. We can only offer those products through other companies of Randstad Group Spain. In order to make this possible, Beatriz Cordero (director of HR) and I, are investing a great deal of energy into a 'social dialogue' with the government and with the unions. And a change may be on the horizon. If the law is changed, the Spanish market will be allowed to develop in full. A conquest of the Spanish staffing market would obviously be great, and yet, I am not sure whether that would exceed my really greatest conquest: I met the love of my life at Randstad, and we'll be getting married in September!"

Rafael Diaz-Cañabate (left) – Institutional relations Manager Randstad, Spain

58

Dagmara's secret

Having risen through the ranks from receptionist to regional director, Dagmara Chudzinska-Matysiak from Poland is a glowing example of how one can build a career at Randstad. Since August 2008, she has been responsible for Eastern Poland, one of the three regions within Randstad Poland. Equally remarkable is that Dagmara has accomplished her ascent up the corporate ladder in just nine short years, two periods of maternity leave included.

"My secret? Well, that's always difficult to say about yourself. I think I'm fairly open-minded; I like people, and I enjoy grabbing new opportunities. Fortunately, Randstad is a company that appreciates that kind of attitude, rewarding it rather than holding it back. You'd be surprised how many Polish companies think they know everything already; they don't take kindly to initiative or input from employees. The strength of Randstad lies in its flexibility. Initially, that would appear contradictory to our conceptual way of thinking and structured processes, but in practice it's not. Flexibility is a part of those concepts; if it wasn't, these concepts would be dogmas instead. Although values such as to *know*, *serve* and *trust* are the guiding principles for our staff, they also leave room for individual interpretation; thank goodness. I am a 'true blue' myself, when it comes to Randstad."

Dagmara Chudzinska-Matysiak– *Regional director*
Randstad, Poland

the Randstad dream

Companies become great by following their dreams. Randstad believes in its values: to know, to serve, and to trust, the simultaneous promotion of interests, and striving for perfection. These values form the bedrock of the company.

Randstad plays an important social role, offering staff and candidates with various backgrounds the work that is best suited to them. Randstad allows them to grow while maintaining a healthy balance between work and leisure; it finds the best candidates for its clients.

continues

The *Shaping the world of work* mission statement is the beacon on the horizon towards which the organization is striving. Randstad wants to be the best and the most valued HR services provider and therefore hopes to grow to become the number one worldwide authority on the labor market. *Shaping the world of work* creates true value for people and society.

Fifty years of Randstad is a story about people and their futures. That story begins here.

timeline

1949 Establishment of the Algemeen Service Bedrijf (ASB, later acquired by Vedior) by Pieter Sturm

1965 Purchase of the first computer: a bookkeeping machine

1969 Vedior establishes itself in the Dutch staffing market

1967 Randstad opens an office in the United Kingdom

1971 Introduction of the term 'intercedent' for staffing consultant

1960 Frits Goldschmeding and Ger Daleboudt found the Uitzendbureau Amstelveen staffing agency

1965 Interlabor Interim branch in Belgium opens

1968 Randstad Zeit-Arbeit opens its offices in Germany

1960 1961 1962 1963 1964 1965 1966 1967 1968 1969 **1970** 1971 1972

1961 Twenty people work for Uitzendbureau Amstelveen

1961 Establishment of the ABU association of staffing agencies

1962 Move to Koninginneweg Road in Amstelveen

1963 Over 100 staffers employed via Randstad

1964 Name changed to Randstad Uitzendbureau

1966 New head office at Oranje Nassaulaan in Amsterdam

1967 Establishment of the Confédération Internationale des Entreprises de Travail Temporaire (CIETT)

1968 Randstad Pension fund is established

1969 German prize for the Randstad logo

1970 New head office on A.J. Ernststraat in Amsterdam

 1972 First Randstad TV commercial

1972 Co-founde[r] Ger Daleboudt leaves Randstad

1967 Introduction of the new Randstad logo

Revenues show a rapid growth of the company between 1973 and 1977: from EUR 51.2 million to almost EUR 137 million

137 million

51.2 million

1979 Introduction of the comprehensive corporate philosophy

1979 100th branch opens, located at the Amsterdam World Trade Center

1979 New head office at Wildenborch in Diemen

1978 Name changed to Randstad Holding nv

1982 The Dutch political system promotes staffing work to overcome economic crisis

1980 Establishment of Randon security services

1973 Activities in France start with takeover of Votre Bureau in Paris

| 1973 | 1974 | 1975 | 1976 | 1977 | 1978 | 1979 | **1980** | 1981 | 1982 | 1983 | 1984 |

1973 By introducing Capac, Randstad now has a second Dutch brand

1974 Cleaning activities start in Germany

1975 Acquisition of Belglas provides access to Belgian sanitation market

1976 Acquisition of Korrekt starts cleaning activities in the Netherlands

1978 Introduction of the 'simultaneous promotion of all interests' principle

tempo-team
1983 Tempo-Team acquired

Revenues more than double between 1985-1990
from EUR 2.3 billion to EUR 5.2 billion

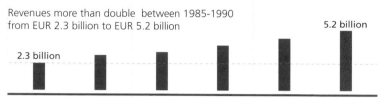

2.3 billion

5.2 billion

1991 The 500th
branch opens

1992 Establishment
of Eurociett

1994 First branch
opens in Spain

1996 Adia and
Ecco merge to
form Adecco

1996 Official
Supplier of the
Atlanta Olympics

1996 Flex accord
signed in the
Netherlands

1985 Frits Goldschmeding
decorated as Officer in the
Order of Oranje Nassau

1993 Acquisition of
TempForce and Jane
Jones Enterprises
means branching out
to the United States

1997 Universal
recognition of
staffing work
by the ILO
convention 181

1997 A first
branch opens
in Denmark

1997 A first
branch opens
in Canada

| 1985 | 1986 | 1987 | 1988 | 1989 | 1990 | 1991 | 1992 | 1993 | 1994 | 1995 | 1996 | 1997 |

1997 Randstad
now has 1000
branches
worldwide

1987 Architect Wim Quist
is asked to design the
new head office

1990 New head office
opens at 25 Diemermere
in Diemen

1997 Beginning
of construction
of the Stad
Amsterdam
Clipper

1995 Activities
commence in
Switzerland

1988 Establishment
of the Randstad
Option Fund for
employees

1990 Randstad IPO
at the Amsterdam
stock exchange

1995 Activities
commence in
Luxembourg under
the name of
Randstad Interim

1997 Randstad
proclaimed
one of four
European
Companies
of the Year

Revenues almost triple between 2003-2008 from
EUR 5.2 billion to more than EUR 14 billion

5.2 billion

14 billion

2000 Activities
commence in Portugal

YACHT

2000 Introduction of
Yacht brand name
in the Netherlands

2004 Partnership with
the non-governmental
organization (NGO) Voluntary
Service Overseas (VSO)

Vedior
2007 Merger
with Vedior

2010
Randstad
celebrates
its 50th
anniversary

1998 A grand 65th
birthday and farewell
party for Frits
Goldschmeding

2004 Activities commence
in Poland

2007 Active in over
50 countries

1998 Hans Zwarts
new CEO

2002 Cleem Farla
new CEO

2004 Activities commence
in Sweden

2007 Randstad 2nd
staffing agency
worldwide

2004 Activities commence
in Hungary

| 1998 | 1999 | **2000** | 2001 | 2002 | 2003 | 2004 | 2005 | 2006 | 2007 | 2008 | 2009 | **2010** |

2000 Launch of the Hedson
and newmonday.com
websites

2005 Activities commence
in China

2008 Acceptance of
EU staffing directive

2001 Legalization of
temp work in Greece;
activities commence

2005 Activities commence
in India

2009 Process integration
of Vedior in Randstad
completed

1999 Activities
commence in Italy

2006 Activities
commence in Turkey

2002 Introduction of
the new entrepreneurial
strategy: building blocks

1999 Activities
commence in Japan

2007 Randstad
formulates its mission
statement: 'Shaping
the world of work'

2003 Ben Noteboom
succeeds Cleem
Farla as CEO

afterword

This study of the history of Randstad was occasioned by the fact that the company is celebrating its fiftieth anniversary. This is a good time to look back. Much has changed in half a century. Staffing in 2010 is very different from what it was in 1960. Of course, the traditional business of placing temporary employees during peak periods and of replacing sick employees continues to exist, but apart from that, Randstad has become active in many other segments of the labor market. An increasing number of businesses can only survive while fluctuating the number of employees along with the amount of work available. This may vary from season to season, by week or even by day. Companies make better profits when they can concentrate on their core activities, while outsourcing activities such as recruitment, selection, personnel management, schooling and training to Randstad. This way, Randstad contributes to increased efficiency, to a more profitable business, and thereby to increased stability on the labor market. The staffing industry has become part of our economic infrastructure, just like the Internet, social safety nets, and healthcare.

The labor market itself also underwent a formidable transformation that can in part be proudly credited to Randstad. A modern employee no longer works in a single job for a single employer throughout his or her entire working life. An increasing number of employees seek to enhance their experience by working for many different companies. Randstad makes this possible. Also, many employees seek part-time employment, or alternatively, full-time employment for limited periods. All these changes have opened the labor markets to workers from demographic groups that used to be on the margins of society. It should also be remembered that staffing is no longer limited to the administrative and industrial sectors, because an increasing number of well-educated people use Randstad as part of their career planning, by acquiring short-term experience in a number of businesses. Today, working through a staffing company clearly works to a person's credit.

The facts belie the notion that temporary employment would only exacerbate the recurring ups and downs in our economy, and that job security in Europe for temporary employees would be lower than that for regular employees. Flexworkers have less trouble finding a new position than other job seekers. The staffing industry prevents wholesale dismissals and allows employers to provide employment opportunities even in insecure times. Moreover, even after dismissal or corporate bankruptcy, Randstad helps employees to find new employment faster.

Has Randstad now fulfilled its mission? The answer is a resounding "no!" There is still a world to be gained in the countries in which Randstad is operating, because the share of the flexworkers still shows significant differences that cannot economically be justified. Moreover, the rapid aging and shrinking of Europe's population require unorthodox measures in order to increase labor participation. In the social and healthcare services sector, the number of jobs will increase significantly over the next few decades. Labor will have to be more mobile than in the past in order to meet the requirements of the great differences of economic growth around the world. In all these fields, Randstad plays an innovative role, and the significance of this role will only increase in the future.

Prof. dr. Piet Emmer
Professor Emeritus for History at Leiden University

acknowledgments

Good ideas often emerge in several different places at the same time. This certainly applies to the idea of this anniversary book. Three years ago, people from various parts of the company suggested that a history of Randstad be written. This immediately led to the question whether it would not be more useful to focus on the future, rather than on the past. The approaching fiftieth anniversary in 2010, in combination with the merger with Vedior convinced us that 'Working on a dream' had to become reality. A study of the past would expose the 'genes' of Randstad, which also determine the future of our business.

We are very fortunate to have found the people of Storytelling Company*, who – along with Piet Emmer of Leiden University – have helped us professionally in adding content and form to our idea. The employees of Storytelling Company have interviewed and consulted many people, internally as well as externally, or involved them otherwise for the purpose of this study. They have sifted through a great number of internal and external archives, and documented everything in an impressive set of original documents, which served as the basis for this book. Unfortunately we have had to make a selection, as the number of pages available to us was limited. We would like to thank all the people, in so many countries, who have so enthusiastically invested their time and contributed to this project by sharing memories and personal experiences, by putting pieces of history into writing, by providing images, and by giving us the very best in logistic and technical support. Even in this summary we cannot be complete. This book is published worldwide in five languages, and we would like to thank our colleagues** for their meticulous proofreading, and for their assistance in the translation effort. Last, though not least, we cannot thank our advisory board*** enough for keeping us on track.

The book is out! It has been a privilege and a pleasure to work on this anniversary publication. Working on a dream can be read as a thrilling book, but… the end is open. That's the nice thing about Randstad: the company is young, and has a whole 'history' ahead of it. Does history repeat itself? Let us hope that the successful history of Randstad may keep repeating itself. Thanks again to everyone!

Fred van Haasteren
Chairman, Randstad Advisory Board

* Storytelling Company: Pieter van Gent, Mathieu Jacobs, Kees de Vos and employees.

** Debra Adamson, Aline Crépin, Christine di Duca, Sharon Gyalog, Sandy Jarrett, Rebecca Johnson, Odette Kamphuis, Rachael Moss, Françoise Orhon, Thalía Ortiz, José Romero, Helene Schmidt, Leticia Serrano, Fred van der Tang, Alberta Tennant, Simone Teufel and Petra Timm.

*** Advisory Board: Frans Cornelis, Piet Emmer, Frits Goldschmeding, Fred van Haasteren, Henk Janssen, Marion Kiewik, Gonda Koster, Sonja van Lieshout, Annemarie Muntz, Ben Noteboom and Wim Vos.

credits

Randstad project management   Marion Kiewik
Randstad design management   Wim Vos

production   Storytelling Company bv, 's-Hertogenbosch the Netherlands
concept   Mathieu Jacobs, Inne van Ussel, Kees de Vos
text   Pieter van Gent, Mathieu Jacobs
design   Inne van Ussel, Nanda Verpaalen
translation and editing   Cloud 9 – Anne Paris, Shunra Media – Daniel Bugel-Shunra
lithography and printing   Lecturis bv, Eindhoven, the Netherlands
binding   Abbringh, Groningen, the Netherlands

ISBN 978-90-71716-12-6

The typography used in the various chapters reflects the house style used by Randstad in the respective periods. Chapters 1 and 2 are printed in the Helvetica font which was used from 1967 to 1986. In that year, Randstad switched over to the Frutiger font, which we have used for chapters 3 through 5.

The Randstad anniversary book is printed on FSC-certified PhoeniXmotion Xenon paper, produced by paper manufacturer Scheufelen in Germany.

FSC
www.fsc.org
MIX
Paper from responsible sources
FSC® C008041

images created for Randstad Holding nv originating from the Randstad Holding nv archives

Arie Versluis & Ellie Uyttenbroek: 53, 285; Cartoonist: Arend van Dam: 18; Ab Koers: 79, 120, 124, 139, 140; Ad van Denderen: 122 (right); Arjé Plas: 25 (left), Jan & Fridtjof Versnel: 127 (right), 141 (top right); Johan de Boer: 206; Marcel Minnée: 132 (top right); Onno Meeter: 127 (left); Peter Marcure: 10-11; Rob Glastra: 84-85; Sherry Kamp: 94-95, 178, 181 (left); Tjeerd Frederikse: 87, 143 (bottom), 146, 148-149, 175, 182 (right), 186; Wim Vos: 181 (right), 240 (top), 248, 249; Vincent Kruijt: 251

images from other sources

ANP: 14 (top left), 122 (left), 128, 132 (bottom left), 134, 176, 192, 236, 253, 273; Bigstock: 116, 215, 220; WFA / Capital Photos: 174; Getty Images: 61, 160, 172-173, 189, 231, 278, 291; Hollandse Hoogte:197, 201, 207, 237; International Institute of Social History / Wimmie Rensen: 71; iStockphoto: 48, 51, 52, 55, 59, 60, 63, 99, 100, 103, 107, 108, 111, 112, 115, 117, 153, 154, 157, 158, 161, 162, 165, 166, 170, 216, 218, 219, 223, 224, 227, 228, 232, 275, 276, 279, 280, 283, 284, 287, 288; Kees Stolwijk: 113; Kontrast-Fotodesign / Bernd Wittesbach: 102; Nationaal Archief / Anefo: 69; Nationale Beeldbank: 56; Nederlands Archief Grafisch Ontwerpers: 141 (left); Frits Goldschmeding, private archive: 17 (bottom), 24, 25 (top right), 66, 68 (bottom), 75, 80 (top), 136, 187, 199; Ben Bos, private archive: 21, 31 (bottom right), 38 (right), 77, 89 (right), 141 (bottom right); Willem Quist, private archive: 142-143; I. Hammelburg, private archive: 78; Private collections of employees/clients: 50, 54, 57, 58, 62, 98, 105, 106, 109, 110, 152, 155, 156, 159, 163, 164, 167, 168, 171, 214, 217, 222, 226, 229, 230, 274, 277, 281, 282, 286, 289, 290; Reclamearsenaal: 135; Reuters / Jon Nazca: 225; Spaarnestad Photo: 14-15; Amsterdam City Archives / Photo collection, images of internal photo service: 67; Storytelling Company bv: 17 (top), 47, 104, 169; Studio Dumbar: 247 (right); Tempo-Team: 130, 255; Tim Eshuis: 45, 101, 114, 221, 233; Vedior: 204

Photography and illustrations not specifically mentioned above were taken from the Randstad Holding nv collection.

For the purpose of creating this book, Randstad has gratefully made use of the many illustrations and advertisements that were created for Randstad over the years by many national and international advertisement agencies and design bureaus.